CATCHING TI

CW00471323

by

Michaela J Loughney

Dedication

Merci, Sainte Thérèse, pour votre amour et d'inspiration.

Contents

Prologue

4th April 2010

Dear JC,

At last, my book is finished. It's as long as a novel, and I don't mind if it is read as such, but it is also a true story. As my mentor and friend, you know me better than I know myself sometimes, and I hope you will be rewarded for the time you have spent listening, guiding and supporting me. Without you, this story would be very different. One of the hardest but most valuable lessons I learned from you was that paying lip service to life doesn't avoid suffering and hardship in the long run. Indeed it prolongs it. You taught me that one of the most important things a person can do is to become intimate with their fears. Facing them is not enough, we have to put our arms out and bring them as close to us as possible. We should embrace our fears as if our life depended on them, and it does, but it isn't easy.

You were right in your prediction about the book. Completion feels wonderful. You said writing would be healing. It has been one of the best experiences of my life, but one of the hardest. Navigating my emotions has always been challenging. The spiritual elements I expected to be harder to write were in some ways easier than the emotional themes, because, on the spiritual plane, I have always felt guided.

The process of storytelling is instinctive, spiritual and necessary for both teller and listener. Our instinct to know what happens next draws us into a story; our spirit finds what our soul needs to know and without stories, our sense of self would be less developed.

Thank you for encouraging me to persevere, and for being such a wonderful mentor, friend, and soulmate.

Yours,

Michaela

4th April 2010

Dear Reader,

About ten years ago, in a vivid dream, I asked God to tell me what my very best talent is. I said to him, 'What do I excel in above all things?'

God simply said, 'You're a good listener.'

I was disappointed with his response; excellence in listening seemed much too ordinary. My dreaming self was hoping for more, so I said to God, 'But listening is easy, there are so many interesting stories to hear: a different one for each person.' He responded with silence. I listened to the silence, and I woke up.

In the days after the dream, I realised that listening may or may not be one of my best talents, but it is one of the most deeply rewarding life activities. I appreciate what an honour it is to be present when someone tells you something about themselves. It is a sacred act to bear witness.

The lives we tell our stories about always hold far more imperfection than we care to admit, many more blessings than we can comprehend, and demonstrate far more courage than we believe we have. My story isn't unique in its form, and it isn't perfect. My countless blessings didn't fully come to light until I wrote about them and the challenges I had overcome.

The proven benefits of writing for psychological, physical and spiritual health are well documented. Less is known about how or why it works. Some theories suggest that through expression we are less inhibited, or we make meaning out of what is written. For me, the healing power of writing comes from taking the time to listen. I learned to listen to my unique self. I heard an inner voice, a whisper at first, but the more I wrote, the more I heard and the more I healed.

No two stories can ever be the same because no two people ever have the same perception, even when the circumstances are similar. Perhaps this accounts for some of our enjoyment of experiencing another's tale? As a listener/reader, consciously or unconsciously, we expect to experience recognition in a story. We look for identification with experiences when we can say, 'Yes, that's how I felt, that's what I thought or did.' But there is always the further fulfilment (to me a deeper delight) of finding, perhaps hiding somewhere within a story, the same challenge or problem we have agonised or pondered over. When we see it from another's perspective, the challenge or problem somehow makes more sense to us than it did beforehand. In telling a story, an author doesn't necessarily tell us something we don't know, but can shed new light and bring longed-for clarity and connection: we learn about ourselves and others and know that we are not alone.

It is a story teller's job to tell the story as engagingly and as truthfully as possible; the rest depends on the heart and soul of the reader.

Here is the story of my journey; it changed my life, and I hope it will touch yours.

Yours,

Michaela Loughney

PART ONE

JOURNAL EXTRACTS

Chapter 1

6th April 2009 to 17th July 2009

Chapter 1

6th April 2009

Yesterday I made a decision to fulfil a lifelong dream, but it terrified me too: I am going to be a writer. That phrase makes my stomach flip, but my nervousness isn't because writing is something new to me. I have written my journal almost every day for the last five years (since I was 40) and as a Freelance Trainer, have written dozens of training courses and manuals; and, during my twenties and thirties, I wrote short stories and poems.

The real significance of this decision is giving up well paid professional work to write full- time. I have wanted to be a writer for as long as I can remember and chose my first degree subjects English Literature and Philosophy believing they would be the most useful for writing. (I read somewhere that one of the most successful British writers did the same degree subjects for the same reasons). However, I didn't study for my second degree in Psychology because I thought it would help me to write (although of course, it is a suitable subject for understanding what makes people tick). My need for psychology was much more urgent than the luxury of fulfilling my heart's desire. Finding out what was wrong with me was what mattered, and it took me another 20 years to do so.

JC helped me to make the 'I am going to be a writer' decision, but circumstances have played a part too. If I didn't feel so exhausted, I would see the funny side of the Stress Management Consultant feeling too stressed to work. JC says I need to practise what I preach. He is always honest and encouraging me with the big decisions in my life.

When I told Terry my big decision, he was, as ever, an entirely supportive partner, helping me to focus on the practical aspects of making this happen. He confessed he has been worrying about the amount of work I do and its impact on my health.

How am I feeling? Slightly better for writing this down but still anxious and looking forward to the exciting prospect of fulfilling a lifelong dream.

15th April 2009

Today is one of my first days as a full-time writer. I woke at 5am as excited as a child at Christmas and as nervous as a child starting her first day at school. It's 7am now as I sit at my desk and trembling at the thought of nothing to do all day but write. What shall I write? I haven't got a clue. What a thought! I have been dreaming of writing full-time for years and years, and now the opportunity is here, I don't know what to write! It might be helpful to have a read through my journals to see if there is any inspiration there.

23rd April 2009

I have spent an emotional day reading through my journals and 'morning pages', one of the best writing techniques I have discovered. Five years ago, after revealing to a friend that I wanted to write, she suggested that I read 'The Artists Way' by Julia Cameron (1995). I had never heard of it, but within 48 hours I had bought and read the book. Julia Cameron wrote the book about her experiences of unblocking creativity. She is a recovering alcoholic and was married to the film director Martin Scorsese. The 'morning pages' technique is so simple and yet so effective. It involves writing three pages of longhand each morning as soon as I get up. It doesn't produce beautiful writing but produces those thoughts that are running through my head at that time. My understanding is that this unblocks any barriers to creativity lurking in our critical minds and frees us to get on with the creative stuff we want to do. It is amazing how over the last five years these daily writings have accumulated into over 20 volumes just through sticking faithfully to the three 'morning pages' per day (although I often write more).

I enjoyed dipping in and out of the written record of my inner life and seeing how far I have come in the last five years. I will never forget how desperate I was when I first started this practice. The primary cause of my unhappiness then was my relationship with alcohol. It was one of the best decisions of my life when I decided to abstain, but also one of the hardest to arrive at; it was a painful separation. At first, I was just happy to be free from an unhealthy partnership, but then I had to face myself without blaming anyone else.

For the first couple of years of sobriety, daily journal-writing helped me so much as I opened up to my repressed and raw emotions. Learning about my emotions is like learning a new language, and I wouldn't have learned to live without alcohol for the last five years without my journal-writing. I hope my decision to be a full-time writer turns out as well as my sobriety journey.

30th April 2009

Preparing to write calms me. Just having a pen in my hand, without writing a single word, makes me feel better. I am not sure what I am going to write about, but I am enjoying sitting down at my desk with the intention of writing.

4th May 2009

I'm struggling to know what to write, I am desperate to connect with a worthy subject. Other writers suggest writing about what you know. I want to write about what I know in my heart, but this is where the problem lies. I am not familiar with what is in my heart and too familiar with the contents of my head.

12th May 2009

I am staying at the cottage at the Tŷ Newydd Writer's Centre in Wales and fulfilling my heart's desire. I am writing all day and every day. I started a story about a family with a secret, written from the perspective of a brother and a sister who both grow up to be childless (like my real brother and me). I am entirely alone and haven't spoken to another person (other than brief telephone conversations) for days. I am the most relaxed and more at home than I could have imagined. Writing alone is wonderful and will be extending my stay.

18th May 2009

JC phoned me to see how the writer's life is going. He offered to read what I have written so far, but I declined. He is teasing me because he knows that (apart from academic and professional writing) no one has read anything I have written apart from one poem published in an anthology years ago and one short story submitted to a competition.

It seems perfectly reasonable to me not to have shown anyone my writing. Why? Because I don't believe it is good enough. I will be ready to show someone my writing when a) I have decided what to write about and b) when I have faith in my ability. And when I do share my work, it won't be with JC if he is going to laugh at me!

26th May 2009

My thoughts are intense. I haven't written anything other than my journal for three days. I have been too busy reading 'How to write' books. The one that made the most sense was about writing spiritual books. I am wondering if I could do that? I have noticed recently that much of my journal-writing is about spiritual matters and includes prayers.

I love reading and have read many books. I don't know exactly how many I own, but Terry counted 80 shelves of books in the house. Someone asked me once if I had read them all, and apart from the stash beside my bed (waiting patiently in their queue), I can honestly say, I have read most of them, if not all cover to cover, and all are treasured.

If I don't make it as a writer, I could always set up a second-hand book shop, but it would be hard to sell any because parting with books is so difficult, even though I love recommending them to people. I have learned from experience how upsetting it is to lend a book and not get it back. These days, if I want to give a book to someone, I usually buy them a new copy.

5th June 2009

Being a full-time writer is harder than I thought. I start a writing project thinking it is the best idea in the world, and then within days or even hours, I decide it's no good. Am I trying too hard? Am I trying to be too clever? Is there anything I could write that is worth reading? I want to write about something that will be helpful to others.

8th June 2009

I am a little bit clearer about my purpose for writing. It can help me be more authentic, more present to my life, and to help others; but I am still unclear about what to write about.

Reading an article about knowing God made me consider the question, if I don't know myself well, what chance do I have of knowing God? My mental picture of God is not so much as a person, but as a supremely loving universal energy which can be present anywhere and everywhere. However, I also believe that God manifests in human form and his spirit is present in many people. I seek to connect with all these different aspects of God.

Sometimes I pray to a father-like or mother-like aspect of God or I ask universal loving energy (Holy Spirit) for help. Other times my prayer will be to the saints, asking them to guide and inform my thoughts and behaviour. Often I meditate on God as a Higher Power representing the beautiful multi-faceted mystery we will never know in our human form in the hope that this human life is not the end of our experience of the divine. In my prayers, I often call God 'Dear Lord'. I have come to the belief that God probably doesn't mind too much what I call him, as it is the feeling and intention of our prayers which are most important.

As I am writing this, I hear an interesting thought in my mind. Maybe it's not about how to know God better that matters, but how God can know us more fully and live more deeply in our hearts and minds? Perhaps through opening up, we will come to know ourselves better. This train of thought brings me back to a familiar question in my journal: who am I?

I am a seeker and have been for as long as I can remember. Seekers are rarely satisfied with their lives and have an inherent need, like hunger making them weak when it isn't satisfied. Seekers search for answers to conscious or unconscious questions, they wish to discover truths, pursue purposes, or surmount missions. Ask a seeker what they are looking for, and they often can't tell you but will describe a sense that something is missing. Seeking can be frustrating, but it is also the most rewarding experience when an answer appears.

From an early age, I sensed that I was far more restless than other people. Throughout my adult life, I have moved from city to city, partner to partner, job to job, religion to religion. What was I searching for? A purpose (the perfect job?) a person (the perfect partner?), vision (the perfect faith?), and the truth (what is stopping me moving forward?). I was searching for me (a perfect me?); the real me *not* the outward me who is so adept at being competent, people-pleasing and approval-seeking, but the real me: the part of me that I have kept hidden all my life, even from myself.

14th June 2009

I have been writing full-time now for over two months, and every few days have started a new writing project. The fresh starts initially are exciting, but the abandoned projects sit discarded on my shelf saying tauntingly, 'You are not a real writer and you never will be'; 'You may have grand ideas, but you can't keep to the same project for more than a couple of days.'

Where is my muse? I imagined the creative process would start as soon as I made time to write. I believed that lack of time was my only obstacle and took for granted inspiration, self-motivation, and self-discipline. I felt these were all within me, untapped, and to some extent, I was right as I am now putting them into practice. But what about patience? If I don't find some inspiration soon that is strong enough to withstand the negative critic in my head, I will give up. I have an obnoxious person living in my mind, and all my good thoughts have been stamped on by Ms Negative.

My writing projects start with head-over-heels enthusiasm, and the all-consuming excitement of 'This is it! I've found it, this is the book I want to write!' But how quickly the ardour fades. Before long the project is found lacking, and all my interest in the subject disappears. My skin prickles with the shame of all the unfinished projects and I lamely console myself with 'Next time will be different; the next writing project will be the winner.'

Initially, all my writing was done longhand as I much preferred the physical activity of writing, but in the last three months, I have developed a distinction between journal-writing done longhand and creative writing straight onto the laptop.

22nd June 2009

I have been writing about my childhood and felt the familiar rush of, 'This is it, I have found my subject', but my excitement quickly waned after a difficult afternoon trying to write about my emotions and came to the inevitable judgment, 'This isn't good enough'.

I am losing hope. Maybe the writing was only ever meant to be a therapeutic technique which helped me in the early days of my sobriety? While therapeutic writing is worthwhile, I want more. I want to be a proper published doing-it-every day writer. Maybe I am too ambitious. I have made progress as a writer with my training work. I am the successful author of a suite of several dozen training courses and manuals. In the field of business psychology training, my commitment is high and proven, but professional writing is much easier and safer because it is not about me. Creative writing is so much harder because I don't really know myself.

1st July 2009

I am at a crossroads, and it feels like a major crisis. My emotions are out of control; my thoughts punish me, and life seems quite miserable. I am surprised at how quickly thoughts defeat me but, on the other hand, a tiny flicker of hope stirs within telling me that all is not lost and this is just a test, and to stick with it, and I will move forward.

When I tune into this hope, I sense a big life question being asked of me but don't know what it is. I have had this feeling before, and problems can arise if I ignore it. The nagging question doesn't go away, it reappears again later, maybe in a different format, but it will always come back. For instance, many times after a disastrous drinking session I asked myself, 'Why am I so self-destructive? Why did I drink to oblivion?' I asked myself this many times, but one morning, after a particularly drunken night, it seemed different somehow, perhaps I was in shock. Detached from myself but strangely calm, I asked the usual question of why I drank in this way, but this time I was open to hearing an honest answer. I surrendered to the truth. I felt hopeless and helpless, but I knew with certainty that I had to stop drinking.

I was wrong to think that nothing could be done to help me and that no one else in the world drank like me. I wasn't beyond hope and redemption. Through the aid of a programme of sobriety and the love and support of a fellowship of men and women with a common desire not to drink, I learned to live without the crutch of alcohol.

5th July 2009

Writing is the best and the most natural feeling in the world. I love it when I am really in the flow and focused; time flies, and I am oblivious to my surroundings. I have often come to the end of a long writing session, ravenous and ready to faint because I haven't eaten for hours. Stiff joints from not moving a muscle other than my fingers and trembling with cold, I find myself in a freezing room, in complete darkness because I haven't noticed the day change to night. This absorption happens often.

11th July 2009

I am recording what happened to me earlier today because it is so significant. This afternoon, sombre and anxious, I lay down on my bed hoping to feel better. Although a summer's afternoon, the stormy weather outside made it nearly dark inside and the rain and wind rattled against the windows. I felt cold and getting up to draw the curtains against the draft from the wind seemed a futile effort.

Pulling the duvet over my shivering body, I tucked it right up to my chin like I did as a child when I was scared or upset. Lying stiffly and still, I tried to ease the throbbing in my head on the cool pillow. Hot tears stung my sore eyes as they trickled across my face into a cold wetness and made my neck itchy. I fought the wave of hurt coming closer and snuffled 'What's wrong with me?' into the pillow.

A ripping sensation in my chest made my heart feel like it was breaking open. I tried to relax but my throat hurt and my head ached, and it was hard to breathe, but I weakly concentrated on my breath as if I was meditating. I inhaled, stopped, and exhaled, and stopped, and waited until I was breathing more deeply. My stomach tightened with the threat of another attack of hard emotion, but a thought arose with complete clarity and uncharacteristic calmness: 'Stop resisting', and an inner voice said, 'Just let go.'

I obeyed both. The distress ready to assault from the depths evaporated into a whisper of 'Thank God', and tears fell freely. I surrendered to the pain, and it eased.

Eventually, the sobs subsided and the tears slowly dried up, and involuntary shudders comforted me confirming I had survived. Emotionally and physically exhausted, my eyelids drooped, and my body relaxed. It was over. I drifted off to sleep.

I woke a couple of hours later, and as I opened my eyes I was surprised to see it was completely dark, and much quieter outside, the rain had stopped, the wind had dropped, and I breathed in the refreshing, after-rain air. I felt lighter but raw, like a layer of my being had been peeled off and exposed to the air.

'I didn't see that coming,' I thought. I have shed many tears and felt much sadness, but this process felt different. I lay in bed wondering what felt different and remembered the thoughts, 'Stop resisting and just let go', and how unusual they felt, but soon the much more familiar thought spiral began.

'You should be more grateful. You now have the time you longed for, and don't have to dash all over the country delivering training courses anymore, but what have you achieved?'

My inner voice chastised. 'You are wasting your time. You can't stick to any particular project.'

I tried to think logically and honestly assess my hope of making it as a writer, and I had to admit to myself at that moment that, unless something changed in my approach, I knew my chances of success were limited.

This realisation took me from the horror of wondering what will I do with my life if I can't be a writer, to the relief of thinking, I'll get a job and just be normal and stop trying so hard. The surrender was as simple as that. I consoled myself with the thought I would still do my journal-writing every day.

I couldn't imagine my life without writing. Writing is my way of coping with and facing the world.

I lay on my bed grateful that some internal storm was subsiding, and my gaze wandered up and down the titles of the stack of 20 or so books piled high on my bedside table. Some of the titles were familiar, as they are permanent features at my bedside, but one of the titles was new. I bought it in a second-hand bookshop a few days ago. I opened the book at a random page curious to see what words appeared. I am a strong believer that books can teach us what we need to know at exactly the time we are ready to learn. This phenomenon had been proven to me again and again, and I believe it to be much more than a matter of coincidence. The book's title was 'Alpha Questions of Life' by Nicky Grumbel (2007). I bought it because the blurb on the front had said it was about the Alpha course which has been advertised on the outside of churches and community halls recently and I had been impressed with the humour and down-to-earth writing style of the author.

I lay on my bed and browsed randomly through the book, thinking about prayer and how important it has been to me at certain times of my life. Then a sentence seemed to shine out of the text in bigger and bolder letters than the other letters on the white page. The sentence was 'Prayer is the most important activity of our lives'. The words continued to shine brightly on the page, and I read on, and as I did the tears started to run down my face again. I was moved by this phrase. I lay back and stared at the ceiling, thinking about what I had just read. I agreed with every word about the importance of prayer. Something significant was happening, and I talked to God as if he was sitting on the bed beside me.

I meant what I said. 'I can't carry on like this anymore. I am sick of feeling like a failure. It is getting me nowhere and making me unhappy. I believe in you, and yet I am trying to run my life without your help. I humbly hand over my life to you Lord, and hope you will make some use of me.' I thought about what had made me cry earlier and said, 'All my life I have wanted to be a writer, and for the last three months I have tried every day, but I can't do it until I have something to write. If it is your will that I should not be a writer, then I am willing to give up my dream. Maybe you have another plan for my life? More than anything I want a purpose in my life. I have always hoped my life purpose would be to write, but now I am willing, with all my heart, to ultimately accept whatever you have in mind for me, and to commit my life to its fulfilment.'

If an angel had appeared to me and said I was required to go and teach French in the French countryside to poor children, I would have done it, willingly even though my French is appalling. I fell asleep again.

When I awoke, I felt more peaceful than I had in ages. I remembered that, just as I was falling asleep, I had made an important decision, and for a few moments, my mind was blank. Then with complete clarity, I remembered my decision and felt relief and comfort at the thought perhaps the Holy Spirit had put the idea into my head, and if he had, I was grateful because it seemed like a good idea. My decision was that although I hadn't been for quite some time, tomorrow I was going to Mass.

As I lay peacefully reflecting on what had happened, I heard Terry creep quietly into the bedroom trying not to wake me. His thoughtfulness touched me. 'I am awake,' I whispered, and sat up gratefully to take the cup of tea he had brought. Terry sat gently on the bed and asked if I was feeling better and I said I was. I didn't tell him any of the details of crying and then reading the book and deciding to go to Mass, and so when he said out of the blue 'Shall we go to the cathedral tomorrow?' I was amazed at the coincidence. This moment I am grateful knowing my Higher Power heard my prayer and in the knowledge that this matter is now in his hands.

12th July 2009

Today I went to Mass at the cathedral with Terry. As we drove past the Anglican Cathedral to arrive at the Catholic Cathedral, it struck me how lucky we are in Liverpool to have two cathedrals, one at each end of the same road, and so aptly named Hope Street. I enjoyed the service, the choir sang beautifully, and I wondered why I ever stopped attending Mass?

Afterwards, I couldn't resist browsing in the gift shop and instinctively headed for the book section dominated by a special display devoted to St Thérèse of Lisieux. I was intrigued. I vaguely recognised her name, but I didn't know who she was. I noticed one of the books in the display had a black and white photo of a nun on the front, and I assumed it was a picture of St Thérèse. But which St Thérèse was she? There is more than one St Thérèse. I remember a song called 'St Thérèse of the Roses.' Was she that St Thérèse I wondered?

'She must have been quite a modern saint if there are black and white photos available of her,' I thought. Trying to recall details about St Thérèse of Lisieux from school days, I remembered the statue my aunt used to have in her house of a beautiful nun holding a crucifix and roses in her arms. I secretly loved that serene figure: it radiated warmth and protection. I was always too afraid to ask who the statue was because I should have known, so in my mind, I called her the beautiful lady. I knew it wasn't Our Lady, and now I'm certain it was St Thérèse.

There was a large stack of St Thérèse's autobiography, called 'Story of a Soul'. The book 'called' to me and I wanted to read it. Usually, that is the trigger that leads me in a beeline to the payment desk digging into my handbag for my purse on the way. I am usually powerless against the urge to buy a book which appeals to me and was surprised by my decision to resist the common impulse to make an immediate purchase. Although I wanted to read 'Story of a Soul', I didn't feel a sense of urgency but was unusually confident that I would read the book, someday, but it didn't have to be bought today. This is unusual, and now I am writing about it, I believe my remarkable restraint and lack of compulsion is significant.

I looked through all the books about St Thérèse and felt particularly drawn not only to her autobiography but also to one written by Carmelite nuns. It felt heavy but comfortable in my hands, and as I inspected it, I sensed someone standing beside me. I turned to see my friend who I haven't seen for months; the same friend who introduced me to 'The Artist's Way' by Julia Cameron who had such an impact on my interest in writing. I know my friend hasn't been well recently, so I was pleased to see her, and we hugged. As we chatted, I looked for signs to see how she was. She seemed okay. I told her I was looking at the St Thérèse books, and as I said it, the impulse to buy both books immediately came over me again.

I studied my friend's puzzled look as she stared down at the books, and she pointed to the photo of St Thérèse on the front of one, and said, 'She looks odd.'

'Yes she does,' I agreed, but not odd meaning strange, odd meaning unusual. This comment from my friend changed my mind again, and I decided to give buying the books a little more thought. I felt torn between my usual, 'must have it now' impulse and 'hold back' habit based on what my friend had said. I felt both confident and slightly anxious at the same time. Probably because I am addicted to books, I am immediately lifted when I come across a book that provides the possibility of a connection. I notice it first in my stomach, then an all-over thrill but it doesn't last long. I soon need another fix. As the buzz dissipates, what I thought was the answer to a prayer or the missing piece of the puzzle, that was going to fix me or change my life forever is found wanting. The sense of discovery soon transforms into another false dawn, and I end up even more confused, but this doesn't stop me thinking and hoping the next book will be the one, the one to make all the difference to my life.

Terry came to tell me it was time to go, and we said goodbye to my friend. We left her staring at a photo on the front of one of the books.

'She is trying to work out why she thinks St Thérèse looks odd,' I told Terry. But I understood; she seemed fascinating to me too.

On the way out of the shop, I noticed a bigger picture of St Thérèse. It was a large colourful poster announcing the first visit of St Thérèse's relics to the UK in September this year. I thought, 'Wow, how exciting' and then my mind jumped in to dampen my enthusiasm when it told me, 'Why are you so excited? It's only a tour of old bones. What use are they?' As I walked out of the shop, I had an intense feeling I had preparation to do. It reminded me of when I was at university with exam revision to do. I would be excited because it was a subject I was interested in, but would also be apprehensive about completing the revision in time and fearful the exam would arrive, and I wouldn't be fully prepared. I picked up a booklet about St Thérèse explaining the purpose of the visit of her relics. With my friend's words, 'She looks odd' running in my head, I studied the photo of St Thérèse on the front, and I smiled. It was a different picture, and she didn't look odd, she looked lovely.

13th July 2009

Last night I read the booklet I picked up in the cathedral shop about St Thérèse and the visit of her relics. I had to know more. It prompted me to do some further research on the internet about her.

St Thérèse of Lisieux was a Carmelite nun born in France in 1873. Her mum died when she was very young. Young Thérèse entered the convent aged only 15 and stayed there until her death only nine years later aged 24 in 1897. She died of tuberculosis after a very painful illness. Unusually, rather than the traditional 50-year wait before canonisation, St Thérèse was canonised by Pope Pius XI in 1925, only 28 years after her death. This unusually early recognition of holiness is said to have been due to popular demand. St Thérèse was called, the 'Little Flower' and she is famous for her 'little way', and her teachings are profound enough to have earned her the title of, Doctor of the Church.

I am clearer now about who St Thérèse is because initially, I may have been confusing my St Thérèse with the earlier St Teresa of Ávila who was also a Carmelite nun who lived from 1515 to 1582 in Spain. I recently read about St Teresa of Ávila in Caroline Myss' book 'Entering the Castle' which describes the moving and incredible story about how the author came to know St Teresa, and the connection she developed to St Teresa.

Caroline immediately stops writing the book she had spent six months writing to start a new project influenced by her new faith and confidence in St Teresa. I remember thinking at the time; I wish I had a St Teresa like Caroline has.

14th July 2009

I am procrastinating about going into town to the cathedral to buy 'Story of a Soul'. Why am I scared of reading St Thérèse's autobiography? I usually want to devour books, rather irreverently. Part of me wants to go and get it and start reading it straight away, but another part of me is resisting. I feel drawn to St Thérèse, and I don't want to spoil it. Will somehow knowing her as a person through her writings reduce her impact on me as a saint? Am I afraid of being disappointed in her? I am considering giving up the writing and getting a proper job. In the last couple of days, I have decided having faith is more important and if I have to choose between faith and writing, at the moment, I want my faith.

I told JC this, and he said, 'Why not have both?' JC said it is through writing I will find and deepen and express my faith.

Terry said something similar when he asked, 'Are you sure you can separate them?'

I wish I had their confidence. At the moment, I have hope in my faith but no confidence in my writing. St Thérèse wasn't simple, but her methods were. Can I learn to love like her? Her vocation was quite simply, to love.

I also read an article in which the author, Michael Whelan (2007) says, 'St Thérèse's life gives us an example of the "hope-despair tension" … hope calls for surrender and abandonment'. I know this. I despaired in February 2005 and surrendered, and again last weekend, and in doing so have found hope for my spirit, but I don't know how I will translate this hope into my writing. Maybe I should pray.

'I surrender my will to you and thank you for St Thérèse and for coming to know about her. Please let me develop my understanding of her teachings and to find the way of letting go for this to be the key to unlocking the love I know is within me, and for me to recognise this love and to release it. I have tried to love others, but not always in the best way. Please keep those I love in your safe hands. Amen.'

I felt better after my prayer but guilty that I haven't written much all week. I am going to go to the cathedral later. I can't stop thinking about St Thérèse's autobiography. I am going to buy the book today.

15th July 2009

Yesterday I bought St Thérèse's autobiography, 'Story of a Soul', and started reading it immediately; I can't put it down. I have read and then re-read certain passages; it is very inspiring.

The 'Story of a Soul' was written out of St Thérèse's obedience to her prioress (who was also her sister) and published after her death in place of an obituary to her short life. She never set out to write a book. She only wrote her story because her superiors asked her, and yet I sense strongly she enjoyed writing and the power of words. She writes with such honesty in talking about her weaknesses and longings. I have often wondered why we have a soul, and what are we meant to do with it. I don't know if I will ever understand my soul, but I am encouraged to write to St Thérèse. In my journal, I often write letters to myself and others. These letters are never sent but usually make me better. So, I have decided I am going to write to St Thérèse of Lisieux, one of the most inspirational women in recent history.

St Thérèse wrote her three manuscripts which became 'Story of a Soul' in the form of letters. I admire the intimacy and purpose with which she writes. I would love to be able to write like that.

Not long before I stopped drinking, I would write letters to my guardian angel and then would write an imaginary reply, and it is amazing how much sound advice came in the responses. I had no idea what I was writing would turn out to be so helpful to me. It was worthwhile and comforted me a lot when in need of support, and didn't know where to turn. I didn't realise it at the time, but those letters to my guardian angel were a type of prayer, and know now those prayers were answered.

I have a sense of urgency about writing to St Thérèse. Her relics are coming to the UK for the first time later this year, and I have necessary preparation to do as if she is calling me. One of the best things to happen, since I stopped drinking, is opening to intuition more. Its voice can be quickly drowned by the bullying self-critical voices within that shout much louder, but I am now willing to listen.

What about my writing? I was in despair a few days ago about finding something worthwhile to write. I have been too busy researching and reading about St Thérèse to do much writing, other than this journal, but St Thérèse is helping me.

16th July 2009

St Thérèse of Lisieux had great humility and inner confidence. She was guided, not by what others have wanted for her, not by what others might think of her, but from her true self, from her deepest yearnings and desires. Could she teach me what I need to know?

Today I researched what St Thérèse's title of Doctor of the Church means. It is an honour awarded by the Church to saints whose writings and doctrines they regard as particularly important. Within the history of the Catholic Church, she is the third of only three women ever to receive this title. St Thérèse is in the company of St Catherine of Siena (1347–1380) and St Teresa of Ávila (1515–1582) both declared Doctor of the Church by Pope Paul VI in 1970; and St Hildegard of Bingen (1098-1179) declared Doctor of the Church by Pope Benedict XVI in 2012. St Thérèse was declared 33rd Doctor of the Church by John Paul II in 1997 after her writings were studied and were found to be almost faultless theologically.

I have discovered some amazing coincidences about St Thérèse relevant to my life. St Thérèse was the youngest child of Louis and Zelie Martin who were devout Catholics and loving parents to nine children: seven girls and two boys. The boys and two of the girls died at birth or soon afterwards. The first coincidence is that Sunday 12th July 2009 (four days ago) was the first ever feast day of her parents (they were beatified on 19th October 2008). It is amazing that 12th July is also the day I decided to return to Mass after at least seven years' absence. The second coincidence is St Thérèse entered the convent on 9th April which is my birthday; and thirdly, that sadly St Thérèse's mother died at age 44, the age I am now.

My connection with St Thérèse is growing, and I am more peaceful than I have felt in a long time. I have said some prayers to St Thérèse to help me with my writing.

17th July 2009

I am reading about St Thérèse's 'little way' which describes her spiritual approach to living as one of love, trust and dependence on God, similar to a child's dependence upon its mother or father. It is also understood to be a simple path to holiness available to anyone.

I wonder if St Thérèse could teach me to love in this way and to help me find the love I know I have buried within me. St Thérèse talks about 'a child's trusting love for its parents' and how we should love like this. When I read this, I was sad because I can't fully relate to trusting love. I am more familiar with the concept of responsible conditional love.

St Thérèse's parents, Louis and Zelie, have offered themselves to me as spiritual parents, and they are guiding me to follow the example of their daughter. Like St Thérèse, I have often been a loving daughter, but I haven't always allowed myself to receive or accept the love my parents have offered to me, or I should have directed towards myself.

I haven't ever really thought about how well I love myself. Today I feel the love of Louis and Zelie Martin and St Thérèse has opened something within me. I told Terry what I have decided, and he said this is profound. I agree with him; it feels deep to me. If St Thérèse's teaching is called the 'little way', mine would be called the 'lost way'.

PART TWO

'A Lost Soul'

Chapters 2 to 18

Chapter 2

18th July 2009

Dear St Thérèse,

You faithfully told the story of your life; I want to tell you mine. Your story is called 'Story of a Soul,' mine could be called, 'Story of a Lost Soul'; about someone who has spent the last 44 years searching and longing to know herself. I believe on 12th July, your parents' first feast day, I was granted the grace of your guidance helping me to understand myself better and moving me to follow your example. You wrote to your sister and prioress; I will write to you.

My uncharacteristic confidence in embarking on such an undertaking is faithful to your example. In the story of your soul, you wrote first about your childhood, and then about your faith and your spiritual experiences, I will start with my childhood but have no idea where I shall end up. My desire is to prepare for the visit of your relics to the UK, which starts in Portsmouth on 16th September and ends in Westminster Cathedral in London on 15th October with a two-day visit to Liverpool from 24th September 2009.

I want you to know who I am, and maybe it will help me to know myself better? Thank you for listening.

Yours,

Michaela

Chapter 3

19th July 2009

Dear St Thérèse,

At Mass today I had an important realisation. My pilgrimage has begun. I have sensed divine intervention in the past and feel it strongly now. These are the same powerful forces I sensed five years ago when I stopped drinking. I believe with all my heart my Higher Power played a part in my getting sober. I couldn't have done it alone; and so far, it is the best thing that has happened to me, and my life has only improved since that day.

I had been praying hard in the months before. It was St Valentine's Day: Monday 14th February 2005. I arrived home from work about 6.30pm, cold and tired and dreading the long night of loneliness ahead. I opened the front door, mentally working out how much wine was in the kitchen and how long it would be before I would need to walk out into the cold night air to buy more. My last alcoholic drink had been in the early hours of the day before. As I walked into my living room, I felt some of the usual dread, but also partly detached, as if some external force was pulling me. I had a sense of watching myself rather than being fully present. When needing to make a decision, I can suffer greatly from procrastination (I was even worse then). I can spend hours weighing up the pros and cons and painting a negative picture in my mind so gloomy I have talked myself out of something by predicting failure without giving myself a chance of success. A major decision like asking for help with my drinking was ripe for at least a few days of procrastination. But it didn't happen. I just walked over to the telephone, and if you had asked me who I was going to call, I wouldn't have been able to tell you. But as I picked up the phone book I knew what number was needed, and without hesitation, I found it and dialled the number. Within an hour and a half of making the call, someone had called me back, collected me and taken me to my first meeting of Alcoholics Anonymous.

In the room full of strangers, I was terrified, but I also intuitively knew I was in the right place. The people I met were unbelievably welcoming. I was hugged and encouraged to come back and felt waves of sincerity and love from these strangers. I had never experienced anything like it before. I felt a glimmer of something reassuring (which I now know as hope) and someone said to me, 'Michaela, remember you are no longer alone!' This simple comment moved me, and I believed it, because, for one of the first times in my life, I wasn't alone.

Until that day, I had thought I was the only person in the world who couldn't handle alcohol and suffered under its influence in the way I did. I drank when I was happy, when sad, because everyone else drank, because it was the only way to celebrate, because my life was difficult, because I worked very hard and didn't I deserve a reward now and then? I drank so as not to face mental and emotional pain and needed a crutch to help me deal with life. I never, ever intended to get so drunk. I always thought, 'This time I will control it; this time will be different; this time I won't drink to oblivion; this time I will stop when I have had enough.' Of course, I never did follow my own intentions. I couldn't. My make-up (physical, emotional and spiritual) dictates that once I have alcohol in my system, I continue to drink until I pass out or become so exhausted through arguing, fighting or crying and fall asleep, or someone hits me hard enough. Having strong stamina wasn't helpful in these situations. It is in my nature to try to do my best in all the things I do, even getting drunk. I excelled at it.

I woke on 15th February without any alcohol in my system. I waited for anxiety to appear as it did every morning but just for a split second there was nothing, no emotional tremor, no dread, no guilt, and no shame, just a few seconds of peace and quiet. I felt different, and although it only lasted a few seconds, it was enough to tell me an important change was occurring. The usual anxious thoughts and churning stomach set into their habitual rounds of my body and mind. If you had asked me at the time what had happened, I wouldn't have been able to explain it at all, but I know now it was a glimmer of hope. I had experienced something special in that momentary insight. If I worked hard enough, things would be different. My heart became set on success.

In the days after my first meeting, I learned so much. Recovery isn't just about stopping drinking; it's about changing my thinking and handling emotions too. This intuitively made sense to me. People don't have to reach homelessness, complete madness and cirrhosis of the liver to stop drinking. We can get off the cycle of addiction at any stage. There is a solution for anyone who wants it and my recovery programme has been called (by Henry Kissinger) one of the greatest accomplishments of the twentieth century. I was relieved to learn alcohol caused many of my problems. For most of my adult life, I had genuinely believed I was mad or bad (or both). It was a relief to meet ordinary people who had the same problem and who were now recovering. I wanted sobriety more than anything I have ever wanted in my life.

JC, the man who was to become my sponsor and dear friend today, was present at my first meeting and within a few days he had made contact with me and bought me as a gift the book we use in our recovery programme. This book was written in the 1930s by the first members and explains what alcoholism is, how recovery works as a programme and provides examples of people writing about their experiences of recovery in their own words. JC has an excellent sense of humour and an incredible capacity for honesty, and he has helped, guided, consoled, and loved me along my journey so far. He has also helped many other people. He is a real inspiration and source of strength. The fellowship encourages us to pass on the message of hope in this way.

When opening the book JC presented to me, and seeing the personal message, 'Welcome to the most expensive club in the world', I didn't understand the inscription. My first thought was, 'I thought our programme was free!' He must have noticed a confused look on my face because he said, 'The inscription refers to how much you have lost in getting to this point.' I understood realising recovery was going to involve a lot of facing up to what I have lost or failed to achieve due to the power of alcohol. I have done a lot of crying in my recovery, but there have been some tears of happiness too.

I could write a whole book about the recovery programme and its success for me and the wisdom it imparts to those who follow its suggestions. We have a tradition of telling our story, it is called, 'our experience, strength, and hope.' It usually follows a pattern of telling people in about 20 minutes what we were like when we drank, how we stopped drinking and what has happened since i.e. how our life has changed for the better since we have stopped drinking. I will leave that aspect of my story for the recovery rooms. I am so grateful for the guidance and wisdom I have received. Its relevance is universal. The best summary of its wisdom for me is the prayer adopted by members. 'God grant me the serenity to accept the things I cannot change, the courage to change the things I can and wisdom to know the difference.'

I am learning today to know the difference between what I can and cannot change. I can't change the past, but I can learn from it and allow it to help me have a more rewarding and fulfilling future. I can't change other people, but I can change myself. I can't change my previous actions, but I can change how I act today or in the future.

Yours,

Michaela

Chapter 4

20th July 2009

Dear St Thérèse,

Yesterday I mentioned hope and how important it is to me. I used to think that hope was for the weak-willed who could only wish for the good things rather than make them happen, but in early recovery, hope became my new best friend. I once read that lack of hope was the biggest predictor of suicide, and it has always amazed me that this fact is not more commonly discussed. I can't imagine how I ever lived without hope. Living with hope introduced me to the joy of finding out about new friends and me.

Why was hope my treasure? There are significant general hopes such as I hope that the future will be better than now and that I will be less of a failure. I hope that I won't miss any significant opportunities and that I will live my life as well as possible without hurting anyone along the way. I hope that my God will know that I am here and that I am aware of his presence. But there is also a precise definition of hope, that is, the hope that I can discover through seeking, and the hope that gives us the purpose for our lives, the hope that tells us the truth: 'hope is born when facing the unknown and discovering that one is not alone' (Kurtz & Ketcham, 1994). How does knowing that I am not alone help? It tells me there is a solution to my problem. It helps me to plan a strategy of action and to find out how others before me have solved similar problems. It tells me what I can reasonably expect from a situation and to face reality. It encourages me to seek to help, and in doing so, I know that I will help myself. It tells me that I can't do it on my own, even if I wanted to and helps me ask the right questions.

The biggest gift of hope is faith. Faith helps me to be courageous and confident. It helps me to address some my lifelong unanswered questions. These matters are described well in the book I was reading when I first went into recovery, 'Six Questions that Can Change your Life' by Joseph Nowinski (2003). When I returned to the book a few months into sobriety, I was amazed to see that one of the case studies was about a professional woman who came to a profound understanding of herself through one of these questions when it helped her to realise that she was an alcoholic. I hadn't remembered reading this part of the book before sobriety. I only recognised it when I returned to the book after I stopped drinking. The author suggests that there are six fundamental questions that we ask ourselves in managing and developing the course of our lives; they typically are: Who should I be? What do I want? Where is my position? What do I own? What am I worth? How can I gain approval? And he suggests that there are six alternative questions which are much more relevant and useful. They are: 'Who am I? Why am I here? Where do I belong? Whom do I love? Who loves me? How can I be true to myself?' I have found these questions extremely helpful over the last five years. They have given me hope and inspiration when I have most needed it.

Hope is a purpose, a feeling, but it is also a way of thinking and acting. In one of our conversations about hope, JC explained that the foundation of his spiritual approach is hope. My understanding of what he said is that hope is much more than hoping for the best in an egotistical way, rather it is recognition of the presence of the best in us and the mystery of the divine in us. Hope helps us to surrender to and embrace our fears. Hope helps us to face the void of the unknown and not to fall into the trap of isolation. You would agree with JC in his thoughts about hope. JC also puts his hope into action. His hope is life changing; I know from experience that he has saved more than one agonised soul.

A part of me would be happy to stay in the places hope shows me, and I could be comfortable forever, safe but unchallenged. But hope guided me and showed me that there is more unexplored land on the horizon and I am still a long way away. There is an empty place within, like a huge void. Sometimes it is sadness that I sense, but I don't know what it is I am grieving. At times I am angry, but don't know why. At other times it feels like loneliness and needs that I cannot meet. It is something that I am trying to reach, just out of my awareness. Is it a place too dark and too buried for hope to reach? It can be an intensely painful feeling, and although the empty feeling is the smallest place within, it is also the deepest place. Hope has touched my mind and heart in recovery but has not yet reached this most important place. People have given this place different names: 'inner truth' – JC; 'deepest place' – Ronald Rolheiser; 'the forbidden city' – Thich Nhat Han. I call it my soul.

Yours,

Michaela

Chapter 5

21st July 2009

Dear St Thérèse,

There is a phrase in our recovery programme which resonates with me strongly called 'soul sickness'. It describes some of the causes and effects of addiction on the person who experiences it. I understand it to mean that my spirit was so weak and lost so deeply that I was indeed sick in the same way that we can be physically and mentally ill. The most fundamental aspect of my 'recovery' is the healing of my soul.

As a child, you were a worrier and had a mysterious illness which may have been a kind of soul sickness because its causes were unknown (probably due to the effect of traumatic losses in your life), but faith cured it. Your family was anxious and prayed for you, and they carried a statue of Our Lady into your room, and when you believed that Our Lady had smiled at you through her statue, you were instantly cured of the illness and subsequently became less of a worrier.

I was born on 9th April 1965, and mum has often said that my sensitivity comes from my traumatic entry into life. I wasn't breathing when I was born and had to be resuscitated. I am the eldest child of two and the only daughter. My name 'Michaela' was chosen to be the feminine of my dad's name, Michael, and was inspired by two Michaela's popular in the mid-sixties, one real and one fictitious. Firstly, Michaela Denis, wife of the explorer, Armand Denis; and secondly Nurse Michaela Large, a character in Emergency Ward 10. I like my name and am grateful to mum and dad for choosing it. Names are important and I know it sounds conceited, but I wouldn't have liked having a plainer name.

When I was old enough to understand the importance of what my parents did for a living I was proud of their occupations. My father was a police officer, and mum worked in an office. It was much more unusual in the late sixties and early seventies than it is now to have a working mum, but instead of seeing this as a disadvantage, I liked the fact that my mum wasn't like other mums.

Both my parents came from strong Catholic backgrounds. My father's mum was from Dublin and spoke with an accent as strong as if she had only just left 'home' but had in fact lived in Liverpool, most of her adult life. My mum's family background also has Irish origins. My brother David was born 14 months after me on 13th June 1966 (feast of St Anthony of Padua), and he completed our little family.

I have always loved my brother David intensely. One of my earliest memories of this love was being on holiday when I was young, perhaps three or four and he was a toddler. I remember the dampness of a warm rainy day, and we were in a big shop, probably Woolworths and perhaps sheltering from the rain. As we wandered, I saw a little blue teddy bear on the shelf, and as I was staring at it thinking how much David would like it, he came up beside me and picked it up. Then as he inspected the toy, I noticed him ever so briefly cuddle the little bear and then put it carefully back on the shelf. Even though I was very young, I felt that I might burst with the intensity of my love for my little brother as he gave a secret cuddle to the little blue bear.

I gently took the bear out of his hands and took it over to my parents and said, 'Please can we buy this for David?' My parents weren't unkind, and when they said no there was probably an excellent reason for refusing, but I felt frustrated because I was too young to explain why it was so important to buy the bear for David. David didn't say anything, but I instinctively knew that he wanted it, and I felt heartbroken that I couldn't persuade my parents to buy it for him.

I told David this story recently and asked him if he remembered that day, and he laughed and said no he didn't but thanked me for trying to get mum and dad to buy him the toy.

Thanks for helping me remember this.

Yours,

Michaela

Chapter 6

22nd July 2009

Dear St Thérèse,

You only lived in three places in your short life. Your home in Alençon where you were born, the family home in Lisieux where you moved to after your mother died, and the convent in Lisieux where you lived (without leaving once) until your death.

I have always been restless. I have lived at over 20 different addresses and in five different cities (Liverpool, London, Cardiff, Glasgow, and Edinburgh). Although some of these were temporary student addresses, each move between cities was an attempt to make a fresh start. But I always took 'me' with me wherever I went.

I don't remember my first move because I was under the age of one when mum and dad moved from a flat near Penny Lane to a brand new semi-detached house in Formby, about ten miles outside Liverpool.

My main memories of our life in Formby, the first six years of my life, evoke little emotional reaction in me now, but I remember clearly the emotions I felt at the time. Is this normal? Surely looking back at my younger self should stir some response of affection, but recalling these memories is like watching a film about someone else, another little girl who is not me.

I remember the shame of my mum insisting that I only needed to wear red ribbed tights and a red sweater to a ballet class. I didn't understand why I wasn't allowed to wear a skirt over the tights and made a big fuss. Dad took me to ballet class. On the way, he tried to reassure me that ballet dancers wore special costumes and that's how you knew that they were special because skirts were too ordinary for them. I didn't believe him, but I like the way he explained it to me. So here I can remember feeling one of the strongest emotions, shame, but I feel nothing today when I recall it.

I remember the distress of discovering a stain on my white dress when I was about three years of age. When I found that I couldn't rub it away, I couldn't stop crying. My mum tried to assure me that it wasn't the end of the world and bought me a glucose lollipop to cheer me up. Today I recognise how upset that little girl was, but I don't feel any emotional connection with her as my younger self.

I remember when I was still at nursery school, sitting in the front seat of the car and finding out from my mum that I was on my way to the hospital to have an operation (it was a tonsillectomy). I cried until my eyes were sore once my mum left me at the hospital. My only conciliation was the brave older boy in the bed opposite who tenderly comforted me and shared his ice cream. During the same hospital visit, I also remember the shame of being made to undress for a bath in front of a stranger (a nurse) who kept telling me that I was a silly girl for being so shy. These events seem like they happened to another little girl, not me.

Around the same time at nursery school, I remember the wonder of the sight of the cat that lay permanently curled around the neck of the nursery-school owner. She wore the cat like a stole. It moved so little that I often wondered if it was dead but on the rare occasion that we were allowed to touch the cat, I knew it was alive because it felt warm. This memory is different; a wave of affection comes over me for the cat.

When I was about four, the marble fireplace that used to be in our living room was propped up against the wall outside our house waiting to be collected, and it fell on me, and I got trapped beneath it. Everyone said it was a miracle that a neighbour was able to lift it on her own to free me and that I escaped without any crushed and broken bones. This memory is perhaps not even a memory at all, I am just recounting what I know to be true.

I remember the intense sadness that came into our family with the death of Nana Burke, my maternal grandmother, but it was also an occasion which meant an exciting 'best-clothes' trip to the pictures for the children while the adults sorted through and packed away her things. When I recall this memory, it evokes present-day sadness for the impact on mum when her mother died, and the usual wave of love when I remember my little brother when he was a child, but nothing for me.

I remember playing with my brother when we shared a bedroom as toddlers, and we couldn't get out because the door was locked (for our safety). During those times we used to play together for hours, but one day a game with David turned into a fight while we were waiting for the door to be unlocked. It felt like we had been locked in all morning and I remember being so frustrated at not being able to get out of the room that I threw David's favourite toy truck against the wall and it broke. Immediately I knew I had done something terrible and, however much I wanted to, knew I could not undo the act. I felt distraught. I must have made such a noise that mum came into the room, and I remember her trying to console us both.

Although I couldn't name it at the time, I know now that guilt was the name of the strong emotion I felt at damaging David's toy rather than one of my own. I asked David about this recently, and he said, 'Of course I remember the day you wrecked my best toy', with a glint in his eye that told me that he had long forgiven me, but the incident had not been forgotten.

One of the effects of this is that I have rarely thrown things or broken things in temper because I learned at such an early age that once a thing has been done, it often can't be undone. Trying to stop my anger swelling to the point of being uncontrollable was a lesson I learned well. Throughout my childhood, I rarely expressed anger and felt that I wasn't allowed to, and if I did, there would be painful consequences. I learned to hide anger.

Repressing normal emotions is not good for us, but I didn't see this when I was young. I remember being keen to grow up as quickly as possible and repressing emotions was part of my plan for growing up. So I just thought I was grown up when I managed to stuff down worry and fear and anxiety. To me being grown up meant not showing your emotions.

This attitude has stayed with me most of my adult life. Managing emotions means hiding the chaos within. Consequently, a lot of my emotions became hidden, even from me, and this made me even more satisfied. I didn't realise how much damage I was doing stuffing them away, and I didn't always do it consciously.

Yours,

Michaela

Chapter 7

23rd July 2009

Dear St Thérèse,

After the loss of your mother when you were only four years old, your family moved to Lisieux where your uncle ran a pharmacy. This was a happy move for your family. I wasn't much older than you were when our family moved back to Liverpool. Dad put me in charge of Ratbag, our huge black cat who sat on my lap in the front passenger seat in the car. I felt so grown up. I loved Ratbag very much and have loved cats ever since.

I remember a poem that mum and I made up.

We have two pussies they both are black,
We like to stroke them on their back,
One's eyes are blue the other's green
No other difference can be seen.
They love to play with a little ball,
And scratch the carpet in the hall,
And then you'll hear my daddy shout,
'You naughty pussies you must go out'.
Our pussies' names are Sooty and Sweep

And all they do all day is sleep,

You'll never see one without the other,

That's because they are sister and brother.

Our new home was a three-bedroom semi-detached house in South Liverpool, bringing us closer to my aunt and uncle, (my mum's sister and father's brother who were married to each other) and my cousins, and my nana who lived with them. I didn't know my paternal grandfather as he died of tuberculosis when my father was only a child. My maternal grandfather 'Pop' lived in Crosby in between Liverpool and Formby until the death of his wife ('Nana Burke') when he moved to a flat in Sefton Park; so by 1971, our small extended family were all living close to each other.

Our new house was older than the one we left and felt much more solid and interesting. The back garden was lovely with a patio and archway, a wooden bench and two beautiful apple trees and a cherry blossom tree. In the front garden was a beautiful 'weeping' tree (Laburnum) with beautiful yellow blossom. The air was full of newness and excitement, and there were lots of visits from my aunt and uncle and cousins and lots of activity going on. I loved people being around because then my parents seemed much happier. Most of all I loved my bedroom with its old fireplace, and I imagined how cosy the room would have been in the days when the fireplace had a roaring fire. There was also an airing cupboard in the corner which made it warmer in the winter. From my bedroom window, I could see the back garden and loved looking out onto the trees. We were close to the railway, and as I lay in bed, I could feel the vibration of the trains. My dad told me that some of the trains went to London, the capital of our country where my mum lived for a while before she got married, and I imagined it to be the most sophisticated place in the world. I could tell by the way that he talked about London that dad liked it there, and I told myself that one day I would go and live in London, and dad could come and visit me like he had gone to visit mum.

The best thing ever about our new home was that the lock on bedroom door was on the inside, which meant no more being locked in; even better, I could lock people out if I wanted when I was older (until then the lock was too high for me to reach). As I lay in bed on one of the first nights in our new house, I felt happy listening to the chatter and laughter downstairs and wished that I could stay like that forever.

I remember our first Halloween 'duck-apple' party. The thrill of my older cousins coming on a school night was immense. Blindfolded, we raced to bite apples on strings, and we pushed our blind-folded heads into the washing basin filled with flour to retrieve wrapped sweets with our teeth. I still love October-time today because the smell of the air reminds me of a time when everything was exciting and happy.

I recall another significant memory from that time which inspired me with a sense of awe and generally happened spontaneously just before I fell asleep, and usually when I was relaxed but still aware of my thoughts. Let me explain. As I lay in bed, my mind would follow a train of thoughts which questioned why we are here. Where do we come from? What would happen if I wasn't here? This last question was usually the trigger. Just when I would try and imagine my non-existence, I would become aware of the vast space not just in our world, but within our universe, and it was as if the whole of the vast universe would be, for a tiny fraction of time, within me. I would try and hold the feeling as long as possible, but after a few seconds, it would burst like a balloon, and as it did an expansion of thought and feeling would occur to me. It didn't last long, but I delighted in the experience.

Yours,

Michaela

Chapter 8

24th July 2009

Dear St Thérèse,

Even though you lost your mother at an early age, you were much loved as a child. You were the youngest of nine children and claimed your older sister Pauline as a surrogate mother when your mother died.

My life between the ages of six and ten consists of the happiest of my childhood memories. When I joined St Anthony of Padua Catholic Primary School the school term was nearly six weeks old. My brother David started in the class below. I was nervous when the Headmistress showed me around the new school and explained that the class teachers had already taken the registers for the day. I didn't understand until a girl with the longest plaits I had ever seen marched along the corridor carrying the big class registers.

'Thank you, Janette,' said the Headmistress taking the registers from her.

'This is our new girl Michaela who will be joining your class.'

Janette smiled at me and walked off to her classroom with her plaits swaying. A little while later, I was taken to my class and introduced as the new girl. Janette smiled at me shyly as I looked out at all the new faces in front of me.

Helen, another girl in my class, also smiled at me with a big mischievous welcoming grin.

These two girls were to become my best friends over the next 12-year period. Firstly, Helen was my best friend during primary school, and then Janette during our teenage years. Ironically, Janette and I didn't go to the same high school, and while Helen and I did choose the same high school, we hardly spoke there, but I am rushing ahead and will get to that later.

Until we left primary school, Helen and I had a close friendship, and if you asked me to sum it up, the theme would be of adventure and exploration. We had many 'firsts' together which stick firmly in my mind.

The first time we ever attempted to skip school together, we got caught. Aged ten, Helen and I decided that we wanted to go to her house for the afternoon. We agreed that we would say that we needed to go to her house to get her swimming kit for the after-school swimming club. The teacher said, 'Okay, but be quick and don't let Mrs Farrell catch you.' Mrs Farrell being the extremely strict Headteacher.

We enthusiastically and angelically nodded our agreement, but we had no intention of returning to school after lunch, we were going on an adventure. In the spirit of daring, we convinced ourselves and each other that no one would notice us missing. On leaving the school grounds, we squealed with delight and ran to the newsagents and bought crisps and sweets.

For me, it wasn't long before the excitement waned and became nervousness. I had never seen the streets around the school so quiet. In our school uniforms, we stood out as being at large during school hours. I felt that everyone we met along the way knew that we should have been at school. My wish that we were back in class grew rapidly, but I consoled myself with the thought that we did have permission to leave. I suggested to Helen that our adventure was perhaps not as much fun as we thought it would be. But Helen, the intrepid explorer, was adamant that we were going to her house as it would be empty, and we were going to eat the strawberry tarts she knew to be in the fridge. I reluctantly carried on walking beside her.

We had just reached the corner of Helen's road when I stopped to look across towards the row of local shops because I felt uncomfortable, as if we were being watched. My heart sank. The Headmistress was standing watching us from the opposite side of the road. I told Helen, and she stopped and stared back. We stood as if frozen to the spot and she stood glaring at us. But there was something wrong. She didn't look right to me. When cross, Mrs Farrell always stood with her hands on her hips, but she seemed to be holding them behind her back. Then I realised what looked out of place when a faint cloud of smoke rose from the back of her head. She was holding a lit cigarette and trying to hide it behind her back. I was wondering who had caught who until she shouted, 'You two, get back to school now! If you are not in the playground in ten minutes, you will find yourselves in big trouble. Move!'

Without even looking at each other, Helen and I turned around and ran as fast as we could and didn't stop until we were inside the school gate. Then we collapsed into each other's arms breathless from the running and the fit of giggles that came upon us.

'How long have we got?' I asked Helen still panting (being literal about the ten-minute curfew).

'About nine minutes left,' said Helen, and then we were almost on our knees with laughter when we realised how quickly we had run back to school.

We hid behind the infant's block and waited to see her car approach the school gate before we ran into our playground and joined in a game as if we had been there all along.

We don't know if Mrs Farrell ever did check the playground that afternoon. My guess is that she certainly would have made sure that we were back at school, but she never said anything to us about the incident. I prefer to think of it now, not as the day that we got caught outside of school, but the day we caught the Headmistress smoking!

Another first with Helen was a forbidden trip to Sefton Park Lake one Saturday afternoon which nearly ended in disaster. I was at Helen's house for a sleepover. We told Helen's mum that we were going for a walk, and she said not to go too far. Sefton Park was definitely out of bounds, but we had planned this trip for weeks. I was wearing brand-new brown cord trousers and a brand-new cream and brown jumper, and Helen was wearing good clothes too.

We hadn't been in the park too long when we decided to cross the dell and jump across several stepping stones over a stretch of what appeared to be shallow water. (I have just realised that Helen's mum was called Del, so we achieved our purpose of 'crossing the Dell' in more ways than one.) I hadn't gone too far when I fell into the water, and as I tried to get up, fell again, further away from the stones and into the deep thick mud. I sank so quickly I was shocked and froze. I just stood there sinking, and I was waist deep before I attempted to escape. The thick mud felt like treacle as I struggled desperately to free myself using my arms to help drag my legs toward the bank. I made slow progress. At first, Helen must have been as shocked as me. One minute we were skipping across the stones with giddy excitement, the next I was disappearing into the mud. She froze for a bit too, and I saw her mouth and eyes wide open in surprise. Then suddenly she lay down on the side of the bank and stretched her arms toward me. She grabbed my arms as I lunged towards her and somehow, with a tremendous effort from us both, as quickly as I had fallen in, I was out, and we both lay on the side of the bank panting.

When we stood up, we found that amazingly Helen wasn't too dirty (although her face was muddy) but I was filthy from head to toe. The mud was everywhere, even in my hair and nostrils. On the awkward and uncomfortable walk home, we had time to decide that we had no other option but to tell the truth about what had happened.

What a picture we were when we arrived back at Helen's house: I was covered in thick, slimy, smelly mud which felt like it was encasing me in all the places it had dried and hardened, and Helen looked like a chimney sweep. I was firmly but not unkindly guided straight to the bathroom, and Helen helped me peel off the ruined new clothes. My mum was called and informed of our misadventure, but Helen's mum must have sensed that we had both had a fright and so wasn't too hard on us after the first reprimand.

In Helen's bedroom later, although it was early, we were both in our pyjamas. (I had no option, and Helen was told to get ready for bed early too.) We felt a little bit sorry for ourselves, but we cheered up when we heard muffled but unmistakable laughter coming from the kitchen when my mum arrived with my change of clothes. When Helen's mum called us downstairs, we could tell we were still in trouble by the quiet atmosphere at the tea table, but when I saw Helen's mum and dad grinning at each other when they thought we weren't looking, I worked out that they were partly pretending to be cross.

Back upstairs later we had great fun recounting the day and laughing hysterically at each stage of the adventure. Helen called me 'Mad, Mud Girl', and I made up a scary story about a girl who fell into the mud but when she tried to wash it off, no matter how hard she tried, it wouldn't wash away. As the mud dried, it got harder and harder, and the girl was trapped inside like an Egyptian mummy. Squealing and laughing, I acted out each scene of the story (running around after Helen like a monster), and Helen acted out her version of what happened (mimicking me with pitiful Penelope-Pit-Stop cries for 'Hayulp' as I flayed around in the mud).

Our game kept us amused until the early hours of the morning. We finally fell asleep with whispers of agreement of what a great adventure we had had and what fun we would have telling about it back at school. My only worry, but I kept it secret, was what mum and dad would say when I got home about ruining my brand-new clothes. I decided to offer to wear them whatever state they were until they were threadbare.

Yours,

Michaela

Chapter 9

25th July 2009

Dear St Thérèse,

When you went to the convent, your two older sisters Pauline and Marie were already nuns there, and you were proud to follow them. I was happy to follow my older cousins through primary school, but I wonder how my younger brother felt as he followed me? We were different but very close, and so if he hurt, I hurt. I was extremely protective towards him which must have annoyed him because we did not share the same fears. From an early age, I convinced myself that the secret of survival at school and home were simple. Be good. At all costs. No matter what. I have often fallen short of this maxim, but I believed in it wholeheartedly. Too much depended on being good and the consequences of not being good were too appalling.

I was always worried about David. There are many incidents I can recall, but one of the earliest is the day David was caught on the school roof. I remember standing in the junior playground trembling. The entire school was watching. The usual punishment was a few whacks of the ruler on the palm of an outstretched hand. On this particular day, David was hit so hard on his hands with the wooden ruler that it broke in half. I distinctly recall the thwack of the wood as it hit his little hand and the split second of numbness waiting for my brain to register the pain and the roaring sting of the heavy-handed teacher's wallop. Then the unified gasp as dozens of pairs of eyes saw the broken wood flying up into the air. I saw his mouth open wide, maybe in pain or surprise or both, but he didn't make a sound. The force of the blow also knocked him off balance, and he stumbled, but he immediately recovered putting his two little feet and short-trousered legs together and thrusting his hand back out to receive the rest of his punishment stoically. I was horrified that the teacher had hit David so hard but proud that he was taking it so well. My mixed feelings were set against a background of the white noise of fear of what mum and dad would say when they found out what had happened. Finally, I felt shame as I saw that as usual, some people had turned to me to see how I would react. I was very predictable. I always cried. Although I should have been used to this attention, I was never able to be as composed as David, and I usually dissolved into tears, but not tears of pity, more dread. On this occasion, as my cheeks burned and hot tears flowed, something else unusual happened. It was as though my mind came right out of my body as I stood transfixed staring ahead. What was going on, in reality, was replaced by what was happening in my mind as if being played on a screen in front of me. In my young mind, I imagined that I marched up to my little brother and grabbed his non-injured hand and protectively pulled him away from the teacher who I was sure was about to complete this punishment with the pieces of broken ruler retrieved from the ground. I didn't care what people said or how much trouble I was causing myself. I just wanted to get him away from the angry teacher. Some of the pupils started laughing and then, as if encouraged by my uncharacteristic display of courage, I could hear them cheering louder and louder as I marched David away from the playground and away from everyone. David, surprised by my unexpected outburst, didn't protest at all to being yanked along needing to trot to keep up with my big angry strides.

'This is going too far David!' I shouted.

'No, it was great!' he shouted, trying to free himself from my grip to go and investigate the cheering and clapping which we could still hear amidst the teachers yelling 'Quiet!' at the tops of their voices.

I stopped and let go of him and kneeled down on the ground in despair. I could hear my usual prayers running around my head, 'Please, let this be over quickly and let David not be in too much trouble.' And then it dawned on me that I would be in trouble too for leaving my place in the playground.

Then I came back to the present, and I realised that I had imagined my rescue attempt. As my mind refocused from its inner world to what was going on around me, I could see that David was still standing in front of the teacher, and I was still standing in my place in the playground. Although I knew the difference between reality and daydreams, my desire to rescue David was very strong, and it triggered a temporary out-of-body experience.

This incident is one of the first times I became sharply aware of the enormous difference between what I wished I had done (or not done) and what I did (or did not do). I knew it was for real when I managed to speak to David when his punishment was over. Even though it would make me late back into my classroom, I was unusually brave, and I went to see him where I knew he would be, standing outside his classroom waiting to be summoned to see the Headmistress. As soon as I saw him, my tears started flowing again.

'Don't worry Chael,' David said, knowing what would be worrying me. I couldn't speak for crying so just tried to tidy his pullover and straighten his hair for what was coming next, and he let me fuss over him.

I didn't even attempt my usual scolding and 'Why did you do it?' conversation. When challenged about anything, David rarely tried to deny or hide the truth. It wasn't in his nature to tell lies to get away with naughty behaviour. In fact, his loyalty often got him into more trouble because he would never tell tales on anyone and was often in deeper trouble than he deserved because of it. This time, I was beyond trying to discover why he had found it necessary to climb onto the school roof. Being in trouble at school was one thing; I was more worried about the trouble he would be in at home, and I was already planning what I could do and say to stick up for him when my parents found out.

Yours,

Michaela

Chapter 10

26th July 2009

Dear St Thérèse,

At Mass this morning there was a notice about your relics coming to the cathedral in September. I was trying to imagine what it will be like when they arrive, and what the casket will be like.

I have always loved attending church services. At primary school, while my classmates groaned in anticipation of long periods of sitting still in silence on cold, hard benches, I loved the solemnity of our little procession, walking in pairs, holding hands, from the school to the parish church. I loved the waxy, incense smell of the church and walking through the massive wooden door and entering the house of God. I never had any problem believing that I was in God's presence and that he would be listening to my prayers.

Before I started school, my Auntie Dorothy took me to Mass one Sunday morning to show me the church beside the school I would be soon attending. On the way, I sat on the saddle of her bike as she wheeled me along. The journey seemed to take hours, and I thought I would never be able to walk all this way to school every day. It seemed so far.

When I entered the church for the first time, I was amazed. The church has a stunning mural of the Last Supper above the altar. I had never seen anything as beautiful in all my life. I looked around at all the people in the church wondering why they were not also gazing upwards in awe at the holiness of the stunning scene above them. The beautiful mural never failed to move me, and I never tired of gazing at the picture of Jesus and his disciples seated at the Last Supper. The image is bright and happy, and the figures seem alive. I used to imagine that Jesus or one of the disciples would turn and smile at each other or peer down into the church to see who was looking up at them. It is with sadness that I tell you, that although it is only a few miles from where I now live, I haven't been in that church for over twenty years. But I know that if I walked in there tomorrow, that mural would still remain one of the most beautiful things I have ever seen.

I was moved when I read about you making your first Holy Communion, and how important it was to you. We have something in common. I took the preparation for my first Holy Communion very seriously, honestly believing that the day when the host touched my tongue for the first time was when I received my first holy personal visit from Jesus. We had several practices in the church in preparation for the event which served to fuel the anticipation. Mum took me to the best bridal shop in Liverpool to buy me my first Holy Communion dress and veil. I loved the full-length cream satin and lace dress with pretty puff sleeves and a high collar that we chose. It felt solemn and special at the same time. It was almost a little wedding dress. I tried it on again at home and just couldn't wait to wear it for real. It sat in mum and dad's wardrobe in its plastic cover waiting for the big day, and I longed to sneak into their bedroom, open the squeaky wardrobe door and push my hand up beneath the plastic to feel the silky satin.

I made my first Holy Communion on 13th June, the feast of St Anthony of Padua (also the feast day of our school, and my brother's birthday) in the church of St Anthony of Padua. Mum had taken the day off work and helped me to get ready. I put on my beautiful long dress and mum did my hair in the most grown-up style I ever had. My long blonde hair was piled up into a bun on top of my head, and my headdress placed on the chignon. The veil stretched behind me. My hair looked just like yours St Thérèse in the photo of you when you changed your hairstyle to make you look older for a visit to Mgr Hugonin, Bishop of Bayeux, to seek permission to enter the convent at 15 years of age.

I was excited and extremely nervous when I arrived at the church forecourt. I saw the rest of my class standing outside waiting to enter in a solemn procession as we had practised. Mrs Farrell, the Headteacher stood beside the children, grinning. It was unusual to see her smiling, and you could see her tobacco-stained teeth. We didn't see her teeth often because she rarely smiled at pupils, only parents. It was time to say goodbye to mum who seemed reluctant to leave me. She was looking at everyone around us with an expression I couldn't read. Then I noticed that all the other girls somehow looked different to me. I was the odd one out. Mrs Farrell approached staring at me and said in her most dramatic voice, 'Michaela Loughney is wearing a long dress! I specifically said, no long dresses allowed!'

Before I had time even to think, let alone speak, mum said in just as dramatic a tone 'Oh I am so sorry Mrs Farrell! I must have missed that memo, but doesn't she look beautiful.' To my complete surprise, Mrs Farrell said warmly, 'Yes, she does!' and then walked away smiling.

'Oh my goodness,' I thought, 'I am the only one wearing a long dress', and all my pleasure drained away. I must have looked like I was about to crumble because mum was saying in my ear, 'Don't' worry sweetheart, you are the most beautiful girl here'.

I didn't say what I was thinking, 'I don't care how beautiful I look; I just want to look the same as the other girls!' When it was time to join the procession in the church, I took my place and kept my head down trying not to meet the eyes of any of the other girls. The ceremony itself was everything I expected, and I felt the holiest ever as the priest put the little host on my tongue. All thoughts of long dresses and short dresses faded into insignificance compared with the magnitude of accepting Jesus for the first time. Afterwards, there was a communion breakfast in the Church Hall, and within a few minutes of sitting at the table, I spoilt my beautiful dress as I accidentally tipped half a tumbler of orange squash over myself. I cried then with the burning hot discomfort of being different, disappointment at spoiling my dress and the joy my first Holy Communion had given me. For one of the first times in my life I felt special and that I belonged, but the belonging did not relate to my classmates, it was something else. It was a wonderful day. No one mentioned the length of my beautiful dress to me again. But later that night, I was standing on the landing of the stairs at home, listening to mum and dad talking in the kitchen. I heard my dad ask my mum if she had known about the 'no long-dresses rule'.

'Of course not,' she said, followed by silence in which I imagined her smiling at my dad, putting her finger to her lips in the gesture of 'quiet' and nodding her head as if to say, 'Of course I did, it was a silly rule.'

Another two childhood experiences that had a similar impact on me (but not quite as intense as the church) were when I saw my first swimming pool (age six) and my first visit to the local lending library (slightly older). They were similar to the church in the wonder and awe they evoked. To this day, I still feel a thrill of delight at setting eyes on a swimming pool (particularly an empty one where the water is still and clear) and entering a library (or even a bookshop) is still exciting. Today I swim regularly and am in a bookshop as often as possible. Sadly, my attendance at any church in the past has been much less regular.

Yours,

Michaela

Chapter 11

27th July 2009

Dear St Thérèse,

Your relationship with God was well established from a young age. You delighted in his presence. When did I first feel God's presence?

When David and I were very young we would often play 'ships' in my bedroom, where single beds became our personal ships, and every bit of visible carpet was the sea, and the dressing table and wardrobe were distant islands. We were each captain of our own ships. I felt safe, as if a presence watched over us, and would survey with pride every inch of my ship (marked by the squares in the checked, brown and beige woolly bedspread). Looking back, I can see that while the ship scenario came from our imaginations, the presence felt real. One time I not only felt a presence, I saw someone too.

I was woken one night when I was about seven or eight by the sound of a child calling my name. At first, I thought it was David calling me from his bedroom along the landing, but then I realised that the voice was coming from somewhere much closer, somewhere within my room. Sleepily I got out of bed, and although my room was only dimly lit by the light from the landing coming in, I tried to sense if someone else was in the room, but couldn't see anyone. Too afraid to disturb my parents by putting the light on, I stood and listened to try and understand where the voice was coming from. I decided it must be coming from the tall toy cupboard in the corner. Only just tall enough on tiptoe to reach the handle to open the door, I was surprised to find a little boy with blonde hair sitting in the bottom. He just squinted a little and rubbed his eyes as he looked up at me. I asked him if he was okay and what he was doing there, and he didn't say anything, but I felt that he was trying to tell me something by the earnest look in his huge eyes. I tried to coax him out of the dark cupboard, but he pulled back from me as if he didn't want to come out, but he looked sad more than frightened.

'How horrible,' I thought, that he preferred to be sitting in the dark cupboard in the middle of the night. I wasn't at all afraid of him. He had a slight golden glow around his features, and he felt warm when I touched his hand to coax him out of his confined space. I wondered who the little boy was. I thought it must be my brother David looking strange in the dim light. I then realised that although his hair was the same golden colour as David's and he looked much like him in size, the boy in the cupboard was too still and peaceful to be my boisterous little brother. I don't remember saying goodbye to the boy and going back to bed.

When I woke the next day, my first thought was, 'I wonder if he is still in the toy cupboard?' and I jumped out of bed to check. The toy cupboard door was open, and I was surprised not to see the small golden figure crouching in the bottom. The memory was very vivid. It didn't seem at all like a dream. It felt real. But in the cold light of day, there was only one possible explanation: I must have dreamed it, but to this day I still wonder about the experience.

You didn't see little boys hidden in toy cupboards, but you did have a premonition when you were looking out of the window as a young girl and you saw a stooped man, who looked like your father, slowly making his way across the garden. Although the suffering stooped man resembled your father in his physical appearance, he seemed gravely sad and walked with his back bent in pain, as if in tremendous suffering. At the time your father was full of vitality and experience of a vision of a future version of your father upset you. I recall a similar experience of sadness which seemed to come out of the nowhere and its effect on me didn't appear to match the gravity of the situation. Did I have a premonition of the loss that was to come to me?

About seven or eight years old lying in my parents' bed in the afternoon – a special treat because I was unwell – I fell asleep crying. When I awoke, it was early evening and dark. I lay in the dark alone and clutching to my side Tina, my favourite doll. She was a chubby baby doll with short brown curly hair and a comfort to me as I lay in bed thinking. I used to think about things a lot, sad things, and that afternoon my mind travelled ahead to when I would be an adult and probably would not have Tina anymore. I remember the intense love for my doll mixed with sadness that she would be lost to me when I was grown up. I cried so hard that I was either heard by my mum or cried out for someone to come. My mum came and sat on the bed and asked me what was wrong, and I told her the truth. I was sad because when I was older, Tina would be gone and I would miss her terribly. Mum comforted me and reassured me that although I probably wouldn't have Tina when an adult, I didn't need to be so sad because I could remember the feeling of love for Tina, and this memory could stay in my heart forever if I wished.

I wonder if this was a premonition.

Yours,

Michaela

Chapter 12

28th July 2009

Dear St Thérèse,

You experienced several significant changes in your childhood. Our family life changed forever in 1975 when I was ten. My brother and I arrived home from school one day to find both my parents and my aunt at home, an unusual event because mum came home a couple of hours after us. Mum and dad didn't hear us come in, so we went to sit in the kitchen as we knew something was wrong. I saw mum's gold wedding ring on top of the fridge. Mum was in the living room, and I heard her say to my aunt, 'It's over, my marriage is over.' My dad was in the dining room alone. I didn't let anyone know that I had heard these words. Later mum's wedding ring was back on her wedding-ring finger, and she and dad presented a united front acting as if everything was normal.

A few days later when my brother was at his friend's house, mum and dad sat me down in the living room and said they had something important to tell me. I felt shocked when they said that they loved my brother and me very much but they didn't love each other anymore, and they would be splitting up. I didn't know what splitting-up meant, but I did know that I was more worried about my brother than myself at how he would react to the news. Straight afterwards, I went in the car with mum and dad to collect David from his friend's house. On the short journey, distressed that I was about to witness my brother's life changing forever, I wondered how he would react to the news that my parents would be splitting up. I felt guilty for not being able to stop it happening and that I was somehow responsible for this awful event. It was a nagging fear that there must have been something I could do to stop this happening.

David recently told me of his recollections of that day and reminded me of something I had forgotten. Mum simply said to David, 'Your dad, and I are splitting up' as if it was something that happened every day and gave him a present. It was a single record, 'Oliver's Army' by Elvis Costello. This song always makes me emotional, and perhaps I now know why. Soon after this incident, mum left the family home and moved to a bedsit a couple of miles away. David and I stayed with my dad. This incident was the end of my childhood because, from that day, I felt somehow responsible for everyone's happiness, least of all my own.

I wish I could go back to that ten-year-old child and tell her that she wasn't and isn't responsible for the breakup of her family because it was that sense of responsibility which dictated the course of the next 33 years of my life. I have read about how children can respond to seeing their parents in difficulty: they experience anxiety, and rather than blame their parents for the family problems, children try to take responsibility for what has gone wrong and then often end up blaming themselves. Of course, it is impossible for a child to take full responsibility for the adults in their lives. They can never meet the needs of their parents. It is impossible. However, it doesn't stop many children trying, and I was one of them. I am sure that many parents don't realise all that is going on with their child's thoughts and emotions. Often they are dealing with their own pain. But I would say to any parent who is going through a relationship break-up, please make sure that your child or children don't take responsibility for what has gone wrong. Don't let them experience failure or guilt because if they do, it is likely to stay with them for the rest of their lives.

I remember the day my mum left our family home as being one of the most painful of my whole life even though I don't remember all the details today. I am sure I have deliberately blocked out some of my memories. I do, however, have the clearest vision of one specific moment. I am lying on my bed, and mum says goodnight and tells me that she is leaving but that we will see each other again soon. I ask, 'When?' and she says she's 'Not sure, but later in the week.' I watch her walk out of my room towards the stairs. I am in tears, and although I can't see her face, I can tell by her voice that she is upset too as she says a final goodbye without turning around. Later that night, unable to sleep, I felt sadness so strong that it was a physical pain, like knives tearing up my insides. My only consolation as I lay in bed wondering what I could have done differently to make sure mum didn't leave, was my decision to ask God to bring her back. Surely if I prayed hard enough, my request would be granted. That night and subsequent nights I prayed with all my heart for mum to come home, until my head was hurting with crying and praying; and I didn't stop praying until I fell asleep.

Mum's new home was a bedsit in a large house in a leafy suburban road. The first thing I noticed standing outside the front door on my first visit was the many different types of trees around and the smell of the air. It was different to how the air smelled outside our house. It smelled salty and earthy. Mum's new home was close to the River Mersey, and maybe that was what I could smell. I felt surprised and then betrayed by the beautiful trees and the freshness of the air. It was as if I expected the place to be as dark and as dismal and to smell as rotten as I felt about the whole situation. It seemed odd to me that mum and dad seemed to be getting on far better than ever, and I felt bewildered by their cheerfulness. I understand now that my parents were both trying to make things easier for my brother and me and that they were probably just putting on brave faces to show us that the world hadn't ended just because they had split up. Perhaps they were also relieved not to be fighting anymore. We soon settled into a new routine where mum would visit us often, and every Friday afternoon after school we would go to her bedsit for dinner with dad. After a cheerful spaghetti bolognese on one of these visits, David was asleep with his head on mum's lap, and I had been asleep with my head on my dad's lap. I awoke to hear mum and dad talking in quiet tones. I didn't move or open my eyes so that they wouldn't know that I had woken.

'How are they really?' my mum asked my dad with concern. 'Are you sure they are coping with it all?'

'Of course they are, you mustn't worry about anything,' my dad replied. I remember being so shocked that even if I had wanted to move, I couldn't because my dad had just told the biggest lie in the world, and I didn't want them to know I had heard, so I pretended to be asleep still.

'We are not fine; none of us are,' I wanted to shout, but I didn't. Although I felt upset at what dad said, I instinctively knew he was trying to reassure mum and possibly didn't consider his own feelings for one second. His aim was to make mum feel better.

Practically speaking, dad took perfect care of us but it must have been hard for him on many levels. For instance, for some years he worked shifts, and he couldn't always be there for us physically, and at those times he had to rely on the help of his mother, our nana. Mum would come to the house often, but she worked full-time. When we were too young to be left in the house alone, nana was helpful preparing food, doing housework, etc. I loved nana very much. She could be strict, but often in the midst of chastising us, it was as if all her energy for being cross would drain away and instead of scolding us she would chuckle, and all her anger would seem to go, and we would be so relieved. Sometimes we tried to bring on this change of heart in her, but as we didn't know what caused it, we were usually unsuccessful.

After about six months, I thought all my prayers had been answered when dad announced that mum was coming home. I was ecstatic, but it wasn't long before I discovered that there was a catch. Although she was coming back to live with us, it was explained clearly that it didn't mean that mum and dad were getting back together again. Mum would be living in the front room. At first, I didn't understand the arrangement. I was confused, but then all that mattered was that mum was coming home because she missed my brother and me so much. I was overjoyed, but I vowed there and then I would never forgive her if she left again. This return was her last chance! How harsh I was St Thérèse, putting these conditions on her return, but I reasoned it would be less painful not to have her back at all than to endure the unimaginable pain of losing her a second time.

Yours,

Michaela

Chapter 13

29th July 2009

Dear St Thérèse,

Your time on earth was short being only 24 years. I can't imagine how you became so holy and so wise in such a short space of time. Time has always been both a fascination and source of struggle for me. As a fascination, there is only one thing in this life that I can be sure about, and that is that one day, in the fullness of time, I am going to die.

I am always fighting and resisting time and rushing trying to do too much. I set impossible standards to achieve, and when I inevitably fail, my inner voice chastises me telling me to just try harder, be better and then I won't be a failure.

'I am running out of time' is one of the oldest and most familiar thoughts running through my mind. I don't know why I have been so mindful of time being short throughout my life. I used to think that it meant that I was going to die young, but now it is to do with appreciating that our life on earth is very short and yet often we act as if we are going to live forever. I don't think about the shortness of time in a morbid way: I just really sense it strongly.

On the day that I realised that I could tell the time, I was overjoyed. It was a real epiphany; I felt as though I had woken up to something very important. I felt alive and connected by my new understanding. Sitting in the classroom at junior school watching the teacher demonstrate how the spikes of the clock were the 'hands' and that the circle with the numbers on it was called the 'face' – I was hooked. Hands and faces usually belong to people, and aren't people always important? Understanding time somehow also gave me a new-found sense of having some control over my life, and that day was also the day that I decided that my approach to life was to be the very best person I could be. It was probably also when the roots of perfectionism took hold within me. Striving to be good became my life purpose, and time was a significant measurement for me. If I was 'on time' I was good, if late, I was bad. I often failed miserably at being good; with an extremely punctual father, my tendency to lateness brought me more than a few reprimands when I was late home from school.

As I got older, my fascination with time progressed from punctuality to the capacity of time. My goal was to see how much activity, homework, reading, praise, work I could cram into my days. This was one of the ways in which I sought approval from external sources. My identity was starting to develop based on how competent or well behaved I was rather than on how I felt about myself. Even at this young age, my self-esteem was low. My excitement about mum coming back to live in our family home was the prospect of having the opportunity to earn her love. Deep down I felt that I was responsible for her leaving in the first place and that if I were just good enough, she wouldn't want ever to leave again.

Mum's return helped develop my faith. I had prayed so hard after mum left that her return was proof to me that God was listening. He had heard my prayers and was sending mum back to dad, David and me. With renewed faith, I worked hard at earning mum and dad's approval and being worthy of God's love.

Yours,

Michaela

Chapter 14

30th July 2009

Dear St Thérèse,

I wonder how you felt when you first went to live in the convent: did you imagine that you would spend the rest of your life there? I know you were happy to be there and to be reunited with your beloved sisters, especially Pauline whom you missed so much when she left your family home to enter the convent six years before you did. I have read descriptions about you saying how brave you were to have suffered so many losses of the people you loved. I identify with these losses in that, although my mum didn't tragically die like yours did, I did lose my mum again after she had returned to our family home, but I am rushing my story again.

When mum moved back in with us, I helped her 'move in' to the room which was to be her new 'bedsit'. Although dad, mum, David and I were all at the same address as a family again, it felt strange, much more formal. Without being told to, I used to knock before I entered her room to respect her privacy. Looking back, I can see that mum's return coincided with the loss of my 'ideal' mum. Believing it was my fault that things were different, I tried not to dwell on it and concentrated on being good and responsible and grown up to ensure that mum didn't leave again.

Around the same time, I experienced another loss and the perceived deserved rejection of someone I loved very much. When I started my first year at secondary school after the long summer holiday, I was nervous but much looking forward to a joyful reunion with Helen, my best friend from primary school. We had seen little of each over the school holidays which was unusual, and I put it down to the preparations for going to our new school. I have never fully recovered from the shock of finding Helen completely changed towards me. Not only did she not want to be my friend anymore, but she was acting as if she didn't know me. I felt confused and rejected. On several occasions, I tried to speak to her as we had when we had been so close as best friends at primary school. These clumsy approaches seemed to make her worse. Her hurtful ignoring of me became openly aggressive. The hostility resulted in us physically fighting each other one day. I didn't want to fight her, but I didn't want to be bullied either, and when she challenged me to meet her outside the school gates, I turned up feeling physically sick with fear and, unlike her, without an entourage of supporters. We fought physically. We pulled each other's hair and scratched each other's skin. The fight was witnessed by what seemed like most of the rest of the school. I didn't care that Helen was deemed to be the victor. It didn't get me any closer to understanding why she had rejected me, and it was the 'why' that was tormenting me.

'What had I done wrong? Why did she seem to hate me so much?' It was so devastating that I wanted to leave the school, but was too ashamed to tell anyone.

Losing Helen's friendship affected me so much that I didn't make many close friends at the secondary school. In time I developed a new best friend outside of school in the form of Janette who I mentioned earlier as the first person I met on my first day at primary school (with the beautiful long plaits). We had been friendly at primary school but attended different secondary schools, so we hardly saw each other. However, I bumped into Janette one day and told her what had happened with Helen, and Janette was very kind and sympathetic, and although we were the same age, I found in Janette someone who I looked up to. Looking back, I can see that she was perhaps more emotionally mature, and was quite maternal and protective of me. We stayed close friends right through secondary school.

Added to the disastrous start to secondary school with Helen, I also felt the weight of being a disappointment for being chubby and clumsy and not at all sporty like my older cousin had been before me. My form teacher in the first year was also one of the PE teachers, and on first meeting, I could see her surprise (and disappointment?) at how unlike my athletic cousin I was.

I have read that you didn't like school St Thérèse, and I felt the same. Although I did try to fit into secondary school, I mostly found it unpleasant and frightening. Things were difficult at home and challenging at school; I felt alone and deserving of rejection. I had two sources of respite in two of the teachers, the English teacher who was strict but encouraging and the eccentric Economics teacher who told me I would be a writer one day. He was an author and presented me with a signed copy of one of his books. I have treasured this book for nearly 30 years. Co-incidentally, I heard only today that this lovely man died last week aged 85. He was a much-loved artist in his retirement, and I have one of his prints which is a charming view of the Albert Dock in Liverpool, one of my favourite places.

During this time at school, my faith was alive to the extent that I believed in God, but I felt undeserving of love. I longed for the loving God I thought existed and might have found him at that age had I not felt so burdened. There was one time when I briefly glimpsed a carefree life, and it happened in the Dolomite mountains, when I was 14, on a school skiing trip to Italy.

The person who left on the coach was hardly recognisable from the one who came back. We arrived at our hotel in the Dolomites in the cold-dark-drizzling night and then, next morning, when we left the hotel to go to the ski slopes I was amazed. I had never seen anything so beautiful in all my life as the land covered in crisp, crunchy snow, and the trees and snow-capped mountains seemed like a wonderland bathed in bright sunshine. I closed my eyes and lifted my face to the sun and its unexpected warmth streaming from the bluest of cloudless skies. I adored the effect of the sunlight reflected on the snow. Everywhere was pure and like nothing I had ever seen.

I had never skied before but found that I loved it and was surprisingly rather good at it. Because I wasn't afraid to fall over, indeed, I rather enjoyed tumbling in the snow, and it made everyone laugh so much. In the first few days, I spent loads of time on my back with my legs and skis all tangled, laughing my head off because it was lovely landing on the soft snow and lying on my back and looking up at the cloudless blue sky. I also crashed into a few trees and gave myself some large bruises, but the whole experience was so enjoyable I hardly felt any pain. Each night at the end of the skiing we would all have dinner and tell tales of who had been the most hilarious, and I noticed that I was getting mentioned a lot.

This holiday is the first time I felt popular. I wasn't used to being the centre of attention and shy-reserved Michaela discovered how much she enjoyed it. One morning at breakfast I had to report to one of the teachers that the wardrobe in my room had broken. I was worried that my taste of carefreeness was going to be short-lived when asked to explain across the breakfast table (in front of everyone) what had happened to damage the wardrobe, and I told the truth. I had been hanging my jumper in the wardrobe when out of the corner of my eye I noticed a furry creature (I hoped it was a mouse) run from under the dressing table towards the wardrobe. I got such a fright that I jumped into the wardrobe, but it fell forwards and toppled over with me inside. In my panic not to meet the mouse, I scrambled out of the wardrobe, but the door got accidentally damaged in the process. While I was telling the story, some of the girls giggled but stifled their laughs because the teachers were looking solemn. When I finished my tale, the teacher who had asked for the explanation just stared at me. For a few moments, she didn't say anything, and I thought, 'I'm in deep trouble here'; she is so angry she doesn't know what to say and then she exploded, into fits of laughter.

'Oh Michaela,' she said, 'that could only have happened to you.'

I was very relieved. My new-found popularity even spread to the opposite sex. On a couple of evenings, we were allowed to go to the disco in the hotel, and there were some older Italian boys there. The best looking was Gerberto, and all the girls admired him, but none of them dared approach him. But guess who he came and spoke to? I don't know what he said when he first approached me because my Italian isn't very good. He probably asked me if I would like some crisps. I was just so shocked that he chose me. I thought at first that he might have been fulfilling a dare, but he stayed faithful to me all week. He was everything I imagined a handsome Italian boy would be.

On the last day, we all took a skiing exam, including the teachers. In the evening after dinner, we all gathered in the lounge to find out who had passed the exam. One of the teachers said that there would be a presentation for the person who had come top in the exam and to my disbelief the prize was awarded to me. I had achieved the highest mark. I thought it was a joke at first but then realised that it was true. I was chuffed beyond belief to have done so well, and everyone seemed as surprised as I was. Hearing the applause of my schoolmates and teachers was one of the happiest moments of my life, and just when I thought things couldn't get better, they did. There was another presentation, and before I knew it everyone was looking and smiling at me and clapping and cheering again, I had been awarded a prize for being the Best Laugh of the Week! I was very surprised and extremely happy.

On the way home the teacher said that the trip had brought me out of my shell. She was right. When our coach arrived back at the school gates at the end of the journey, I saw my mum and dad waiting on the pavement, and they looked so serious that my heart sank. 'Something bad has happened,' I thought, but when I climbed off the coach they were both beaming and hugged and kissed me like they had never done before. They told me later that they had been worried sick all week because I had promised to phone them and I didn't. Usually, I was vigilant and doing what they asked, but it must have gone out of my head. When I told them how much I enjoyed myself and they seemed to be pleased, for once I didn't feel guilty about not thinking about them all week.

This was an important event for me in the path to me finding my true self. It was my first time away from home on my own for so long and to another country, and I had thrived! If only my life had continued in this vein.

Thank you for listening.

Yours,

Michaela

Chapter 15

31st July 2009

Dear St Thérèse,

It was inevitable that as mum and dad were living separate lives that sooner or later one of them would meet someone else. I guessed it wouldn't be dad, but I was still surprised when mum announced that she and her boss were 'going out together'.

In 1979, we lost mum for the second time when she moved out again, to live with Paul, who became her husband in 1980. It wasn't such a shock this time, I was 15, and I wanted mum to be happy. I coped by pretending I was okay and didn't confide in and be honest with anyone about how I really felt. I tried to be good, but often I was only pretending because my real motivation wasn't a strong morality, more a fear of being found lacking. The worst thing that could have happened would have been for someone to see through the role I played, and yet this is what I yearned for: for someone to see how lonely and disconnected I was. So the very thing I worked hard to prevent happening (that people would see the 'real me') was the very thing I longed for.

Most week days my brother and I woke to the sound of the telephone ringing in an adult-free house. It was the telephone 'wake-up call' from my dad which he made daily from work at about 7.30am (he started at 7am and left the house at 6.30am).

It became a battle of wills between David and me as to who could ignore the phone ringing the longest without giving in. I would usually crack first, fearful of annoying dad that he had been kept hanging on and waiting for us to answer for too long. I usually knew when we had left the 'who will resist answering the phone the longest' too long because when I picked up the phone, I would hear a click telling me the phone line had been disconnected.

At these times my heart would sink, and I would shout up the stairs to David who would still be lying in bed, 'We've had it now, dad didn't speak!' Dad was probably just relieved to know that we were up, and didn't have time to talk. As time went on, I took responsibility for being the eldest and tried to be ungrudging about getting out of bed first and answering the phone and making breakfast for my brother and myself.

Yours,

Michaela

Chapter 16

1st August 2009

Dear St Thérèse,

The summer I was 16, I uncharacteristically and confidently announced to my family that I wouldn't be returning to my convent school to enter the Sixth Form. I decided that I wanted to study theatre and drama so I applied to go to a technical college to do Theatre Studies but found the course was full and the auditions had all finished. Bravely, I went and appealed to the Principal of the college, but he said he was sorry and that I should apply again next year. I accepted this decision with disappointment but felt sure that there was nothing else I could do other than wait for another year.

One of the most significant incidents of my life was my mum's refusal to accept this decision on my behalf. At first, she encouraged me not to take no for an answer, but it felt pointless to me to resist the decision because the course was full. This was something that I couldn't change, but mum had other ideas. A battle began and lasted for the next couple of weeks up until the day of enrolment. Although I wasn't expected at the college, my mum had 'persuaded' me to attend and ask for a place and asked my eldest cousin to accompany me (or make sure that I went). It seemed to me to be the most embarrassing thing in the world just to turn up and ask to join the course.

All my protestations about the need to pass an audition were futile. 'Just go,' she kept saying, 'they'll take you when they see you.' I didn't dare disobey, but on the day of enrolment, I felt terrified as I turned up at the college and searched for the right classroom. My knees were knocking, and I was shaking like a leaf when I found the right room and stood outside with my cousin beside me who tried to calm me.

'Go on,' she said, 'now or never.' Perhaps she felt sorry for me maybe believing my attempts to be as futile as I did. My recollection tells me that my cousin opened the classroom door and almost pushed me into the stuffy room (in reality she is too gentle to have pushed me, it was my mum metaphorically pushing not my cousin). As I 'fell' into the room I stumbled and stood with my back right against the door which had slammed behind me. It drew everyone's attention towards me. I saw a room packed with people seated around tables and not a vacant chair in sight. A tall, well-built man with a booming voice and a grey beard stood at the front of the room. Everyone turned towards me as I trembled in the doorway.

'You're late,' boomed the loudest voice I had ever heard from a man with the bushiest beard I had ever seen. He turned away as if he expected me to sit down quickly and quietly to avoid any further interruption, but I just stood there. I didn't move because I didn't dare just sit down and pretend that I was an authorised student.

'I ... I ...' I stammered.

'What are you trying to say, girl? Speak up,' he boomed.

In terrified obedience, I found the loudest voice possible and shouted, 'I want to join this course, and I know it is full, but thought that someone might not have turned up, so came just in case.' And then I breathed. My fate was in his hands. I surprised myself. Even with all my mum's cajoling, I didn't believe that I could have stood up and told the truth in front of so many strangers with the possibility (or certainty) of rejection, and yet I had done it, and for that, I felt relieved. The whole room seemed suddenly silent and like me, waiting to see what happened next.

'Hmm,' said the beard. The silence which followed although probably only lasted a few seconds seemed to last forever. I had time to tell myself to turn around and walk out of the door and to try and pretend that I had walked into the wrong room by mistake and that there was a warm welcome waiting for me in the right classroom further up the corridor.

'If you can tell me the difference between the meaning of the words objective and subjective you can stay.' I breathed again and gave my answer, fairly confident that it was right but not convinced that I wasn't being used as improvised entertainment.

After I had given my answer, the beard smiled and said, 'You can sit down. You are in.' A couple of people close to where I was standing made room for me, and I sat down between them. They both smiled warmly, and I felt something I had rarely felt before. Maybe it was acceptance, perhaps an achievement, maybe happiness, perhaps relief; whatever it was, it felt good. I later learned (a few months into the course) from the beard (Course Director) just how lucky I was to pass this audition as the course was oversubscribed and that there was a long waiting list. When I asked him about the spontaneous audition he told me that he was impressed by my daring to show up on the day without a place, he thought I had 'worthy assets'.

In the days preceding 'the audition', I resented my mother's 'you can't win if you don't try' lectures, convinced that there was no way I would be able to enrol in the oversubscribed course. However, I was glad that I had been too afraid to disobey her. When I ecstatically reported that I had got onto the course, she just said, 'I knew you would.' I could still shudder at the potential humiliation and disappointment that was in store for me if I hadn't succeeded, and at how oblivious my mum seemed to be to the risk of this for me.

I have always given my mum credit for me getting into college, saying, 'If she hadn't pushed me …' and 'She was right, I was wrong …'; but in hindsight, I can see another dimension at work. It was more than my will that got me into college that day. I look back and see a terrified teenager and her patient cousin and another presence that gave me the courage not to run away but to go and ask for what I wanted.

Thank you, for being with me, as I recall and record this turning point in my life.

Yours,

Michaela

Chapter 17

2nd August 2009

Dear St Thérèse,

At Mass this morning, I felt peaceful to be in the cathedral with Terry. The choir sang beautifully and afterwards, we went to have a bowl of soup in the café and then to the gift shop. The collection of books about you has grown. I want to read them all!

I have almost finished reading your autobiography 'Story of a Soul', and the lessons and insights from your writings are inspiring. I am learning about your wisdom in matters of faith and psychology. Your doctrine teaches that God doesn't want us to be guilty. We should view God as a loving parent who loves us whatever we do. All we need to do is to trust. One of my biggest problems lies in trusting. When I was a child, I believed in God, and had I kept him as my foremost authority I might have retained my confidence, but unfortunately, I felt responsible for others and things that weren't my responsibility.

So much has happened in the last ten days in the form of powerful coincidences. The first coincidence I have already mentioned, about hearing the news that one of my favourite teachers, Frank Hendry, has sadly passed away. I have also written about the sadness of losing my childhood friend Helen, but then, out of the blue last week I was invited to a reunion lunch with her – my best friend at primary school and main adversary at secondary school. I hadn't seen Helen for 28 years, and she is home for a holiday. Now she lives in Houston, Texas with her husband and son. It was unbelievable to meet up with her again after all these years. I am sure that you are arranging these 'coincidences' of people from my past coming into my life at this time. It is healing.

Let me tell you what happened with Helen. Amazingly, at the very time that Frank Hendry's requiem was taking place at the Liverpool Metropolitan Cathedral, Christ the King (on Friday 24th July 2009 at 12.15pm), I was standing outside Barclays Bank on Allerton Road waiting for friends, Maureen and Helen. Except for one meeting with Maureen four months ago, I hadn't seen either of these women for 28 years. 'Blimey,' I thought, 'between us, we have got nearly 90 years to catch up within the next couple of hours!' I felt excited at seeing Helen again, and as we came face to face and threw our arms around each other, I knew that I wasn't going to be disappointed. Helen looked amazing. Despite the years, I could still see my childhood friend in the sophisticated woman. I had loved Helen like a sister, and as we held each other, I sense the love of that friendship returning and enfolding us in our embrace.

'I have waited over 30 years for this hug,' I thought.

'That was worth waiting for,' I said to Helen about our hug, and she kissed my cheek, and we grinned at each other. My heart danced with joy at our reunion, because what had happened between us as young girls and teenagers had broken my heart and had not been fully healed by time. It was as if the years just rolled away as she teased me, 'Do you remember when you fell into Sefton Park Lake, and I had to pull you out?' I was amazed that Helen remembered the incident so well. She could even remember what my mum was wearing when she came to bring me fresh clothes. Mum had been playing tennis when she got the call Helen remembered that she was still in her white tennis dress. The picture of a perfect mum!

As we were walking across the road to the restaurant, Helen said something in a fantastic Texan drawl that made my heart jump.

'Honey, why did we fall out?' I had anticipated meeting Helen with excitement for our happy memories and sadness for the friendship we lost, but I had no intention of quizzing her about why she had fallen out with me. But when she said those words, it all came back to me as if it had happened yesterday and not over 30 years ago. As we walked beside each other, and she linked her arm through mine, my mind replayed like a fast-forwarded movie the following scenes. Being told by my parents to choose my secondary school, and although I had passed the 11-plus entrance exam to a better school, choosing to stay with Helen. I saw us starting school, and although we were in different classes, I saw myself naively thinking that we would meet at break and lunchtime, and the reality of Helen making it clear early on that I was her ex-best friend. I remembered the upset at knowing she didn't want to know me anymore as one of the saddest things that had happened to me after mum and dad splitting up. I saw my 11-year-old self wandering around the school alone scared and rejected because Helen didn't just ignore me, she became the 'cock' of the school and had it in for me. I saw us fighting at the school gates and spending the following five years of school wondering what I had done wrong and the torment of not knowing why my best friend acted as if she hated me. Helen then solved a mystery for me that I had lived with for over 30 years. She explained that I hadn't done anything at all to upset her; she had just rebelled against everything when she got to high school, including our friendship. She explained some of the reasons for this rebellion, and I completely understood.

If only I had known then, I might have been able to help her and would have saved myself years of heartache. But hindsight also showed me how much I just assumed it was my fault and took responsibility for Helen's unexplained and sudden adverse reaction to me. It was never my fault. It was never about anything I had done to her; it was for her personal reasons. How often have I made this mistake in life and caused myself untold heartache by assuming that something has been to do with me, has been my fault, when in fact it has been nothing to do with me? In fact, it is egotistical to think things are of my making (good and bad) when they aren't.

Please, help me see the blessing of this understanding. Thank you for healing my relationship with Helen and please help me to be less sensitive and less focused on myself and more focused on helping others in future.

Yours,

Michaela

Chapter 18

3rd August 2009

Dear St Thérèse,

You loved to perform plays. The theatre and music school was an exciting hub of musicians practising, actors rehearsing, and dance classes. We were living our 'Fame Academy' (a popular American TV programme at the time). The old building had a unique smell of sweaty leather dance shoes, musty wardrobes of stage costumes and props, wooden floors, books and the resin and waxes the musicians used for their instruments. College routine and its atmosphere was so much different to school, and I loved it! I woke up looking forward to the day rather than dreading it. On these mornings I would play my OMD or Queen, or John Travolta records; or David would play his Elvis Costello. David left the house earlier than me, and once I was alone, I was free to dance around the dining room as I ate my breakfast. I see my teenage self with big eighties hair and punky clothes dancing wildly around the room with my arms in the air, waving my piece of toast like a flag. I loved OMD's songs about the Maid of Orleans and used to wish that I would grow up to be such a heroine like Saint Joan of Arc.

I read that you loved Joan of Arc, and you even wrote and acted in a play about her. I have seen the photo of you dressed as her. I love that image because it reminds me so strongly of my younger self. Isn't it a coincidence that we both loved Joan of Arc and isn't it ironic that just as my young self wanted to be like her, I now aspire to be like you? I know that I could never in my wildest dreams aspire to be a saint, but I can strive to follow the example of your loving, kind, patient, calm disposition.

At college, I felt so grown up. We smoked in the canteen and often went to the pub at lunchtime. My fellow students were all aspiring actors and stage managers, and we got on well, and after five years of being an outsider at the convent school, it was wonderful to feel that I belonged. I loved the sensitivities and eccentricities of the people (students and lecturers); I loved the classes, and I even liked the homework. Standards were high, and so the workload was heavy, but I felt alive and happy and enchanted by the world of drama and creativity. Some of the group went on to huge success in their craft, becoming household names and remaining extremely successful and well-known today. One of the most baffling things that I noticed about this group at the time was their sense of purpose and their self-confidence and commitment to success. Like you, many students felt they had a vocation, a calling to their craft. I listened to my fellow students in awe of their self-belief as they talked enthusiastically about their plans for their career and how they knew what they wanted to do with their lives. If anyone ever asked me what I wanted to do, I would make a joke about being into animals and hoped that I didn't end up as the back of a pantomime horse. Interestingly I had just realised that two of my starring roles came when I was cast as a mynah bird (quite a big part in a serious play but played offstage) and the wolf in the pantomime spoof of 'Little Red Riding Hood'. Also, I still make a great impression of an anxious cat and an excited crow.

Although I didn't want to be an actor and was far too shy even to try to be any good at it, I was enthralled by the plays and books we studied and theatre productions we attended. I never told anyone about my secret desire to write (novels or plays) and didn't even try, and just assumed that I wasn't good enough. Hindsight shows me that there is no evidence in my academic career to suggest any truth in this. Indeed, perhaps the opposite is true. I came first in English once, and was in the top set once with a 98 per cent score in an exam. I went on to read English Literature at degree level, my essays were always far too long, and I read avidly. I was wrong to believe that I wasn't good enough. The truth is that I didn't dare to believe I could be a writer and didn't even try because I had zero self-confidence. If I could go back and add the characteristic of confidence to my 16-year-old self and ask her what her vocation was, she would proudly and confidently announce that her life's purpose is to be a writer. Perhaps?

One of your amazing characteristics is self-confidence, and I realise how important it is for everyone, particularly younger people to be taught how to develop confidence. Is it confidence that helps us to change or do we build self-confidence through the act of changing?

Yours,

Michaela

PART THREE

'Soul Sickness'

CHAPTERS 19 TO 38

Chapter 19

4th August 2009

Dear St Thérèse,

You had a very close relationship with your father. He called you 'His Little Queen'. To this day, I am very close to my dad, and he still calls me 'Sugar Plum'. I have seen a picture of the beautiful white statue in the garden of your family home in Lisieux. It commemorates the day that you told your father that you wanted to be a Carmelite nun. Although your father was aware that you didn't want to wait until you were older – as was the custom – and he would miss your presence in his everyday life, he agreed to support you and willingly made the sacrifice because he was keen to follow God's will and for his daughter to follow her calling. In my mind's eye, I see the delicate little white flower like the one your father plucked with its roots intact from its unlikely home growing out of the garden wall. He used the flower as a symbol of your being transferred from one life to another. You became known as the 'Little Flower', a beautiful symbol of resilience forged through embracing vulnerability and developing the strength to succeed against all the odds.

If I were to have the equivalent name, it would have to be 'Little Weed' to reflect my perceived lack of courage. I remember watching as a young child the 'watch with mother' programme, 'Bill and Ben the Flower Pot Men'. The sunflower/dandelion character 'Little Weed' grew between the two flower pot men. It is interesting that when the 1960s/1970s programme was re-launched in 2001, 'Little Weed' was no longer a weed but an enormous sunflower that often helped Bill and Ben in a maternal way.

At 16, in some ways, I was well beyond my years, and in others, I was still very childish. For example, my competence at accurately reading the emotions and moods of others and appropriately responding was well developed, but in other ways, such as understanding my feelings, I was naïve, especially in the romance department.

You didn't need human romantic love. You were Jesus' 'little spouse' and felt complete in this. I spent a lot of time seeking a soulmate. I didn't give up believing that a true soulmate existed for me. My challenge was to find this person, and throughout my life, I tried out several potential soulmates, but I can see that even if the people I picked were not unsuitable, my expectations were.

Yours,

Michaela

Chapter 20

5th August 2009

Dear St Thérèse,

Eager to make a fresh start, I never doubted my decision to go to London to study English Literature and Philosophy aged 18. Compared to the close-knit community of the technical college of my A levels, the London College felt flat and uninviting, and at first, I felt alone. I was absent for the first few weeks of the first term through an illness and missed the opportunity of bonding with other students in my classes. Consequently, I felt like an outsider.

After a slow start, I grew to love my course, and my passion for learning came into its own. I discovered an inner realm of powerful instincts and intuition through the great writers and philosophers. My absolute favourite was DH Lawrence and my thesis on 'The Dominating and Destructive Force of Mother Love in DH Lawrence's' Novels' was one of the most enlightening things I have ever studied. I also loved Shakespeare, although it took me a while to get into the mindset of the man, who helped me understand the depth of emotions as motivators for our behaviours. I also really enjoyed studying Freud as a philosopher (rather than a psychologist), while Jung and my thesis on the 'Dreams as the Royal Road to the Unconscious' were life-changing for me as I discovered the power of dreams and their symbolism. The psychoanalysts also introduced me to the fantastic concepts of the unconscious and defence mechanisms. I recognised (maybe not entirely consciously) that I had a habit of repressing feelings and that the emotional energy that I tried to pretend wasn't there, didn't just disappear. An excellent course called 'States of Consciousness' introduced me to astern philosophies and I loved the eastern approach to understanding the mind as opposed to the western approach of trying to understand behaviour.

So in my first year in London, external circumstances reflected what I was discovering internally: a taste of freedom. I loved exploring the vastness of the capital, from the theatres and bookshops in the West End to the vibrancy of the cosmopolitan community of North London. I never tired of walking along Haringey High Street in the evening and going into the Greek–Cypriot bakeries and grocery shops. Once shop owners got to know me, they would invite me to sample delicious cheeses, bread, and pastries I had never seen before and I didn't know the names of many of the brightly coloured vegetables and fruit on the stalls that spilt out onto the pavement. Today, the smell of baklava or a particular bread can take me right back there over 25 years later.

In the road where I lived there weren't any other girls living alone, so I was noticed, and I enjoyed the attention. I made good friends with my neighbours, and I will never forget them. When I was ill and fainted in the phone box at the end of the road, I was picked up by two strangers and carried home, and then neighbours brought me food for days afterwards helping me to recover. One of my favourite friends was Peter from Africa, tall and athletic and he had a deep rich voice and an imposingly posh English accent. He was well educated but unable to work in London in his profession, so he retrained and was working as a nurse. He spent most of his spare time renovating MG sports cars in a garage at the end of my road. We became good friends, and I sat for hours in his workshop preparing for my essays while he lay under a car soldering and repairing. Often I read my latest essay to him while he worked and, if I was stuck, he would help me because often he would have read the novel or play I was critiquing. He was brilliant, and his knowledge of English literature and language was incredible. It wasn't unusual for him to correct me on my grammar.

'What are they teaching you?' he would say. 'Surely the English language is part of your course.'

'No Peter, it's an English literature course I am studying.'

'Well aren't all your novels and plays written in the English language?' I couldn't argue because he had a valid point.

Two other lovely friends I made at college were Nicky and Phil. Nicky introduced me to the delights of dark rum and Edgar Allan Poe and gave me the desire to visit San Francisco after sending me a postcard from there while she was on her American placement year; and Phil, being a Londoner, was a fantastic guide to cultural London and ironically introduced me to Beatles' music. Until then I hadn't been much of a fan, but Phil's passion rubbed off on me, and to this day certain Beatles' songs take me back, not to my hometown of Liverpool, but to sunny days as an 18-year-old in London.

With genuine friendship and a passion for learning, I made the beginnings of many exciting journeys as I opened up inwardly and outwardly during my first year in London. I loved hopping on and off the big red-route-master buses and the London Underground 'Tube'. Life was exciting, interesting and great fun; and although unconventional, I felt the burden of inner and outer tension replaced by the taste of internal and external enjoyment.

Yours,

Michaela

Chapter 21

6th August 2009

Dear St Thérèse,

After the first academic year, I went back home to Liverpool and stayed with my dad for the summer holidays. One day, feeling quite lost and wondering how to make myself useful until it was time to go back to college in London, I got a shocking telephone call from the Dean's office at the college. One of my lecturers had accused me of plagiarism. The English tutor for my module for the 19th-century novel had found me guilty of copying word-for-word her description of the importance of the candle as a metaphor in George Eliot's novels in a thesis I had submitted. When I got the initial call, I didn't know all these details, just the allegation and the date of the hearing. The Dean's office informed that I didn't have to turn up to the hearing (as it appeared to be a cut and dried case) but I had the right to do so if I wanted. So I gathered all my lecture and essay notes and trembled on the train all the way to London not knowing what would happen, but only knowing I had never knowingly plagiarised and indeed had been careful not to do so.

On the day of the hearing, I turned up at the deserted campus, terrified of not just failing the course, but of being branded a cheat. The only person I recognised on the plagiarism panel was the course tutor. I smiled at her in acknowledgement, but she just glared at me looking hostile. The chairperson of the hearing explained that I was accused of plagiarism in my thesis because I had written an explanation of the candle metaphor as if it was my original thoughts. This description had been written by my course tutor and published in a book, and I had failed to attribute the candle metaphor's author in my work. The chairperson asked if I had read the book (which I can no longer remember the title of) and I said that I most definitely hadn't. When I understood the details, the allegation started to make more sense, and I felt a little more confident about explaining myself. I remembered my tutor explaining her thoughts about the candle metaphor in a seminar because I had been fascinated by it and I thought that this was a universally accepted theory of the candle metaphor, rather than the lecturer's personal hypotheses. I also took copious notes (as I did in every lecture) and had my lecture notes in front of me and was quickly able to find the description of what the lecturer said. I handed my lecture notes to the chairperson. There was complete silence as he read, and then he stood up and showed the panel my notes.

My lecturer said, 'You have written what I said, word-for-word as if verbatim.'

'I do write very quickly,' I said, 'but that's not plagiarism, it's what we are taught to do throughout school: remember what the teacher has said and regurgitate it in an exam.'

So it was finally agreed that I wasn't guilty of plagiarism, my crime was of reporting a lecturer's verbal explanation too accurately. The lecturer had verbally explained in a lecture her thoughts about the meaning of the candle metaphor in a similar way to how she had written about them in the published chapter, and I had written this in the thesis without knowledge of the source. Therefore the panel judged that I wasn't guilty of the original allegation. I had successfully proved that I hadn't copied the description in the book. The chairperson informed me that although the plagiarism charge was no longer an issue, my thesis couldn't be accepted so I would have to sit a customised exam to pass the module. After the hearing, I was relieved, and on the train home reflected that sometimes to make progress we have to unlearn certain truths, and not only did we have to do things differently, it would get us into trouble if we didn't adapt. I took the exam a few weeks later and passed.

This event happened in 1984, and little did I know the impact it would have. That essay was the last piece of non-professional writing done in blissful ignorance of shame and fear of what could happen when people read my work, and what they might say or think about me. For the next 28 years, I did not let more than a couple of people read any of my creative writing. I buried the incident in the back of my mind. It was only recently when JC was teasing me about being the only writer in the world whose work was never read by anyone that I wondered about it. But still, it felt normal to me to write and not to want anyone to read what I had written.

All became apparent only recently through the healing work of the other JC (Julia Cameron) when doing one of the exercises in her excellent book, 'The Artist's Way', designed to discover what might be blocking creativity. The exercise is simple (write an affirmation ten times, and by the time you have finished you will know what is blocking you). I felt quite cynical when I was doing it and even when I had finished my affirmations I was still thinking this won't work, and then I felt a wave of emotion flooding me. What is that I wondered? I recognised it as shame (an all over burning sensation), and then I was astonished as I realised the exercise had worked: as well as shame felt at the time, I felt a wave of anger towards a particular lecturer who had accused me of being a plagiarist.

I realised that 28 years earlier I had buried my anger about the unfair accusation underneath the shame but now wondered if my subconscious had kept me safe from any further criticism by making sure that no one else got the opportunity to criticise me again? If so, what a price to pay, not letting anyone read hardly a word I had written unless it was work-related. With professional writing, I felt protected by the validity and excuse that it was not 'real writing' because it was for work. I also realised that all the training courses and workbooks I had written usually came from the rational, logical part of my brain; again protecting the exposure of anything real that might be written from my heart.

Yours,

Michaela

Chapter 22

7th August 2009

Dear St Thérèse,

My first year in London was my first taste of emotional and physical freedom. Instead of gulping down life in suffocating swallows, I sipped at the lightness of being and breathed in new hope for the future. Living alone and away from my family, the thick, tight umbilical cord to my parents started to loosen a little, and I felt less uptight and more comfortable in myself. For the first time in my life, I had space and wanted to get to know myself. I consciously wondered about whom I was growing into as my adult self. I had some ideas of who and what I didn't want to be and the potential and positive aspect of who I did want to be.

The best part of tasting freedom was being more in charge of my life, and the growing belief that I could make choices about which direction my life took. But when adversity came, the tiny tender shoots of my new autonomous self weren't robust enough to maintain their growth; indeed, they didn't stand much of a chance of survival. I let them (even invited them to) be trampled well into the ground. These are the events that happened.

I returned to London at the start of my second year, relieved that the plagiarism allegation had been resolved. I was eager to go back to my studies. I nurtured my love of learning and enjoyed the time and space to think and explore the new dimension to my inner life. I enjoyed exploring the outer world without anyone watching or inhibiting me and thought that these new-found freedoms would be with me forever. In this spirit, I found the strength to try and support mum who was writing to me about being unhappy in her marriage. We exchanged long letters where I tried to send her some of my newly-found strength to support her. Then I made a decision which brought consequences which changed the course of my life. I suggested that she come and stay in London for a while. At the time, I believed that I made this decision out of love for my mum, but now I know that it was also made out of feeling responsible and trying to please her and gain her approval.

So, on a sunny autumn Saturday afternoon in Haringey, I found myself standing on the pavement on the noisy High Street waiting to see my mum's car appear in the busy stream of traffic. I 'guarded' a parking space for her as long as I could but lost it several times when people just ignored me and parked in 'my' space. I waited anxiously to see her car and wondered what mood she was going to be in when she arrived. I knew she would be more than a little bit stressed after her five-hour journey and it was in my mind that she had just left her husband and her son in her old home and was starting a new life in the bedsit below mine.

After about an hour of waiting on the pavement, I spotted her car coming towards me. I jumped up and down and waved making sure she could see me, but someone had just turned into the parking space I had been guarding (again!). So I shouted to her to turn into the side street, and I would meet her there. She nodded in acknowledgement, and I ran ahead to try and help secure a parking space for her around the corner. As she drove into the space and parked her car, my mum looked tiny and lost amidst all her possessions packed high around her. What mixed feelings I had on that memorable day. I knew that from that point hence, my life was going to change forever. So far in my young life, that 'life-changing' experience had brought the nagging sense that when things didn't turn out well, I only had myself to blame. This situation was no exception because mum's move to London had been my suggestion. I felt entirely responsible.

I was mistaken to feel so responsible and know now that I was acting on my conditioning to believe that loving someone meant taking responsibility for them and unselfishly providing help. Mum used to say whenever I complained about the burden of responsibility, 'Michaela, you must help others without counting the cost to yourself.' I didn't think I had any choice. I was nervous about the future, but I was used to tightness in my gut, and the feeling of my options being limited wasn't abnormal. Until recently, I thought that the highest price I paid was the loss of carefree days taking on the role of trying to be a supportive daughter to a stressed-out mother. Now I am wondering if the price was more than I have ever realised. Apart from staying with her and her husband for a few months before I moved to London, I hadn't lived with mum full-time since I was 14 when she had left us to re-marry, so it took a while for us to develop a routine. In name, I retained my independence as, technically, I was free to come and go as I pleased, but emotionally it was a different matter. My response to being stressed and unhappy at my change in circumstances only made things worse. I tried hard to keep my emotions in check until I had a couple of glasses of wine and then we would row. I always took full responsibility for these upsets; always convinced that they were entirely my fault.

How I regret suggesting that mum came to London because it wasn't a healthy situation for either of us. I ask myself what could I have done differently, and conclude I could have prayed for the guidance to have advised mum more wisely. But I didn't even realise that I needed guidance. There was no other option than for me to take charge. I was mistaken in believing I could control certain circumstances. Today I know the dangers of this illusion, but it was to take nearly another 20 years for me to see the dangers of trying to influence things beyond my control. Although made with good intentions, it was disastrous in the outcome and harmful to both the person I was trying to help and me. I can see how lost I became after having such a strong faith in my early childhood to having little faith. I felt so alone and isolated, but I recognise the courage of a young adult who didn't want to let herself or her mother down. I can also see that I was far more of an anxious child than a trusting child who would seek the comfort she needed from the adults in her life. Indeed, she felt more responsible for giving love than receiving it, but how can a person truly give something to others that they cannot ask for or give to themselves?

Mum lived in the bedsit below mine until I finished my degree. Although I had toyed with the idea of returning to Liverpool when I completed my studies, I decided to stay. Also, I would have felt guilty leaving mum in London on her own, so I managed to get a full-time position at a prestigious location in Liberty House above the shop Liberty's in Regent Street. While the pay was low, I stuck at it for nearly a year mainly because I had a wise boss who spent several hours trying to help me with my self-confidence, but I was more interested in the friendship that was developing with a lovely colleague called Louise. Most evenings we went to Bentley's Champagne and Oyster Bar for a couple of hours after work. Louise could drink wine and champagne and be merry and not suffer much the following day, but I got drunk on more than one occasion and then suffered terribly with hangovers the next day.

I made a decision to move. In recovery, we talk about 'geographicals' to explain the pattern of behaviour where we make a physical move to a new place in the hope that the change of location will make things work out differently. I left London to commence postgraduate studies in psychology at Cardiff University. I had studied some Psychology in my first degree and had enjoyed it, so I looked around at the postgraduate courses on offer and found one which looked interesting: 'Postgraduate Diploma in Applied Psychology'. It was a one-year 'conversion' course for graduates who hadn't studied enough psychology to earn Graduate Basis of the British Psychological Society. It provided a qualification which was the equivalent of having a degree in Psychology. It was a successful move in creating the sense of belonging and happiness of being immersed in studies, but unless we change our behaviour, eventually things will turn out the same and often worse.

Yours,

Michaela

Chapter 23

8th August 2009

Dear St Thérèse,

After the first year, I decided to carry on as a postgraduate student at Cardiff University and lived in another shared house with a new set of people. On the surface, I appeared to be progressing well in life. I enjoyed studying, had a career as a psychologist in sight; I had good friends, and my drinking was only excessive on occasions when I tried to convince myself and others that I was just over tired, or studying too hard and needing a blowout. But underneath the surface, was I searching for a deeper connection when I started praying regularly again?

Although I initially enjoyed my life in Cardiff, I was aware of being lonely quite often. I felt somehow different to the other students. They seemed so carefree, and I often felt as if I had the weight of the world on my shoulders and I felt less deserving than them in some way. Was I attempting to reconnect with the strong faith I had experienced in my childhood? I went to an evangelical church and enjoyed the enthusiastic, charismatic services, and in an attempt to fit in I agreed to participate in a second baptism on 3rd September 1989. I prayed regularly and listened for guidance. I had a memorable and unusual experience when I heard a phrase from scripture being spoken to me when I was praying one day. It felt like an external voice had spoken the words to me, but logically I knew they were coming from within me. The words were, 'Don't pour new wine into old wineskins.' I tried to work out what significance they might have in my life, but nothing seemed to resonate as appropriate, I asked other people in the church, but they seemed more interested in how the words had been spoken to me, rather than what they meant. Although I didn't discover its meaning at the time, I never forgot this experience. It was one of the first times as an adult that I felt that there was a God who loved me personally, and who knew me and through whom I hoped I would learn to be accepted for who I was. My attendance at that church didn't last. Although I was made welcome, after a while, I felt the pressure to convert friends to being 'born again' (although I did introduce some people to Church who I know are still Christians today). I have just realised how much there was a definite pattern of me leaving situations because of the fear of failing to meet perceived expectations. My response on this occasion couldn't have been more radical. It was time for me to move out of the shared bedsit and I needed somewhere to stay for a few months while I finished my Master's thesis.

I wasn't consciously rebelling when I moved into a Buddhist house. I now believe I was subconsciously seeking an answer to the fundamental question of 'what is wrong with me?' My new home had been the marital home of a Tibetan Buddhist Lama and his wife whom I met on the Master's degree programme. When she separated from her husband, she was looking for lodgers, and I became one of them. I was fascinated by her bohemian non-conformist approach to life as a successful psychotherapist. Was this another example of my searching for emotional guidance and wisdom? The room I moved into had once featured in a glossy Sunday-supplement magazine as an authentic Tibetan-Buddhist shrine room, complete with thigh trumpets and human skulls. I wonder how I had managed to stray so far from my faith but I was leaving no stone unturned and if eastern philosophy held the key to my soul, so be it.

Not being able to do anything by half, the attraction of Buddhism went beyond philosophy and, encouraged by new exciting Buddhist friends, I started to follow it as a religion. I went through a painful period where I felt immense guilt about losing my Christian faith and then attempted to become self-sufficient on a diet of meditation. I hit a low point feeling fundamentally flawed, and I craved peace of mind. I misunderstood Buddhism when I meditated for hours trying to become a detached intellectual being, with no need of emotions. How wrong I was. I now believe that my soul lies in the space where I connect my heart with my head; but, instead of bringing these entities closer together, I was driving them further apart. At first, Buddhism seemed so simple, and I loved teachings on the compassion of the Dalai Lama, and I felt sorry for the plight of the Tibetan people: both those living in exile having to leave their home and loved ones, and those people who remained in Tibet without their beloved leader.

Samye Ling Buddhist centre in Eskdalemuir is one of the most peaceful places I have ever been too. The first time I went I was in my late twenties. I couldn't believe the splendour of the authentic Tibetan monastery in the middle of the Scottish countryside. The colourful and archetypal sloping roofs made it look as though the temple had been plucked off the top of a Tibetan mountain. The inside of the shrine room was even more splendid with a huge gold statue of Buddha and candles and offering bowls and colourful cushions presenting an atmosphere of both solemn ritual and sacred openness. I imagined that all who spent any length of time there would surely be on a fast-track to enlightenment. Monks, mortals and friendly sparrows sit on the wooden seats and tables at the outdoor café serving delicious vegetarian food. A short walk took me to the river where I sat and wondered what it was like for the dozens of people in solitary retreat. I knew I wouldn't last an afternoon let alone three years, three months and three days without someone to smile at and smile back at me. My lasting impression was of holiness and a sense that everyone there wasn't *creating* sacred spaces but rather *clearing* them. I visited Samye Ling again in my thirties and forties and each time lay on the riverbank, looked at the cloudless sky and meditated on the sound of the bubbling water, and each time my impression of its intrinsic goodness and compassion was strengthened.

To this day, I have tremendous admiration and respect for the Dalai Lama. I had attended his talks twice, in Cardiff in 1993 and Glasgow in 2004, and saw him when he visited Liverpool to deliver the Roscoe Lecture at Liverpool John Moore's University in 2004 and each time I felt that I was in the presence of immense holiness. Two of my most treasured memories of being in the presence of the Dalai Lama are his amazing laugh which invites the listener to join in pure delight. It is so infectious, almost childlike. Just recalling the Dalai Lama's laugh or seeing him laughing on TV, I wonder at the ability to laugh so wholeheartedly and simply. Such a genuine sound must surely come from a pure and free heart and soul. The other memory is of attending a talk by the Dalai Lama in Glasgow. At question time, at the end of his lecture, the Dalai Lama was asked an immense question that we all might wonder at, but so complex that he wouldn't ever be able to answer in a sentence or two. I don't remember the exact question, but it went along the lines of 'What is the meaning of life?' The Dalai Lama struck me as so genuine and full of truth and humility when he took a long pause, and it seemed as if complete silence descended on the arena; my ears were ready not to miss a word of what he said. He looked over the glasses on his nose very seriously in the direction of the questioner, and it felt like the whole audience held its breath, as I did in anticipation of the wisdom of the answer he appeared to be preparing to deliver. Eventually, the Dalai Lama broke the tension when he said, quite simply, 'I don't know' and then burst into peals of laughter which continued until it seemed that everyone in the room was laughing along with him, myself included. What a sound! What joy his holiness gave me to treasure in my heart. On that occasion, my friend who was studying to be a priest came with me and agreed that the Dalai Lama was indeed a Holy man with loving teachings.

However valid as a philosophy and psychology, Buddhism is, for me, as a religious practice I tried and failed. I need to stay connected to the faith of my childhood. It is a part of me. In fact, I have read many books written and forwarded by the Dalai Lama and have noticed how he advocates that we practise the religion of our childhood. I still meditate, and its benefits are enormous. It seems entirely contradictory now that I thought my intellect and academic achievements qualified me to be a good Buddhist, when I can now see how much Buddhism is a religion of the heart, of compassion. It felt as if I was trying to make a journey upside down: like trying to get somewhere walking on my hands instead of my feet. When we are walking normally on our legs and we stumble, our knees break our fall, but if we are walking on our hands and we stumble, we just bash our heads.

I became disillusioned by my lack of progress in becoming a good Buddhist and drowned my sorrows in the culture of heavy drinking within the household (which included non-Buddhists), but as usual, I found I was unable to drink like normal people. I was incredibly miserable, and I started to lose what little I had left of my self-worth. I didn't know how to get back to where I had begun my life in Cardiff, full of hope and faith. I was also trapped financially into a house I had bought into but couldn't afford, and stuck in unhealthy emotional relationships.

In the midst of these circumstances, mum moved to Cardiff temporarily. She swapped flats with one of my friends. He lived in her flat in London, and she lived in his flat in Cardiff. Overall I didn't react well, even though I had encouraged her. I felt over responsible for her. After several months she returned to London, and I became depressed. I ended up working for a nursing home as a care assistant. I am not diminishing this job, and I admire anyone who does it, but it was the wrong choice for someone who could hardly care for themselves to hold responsibility for caring for vulnerable adults. My self-esteem was extremely low. In hindsight, I took this work because I was desperate for money and didn't feel capable of securing for which I was qualified. I felt like a fish out of water, but because I was invited out socially by the other care workers (all women) often, I went. I clung to this sliver of belonging, but I always ended being ashamed of my behaviour when I did go out. Most days on early shifts and days off were spent with colleagues drinking.

I got so sick of myself and desperate for things to change that my mind felt like it was always racing and the only relief was the numbness that alcohol brought, which just made things worse. I tried to meditate, and sometimes it worked and the dread that lived with me most days would be temporarily relieved. There was one special experience that I will never forget. It was a rare day off that I wasn't creating or nursing a hangover (my dad was coming to visit, and I was on my best behaviour in anticipation) and I placed cushions on the floor of my room and sat and meditated. I had been taught by Buddhist friends to chant various mantras, and I found the repetition of the sound calming. Unusually on this day I wasn't easily distracted, and I spent a long time chanting and in silent meditation. For once my mind wasn't racing ahead worrying about the future or picking over past painful memories, I felt aware of the present only, sitting comfortably on the cushions in the position I had been shown to help stay awake and alert while meditating. Rays of bright sunshine lightened the room and my spirits, and a warm breeze was pleasantly welcome through the open window. With my eyes closed my mind wandered and I imagined that I was in a country far away, from where all I had to do all day was meditate, and my depression was as insignificant as a small cloud in an otherwise cloudless sky just momentarily blocking out the sunlight.

I was deeply absorbed in the meditation when I became aware of a distinct symbol in my mind's eye, and instinctively opened my eyes to refocus, but the symbol which I had expected to disappear remained, hovering gently in space before me. It was a shape I didn't recognise and a distinct colour green. I blinked several times. Surely the vision would disappear when my eyes adjusted to the bright sunlight? But there it stayed, even bolder. How unusual I thought and closed my eyes and relaxed into the presence of the symbol and carried on meditating. Eventually, I finished my meditation session, and gradually the symbol faded into nothing more than a pale-green light which only slightly hindered my sight like the black-spot effect we get behind our eyes when we have been staring into the sunlight.

I got up and moved about my room and found that the session had relaxed me and lifted my spirits. I made a cup of tea and placed it on my dressing table, and I sat and pensively brushed my hair, enjoying the rare moment of tranquillity. Suddenly the open window blew shut with a bang and made me jump, and I accidently knocked over the cup of tea. It spilt all over the dressing table. Irritated at my clumsiness, I wiped the surface and everything that had got wet.

One of these objects was a small box covered in a beautiful ornate-patterned silk fabric. A Buddhist friend had given it to me as a gift and inside the box were two heavy, silver-coloured-metal Chinese 'stress balls' in a display setting covered in blue silk fabric. I liked to take the balls out of the box and gently shake them to hear a soft, tumbling, bell-like sound. I don't know what was inside the balls to make the sound or indeed if the balls were metal, but I liked their heavy coldness and the soothing sound they made.

When I opened the box, I found that the spilt tea had got inside, and the blue silk fabric was wet. I removed the balls and then tried to lift the display packaging out. It was hard to remove as I didn't want to tear the fabric. I also noticed the bare and rough wood of the interior which was also a bit wet. As I successfully removed the last corner of the fabric out of the box, I noticed an amber cord the thickness of a shoelace at the bottom. I wondered if there was something attached to it. I pulled out the cord, and as it unravelled, I was holding a beautiful bronze pendant which I had never seen before. It certainly didn't belong to me.

I looked at the pendant closely and realised with surprise that the symbol embossed on one side was the unknown symbol I had seen in unusual circumstances during my earlier meditation session. As much as I hoped to recognise the symbol, I couldn't. On the other side of the pendant was the image of a woman who looked like a female Buddhist deity, but again it wasn't familiar enough for me to name her. I wrapped the cord around my new-found treasure and put it in my pocket. How did it get inside the box? Somebody must be missing the pretty pendant. In the next few hours all sorts of possibilities crossed my mind, but no firm answers, except the certainty that the symbol was the same one I had seen during my meditation session.

Later that evening I showed the pendant to one of my Buddhist friends, and he immediately recognised the symbol and explained its meaning to me. It was the seed syllable of a mantra for Green Tara, and the female image was of Green Tara, the goddess of compassion. I told him the story of the symbol and the discovery of the pendant and he declared, as a matter of fact, that I must have a connection to Green Tara and advised me to learn and to practise her mantra as often as possible. After a time I stopped wondering how the pendant found its way into my possession and accepted it as a blessing. I also followed the advice and learned Green Tara's mantra and practised it devotedly for as long as I was a Buddhist practitioner. To this day, the pendant remains a treasured item.

However, the specialness of this day was too rare to save me and only serves to contrast more starkly with the reality of my day-to-day behaviour which deteriorated to the point of crisis. Not long following this event, after a spectacularly long day of drinking, I returned home, and instead of opening the wood and glass front door I chose to bash my way through it. Covered in glass, wood splinters and blood, I was arrested and taken to a police cell, and the following day I was admitted to Sully psychiatric hospital, an old TB sanatorium on the Welsh coast near to Cardiff. Fortunately, the police treated me with compassion, and I never faced any criminal charges for my unacceptable behaviour.

Yours,

Michaela

Chapter 24

9th August 2009

Dear St Thérèse,

At Mass today there was a notice in the newsletter asking for people to volunteer to be stewards at the cathedral for when your relics come to Liverpool. Uncharacteristically, I didn't hesitate; as soon as I got home, I sent an email to volunteer on both days.

At Mass, I was thinking about what I have been writing about and meditating on the question of how did I get from happily making a fresh start in Cardiff to being a hospitalised and a completely broken person in heart, mind, body and soul in the space of a few years? This emotional breakdown was initially one of the most terrifying events of my life, and it is probably not just a coincidence that it happened when I was drinking heavily and the most out of touch with my faith. Today I am grateful for the experience because I understand it to be part of my spiritual journey.

Unexpectedly, after the initial shock of realising that I was having a 'nervous breakdown', I had times of great peace while at Sully Hospital. As an old TB sanatorium, it was located on the coast and set in beautiful grounds which led to a secluded beach. Being there at summertime, I had the opportunity to walk on the beach every day and to this day walking on a beach (at any time of the year) can bring me great peace of mind. I believe it goes back to the healing time that I spent in Sully. The psychiatrist who treated me told me that I wasn't psychotic, I just had problems handling my emotions and that the cause of the 'nervous breakdown' was a build-up of pent-up, repressed emotion. The psychiatric staff didn't give me any advice on how to handle my emotions more effectively. My prescription was simple: rest. While I didn't see alcohol as a huge causal factor to my problems, I intuitively knew that it didn't help to drink with the intensely painful emotions that I experienced. My family and friends were incredibly kind to me during my hospitalisation. Mum arrived from London within a couple of hours of admission to support me. Dad travelled from Liverpool most weekends to visit, and my brother came several times too.

Often at the weekend at the hospital, there was a cricket match in the grounds. As a teenager, dad used to take David and me to the local cricket club at weekends where we met my uncle Frank and Granddad, and I used to enjoy the social atmosphere (and the glasses of coca cola/half lagers and crisps). So the sound and smells of a cricket match are soothing for me and evoke a sense of belonging and safety. I have an abiding memory of lying on the grass with my brother watching the match and noting the irony of being the most relaxed I had felt in years, and it was due to being a patient on a psychiatric ward.

Once I had processed my new reality, I soon picked up the hospital routine. I simply obeyed the staff and did what I was told when I was told: when to sleep when to eat when to take medication, when to rest and when to speak to others. At last the 'mask' came off. I didn't have to pretend that everything was okay anymore. I reasoned that I wouldn't have been an in-patient on a psychiatric ward if it was. I was shy with the other patients and kept myself to myself, but I wasn't rude if anyone approached me. I was as friendly as possible.

The woman in the bed opposite me was an alcoholic detoxing but told me that she had a secret stash of alcohol and that I could have some if I wanted. I declined. Alcohol was the last thing I wanted. I spent the days walking alone on the beach in the sunshine or walking in the gardens or sleeping or reading. I started to 'enjoy' the mainly calm atmosphere.

The highlight of each day for me was the bedtime drink. We would queue up at the nurses' station for our medication, and then the drinks trolley would be rolled out by fellow patients who had made the bedtime milky drinks. I drank Ovaltine. I looked forward to this because I knew that after drinks, I would be able to go to bed and find some peace in sleep. After a couple of weeks, I became one of the night time drink volunteers. Four months after I was discharged from the hospital, I continued the Ovaltine routine at bedtime because it was so comforting.

After spending six weeks in Sully Hospital, I never returned to my Cardiff home again. My belongings and my beloved cat, a ginger tom called Ollie were retrieved, and we went back to live in Liverpool with my dad. I moved into the room that had been my childhood bedroom, and dad looked after me with extraordinary gentleness. I slept peacefully and my days were spent walking and reading. But when the old anxiety started moving within me, I 'ran away' again and returned to Cardiff to a new home.

This is one of my main regrets in my life: that I left Liverpool at this time, because it was to be nearly another ten years before I returned. I felt safe living in dad's house, but the restlessness and searching within told me that I needed to keep moving. I don't know what I was seeking, but ever since I can remember I have sought something outside myself. I didn't realise that the solution was internal rather than external. I felt aware of problems within me, but not solutions. I never felt good enough; I felt too anxious.

Moving back to Cardiff for the second time was another fresh start. As ever I put on a brave face and put my heart into my new circumstances. At first, I was happy. I felt a sense of relief that I had reached a 'rock bottom' and survived. I believed that I would never let things get so bad that they would take me back to a psychiatric ward. I found a job that I loved. I worked as a sales researcher for an international hotel chain. I loved the team spirit of the hotel environment and felt at last that I had found a job where I belonged. I was successful at it and got great feedback and rewards. One of these rewards included winning a sales performance league table with the prize of an all-expenses paid trip to New York. I took the hotel secretary with me, and although we went in February and it was freezing, I was mesmerised by New York. It was so vibrant and alive and energetic.

Some of the emptiness I had always felt started to be filled with work. Work became everything to me. However, it never occurred to me to question if I was in the right career. My dreams of being a writer were long forgotten, and I seemed to forget all the effort that had gone into my psychology studies. I was just pleased to be a valued part of a team where the values were about high standards, excellent customer service, and hard work. It was a demanding, all-encompassing 24-hour, 365-days-a-year operation and became my ideal environment.

I knew how to make others feel loved, and this attracted people to me, and I then felt responsible for them, but I had little love or compassion for myself; there was a big hole in me where the loving myself activity should have been.

Yours,

Michaela

Chapter 25

10th August 2009

Dear St Thérèse,

You might have appeared to have made swift decisions, but you weren't impulsive. You knew your heart and mind. Although it might have seemed to others that I knew what I was doing when making certain decisions, I didn't. On a whim, I agreed to follow my boss who was moving from Cardiff to Glasgow when he offered me a job. I left my home and job and a relationship in Cardiff, to work in a brand-new city-centre hotel which was being converted from an old office tower block and wasn't yet open for business. It didn't take long for me to realise that, yet again, I had made a big mistake.

I arrived in Glasgow late on a Sunday evening after a long train journey, and although the directors agreed that I could live in the hotel until I found somewhere to live, there wasn't a room ready for me. It was as if I wasn't expected (and yet this was the date I was told to arrive). If it hadn't been for the warmth and gentleness of the housekeeper – apparently mortified that she didn't know I was coming – I might have left immediately, but where would I have gone? The reality was that however unwelcome I felt in Glasgow, I had burned my bridges with Cardiff, and other than going back to Liverpool, I had nowhere else to go.

The housekeeper showed me to a newly refurbished room, and as it was dark outside, she suggested that I didn't turn on the light because there were no curtains on the windows yet. I didn't see the logic of this because the offices I could see through the bare window were obviously empty at night, but I did as she suggested. I might have moved the bed from its position right in the centre of the room, but being so tired, I didn't even bother to search for my night clothes; I took off my clothes and lay on the bed.

When I woke I knew it was late morning by the brightness of the winter sunlight streaming into the room and felt disorientated until it came back to me, I was in Glasgow probably having made a dreadful mistake. I lay in bed with my arm over my eyes letting them adjust to the light and the strange sense that I was being watched came over me. Instinctively, I sat up suddenly wondering if there was someone else in the room. I was wearing only my underwear and quickly realised that I was right, I was indeed being watched, but not from eyes within the room but the dozen or so pairs of eyes from the people working in the office block opposite. I froze in horror and stared back until I realised that the longer I didn't move the longer the audience had to take in my half-nakedness.

'I hope they can't see me as clearly as I can see them,' I thought, noticing the brooch on the scarf one of the women was wearing. After a few moments of me watching them looking at me, the urge to run activated and I bolted to the bathroom with my mostly naked body burning red with shame. I stayed in the bathroom for ages until I found the courage to open the bathroom door and crawl along the floor out of the audience's view and grab some clothes from my yet unopened case. Looking back, I can see the funny side of that event. But at the time I felt mortified, and there was worse to come. I was soon to discover that the position that I had been recruited for so swiftly had never been mine to take, it had already been filled by someone else. But I agreed to stay and take a less senior position.

I don't blame anyone other than myself for how things turned out, although it didn't change how unhappy I felt. But instead of admitting that I had made a mistake and leaving the situation, I did what I always used to do, thinking, 'I can make this better' and 'I can make this turn out well', but some circumstances are not within our control. Today I know the dangers of living on 'self-will', and I live by the principle of focusing on what I can change and accept what I can't change. It works well, but back then I still tried to change what I couldn't change and ignored those things that were within my control.

Good Friday was a key date in your life when you realised you were ill – when you coughed blood – and how well you accepted the challenge of your adversity. I can't imagine how you must have felt and yet you took the situation as part of God's will for you. One of the lowest points of my life was Good Friday in 1995 during my first year in Glasgow at the new hotel. I was scheduled to work which felt wrong as I was used to it being a holy day and I felt guilty being at work and it didn't seem like Good Friday. It seemed that everyone around me had family and friends visiting them and I felt sad not to be spending Easter with my family as I usually did. I sat at my desk and couldn't remember ever being so downhearted. I was still living in the hotel, which meant that I couldn't escape from the situation. After work, I went to my bedroom and lay on the bed and cried. I had never felt so lonely as I did then. I rationalised that I was grieving for the 'new start' which hadn't turned out as I expected. I knew things had to change and that it was time for me to move on but I had nowhere to go. I wish I had prayed St Thérèse; my prayers would have been answered, but I just let the misery and grief overwhelm me. I felt too ashamed and too unworthy of help to pray.

You never gave up your faith. Even when your prayer life felt 'dry' you carried on praying as if your heart and soul were still completely intimate with Our Lord. I admire you so much for this. Often whenever I felt lost and alone and should have reached out for a connection with God, I became isolated even more, believing myself to be utterly unworthy of his love. Today, I know that it was wrong to feel so unworthy and that I based this unworthiness on false pride rather than humility. Today I try to practise humility by praying on a daily basis for knowledge of my Higher Power's will for me and the power to carry it out.

In Glasgow in 1996 for the first time in my adult life, I lived without practising any faith at all. I was neither a Catholic nor Buddhist. My new religion was work. While I had always been conscientious and a perfectionist, I had never been obsessed with work until then. Workaholism is one of the few addictions that can appear on the surface to be almost virtuous. It makes us think we are right, unlike other addictions which can lead us into shameful situations more often and more quickly. Workaholism doesn't lead to as much immediate remorse, although long-term regrets might come with a vengeance when we realise how quickly our lives have passed and we understand what we might have missed by putting work first e.g. some people miss 'being present' to their children growing up.

People often say at the end of their careers that they wished that they hadn't spent so much time worrying about work and that they had focused on more meaningful aspects of life, such as time spent with their family, etc. As I read somewhere, no one on their deathbed reviewing their life will say 'I wish I had spent more time at work.' They might, however, say, 'I wish I spent more time living my dreams, being joyful; or with my children; or being in nature, etc.'

Workaholism doesn't lead to the same overt judgment from others as say alcoholism or a gambling addiction. Often because although we might be with our families 'in body', it isn't always as obvious as with other addictions how much we are missing 'in spirit'. Again, the impact seems only to become evident on a much longer-term basis, for instance, it might only be when a person reflects back on their childhood that they fully realise how much they might have suffered from the emotional absence of one (or both) of their parents. This lack of immediate or obvious impact of workaholism can only make things worse in the long run.

As with most active addictions, the soul seems to deaden or become 'sick', at best resulting in a lack of vibrancy within and at worst resulting in a complete state of hopelessness. My soul sickness at this time was reflected in my powerlessness, particularly over my external circumstances. There was nothing at all forcing me to live in the hotel in which I worked, and yet I felt compelled to, even though there were no staff quarters in the hotel. For over a year, I lived in an ordinary hotel room relying on the hotel kitchen for food. Often, at the end of a busy shift, all I wanted was a cup of tea and a piece of toast, but I didn't have any self-catering facilities at all, other than a kettle. Being permanently on site also meant that I was 'on-call' even when I wasn't on-duty. I never felt relaxed, and any small amount of free time I allowed myself was spent sleeping, lying on my bed or in a bar somewhere along Sauchiehall Street. In my sorry dejected state, the hotel chef took pity on me. When I went to the kitchen to collect my evening meal, he was often waiting to tell me some little story to make me laugh. I appreciated his kindness and his cooking. When he asked what I wanted to eat each evening, I would ask for something simple – not wanting to cause any bother – but when he wasn't too busy, he would ignore my request and produce tasty, delicious meals using the best ingredients in the kitchen.

After a while, I used to hang around the kitchen while Chef was preparing my meal, and we chatted. One evening Chef confided in me that he was a recovering alcoholic. He was full of life and vitality. We became friends, and I will never forget his kindness in trying to cheer me up. Our friendship ended abruptly after he went away to Australia for a month: I found a new boyfriend and moved out of the hotel.

My new boyfriend was and is one of the funniest men I have ever met, almost a comic genius in what he could say to make people laugh. I often felt unhappy and worried about something, and he would say something funny, and I would be helpless with laughter. We each had our own challenges, so the emotional difficulties didn't go away, but humour made them easier to cope with; he also encouraged me to use my psychology qualifications, and I found a job with an international hotel chain and embarked on a more planned career in Human Resources, which I enjoyed.

As I look back now, I am so sad to recognise the patterns I followed in relationships. I had a knack for recognising people's suffering and offering help. I felt responsible and powerless over a compulsion for wanting to help anyone I met who showed me their pain. I now know that while trying to fix someone else's problems, it gave me an excuse to avoid dealing with my own. It was classic co-dependent behaviour, but I didn't see anything wrong with this because I had done it all my life. I didn't see that it was using up a lot of my energy, which I should have been using better by putting the spotlight on my faults and shortcomings. I didn't think I was a saint, far from it, and didn't realise how much more I could have helped myself had I just known that it was necessary.

I drank little during this time. I feared alcohol. Through a colleague's alcoholic behaviour I saw at close hand the chaos it caused when he lost his job. We stayed in touch, and he subsequently lost another job but went on to make a decision which was to change his life, so much for the better. He stopped drinking and to this day, over ten years later, he has bravely stayed sober. I also can see the crucial lesson (the possibility of sobriety) I learned from this friend although I didn't put it in into practice until I had experienced a lot more pain and madness myself.

I needed to follow my friend's example and to abstain from alcohol completely, but I couldn't see that alcohol caused my problems. I thought my problems were caused by my mental defects or other emotional problems and that the only cure for me was the force of willpower. I just needed to be stronger and try harder, and everything would be okay. But everything wasn't okay, alcohol got me into trouble at work, and I faced serious consequences. This event was typical of the pattern I had developed of only turning to God when I was in deep, deep trouble and it became the only times that I prayed. It would be a desperate prayer where I would plead and bargain with God by telling him that if he just got me out of this mess, I would renew my efforts to be a better person and to stay in touch. I was not insincere in these prayers, but it was the only time when I thought God would be listening. I would pray for divine intervention into the humiliation I felt when I said and did outrageous things while drunk.

During this time I often longed for the comfort of my faith but, because of my behaviour, I felt unworthy of a relationship with God. Maybe it was as a substitute that I developed a friendship with a seminarian who went to Salamanca in Spain to pursue his calling. I was fascinated by his vocation. It reminded me of my childhood when I read about saints, and I remember praying that I would be chosen and receive a vocation.

Interestingly, like you, I wanted to be a priest rather than a nun, and if it had been possible for me to pursue a particular career path, this is what I would have chosen. I told my friend that deep within, like him, I also felt called to a spiritual life, but now I know that my drinking was holding me back. He said, 'Follow your heart.' I didn't. What stopped me? I felt too unworthy. I felt flawed. I felt overwhelmed by inadequacy. In reality, the truth was that I was too trapped by my drinking and the shame it produced in me. But it is a comfort to me now to know that this faith, this desire, has always been a part of me, however much repressed.

Yours,

Michaela

Chapter 26

11th August 2009

Dear St Thérèse,

My pattern of leaving a city to make a fresh start was well established, but the circumstances of each move were deteriorating. I left Glasgow after letting myself down so badly that I felt compelled to leave my job, my home and my relationship and all because of a few hours of alcohol-induced madness. Full of shame and remorse I attempted to settle into my new home outside Edinburgh and, although close to the city, it felt rural. It was a studio flat in an old farm building which used to be a distillery beside the Union Canal, but I barely noticed any of the natural beauty. My 'flat' was tiny, and I called it 'the cave'. The old walls were bare stone, and in subdued light, it did look much like a cave from within.

After I had moved in, I found out that I was living in the part of the old building which in 1864 had been part of the scene of the murder committed by Geroge Bryce, who was the last man to be publicly hanged in Edinburgh. His victim was a nursemaid (Jane Seaton) who had lived at the big house close by. At the time of her murder, Jane Seaton had been running to safety after having been attacked and partially strangled in the 'big house'. George Bryce caught up with her at the threshold of my building, and he finished the job by pulling out a razor and cutting her throat.

My imagination ran wild about the ghost of Jane Seaton haunting my tiny bedsit. I imagined her running for her life but not quite making it to safety. I was scared by the thought of, but grateful that I hadn't faced, the fear she must have felt with such a horrific death. It was as though I was able to identify more with tragedy than happiness.

The secluded rural setting of my home would have been a perfect place to find some peace and serenity away from the intensity of the city, but I was unable to appreciate it. The canal would have been lovely for long walks. Instead of avoiding the happy people walking across the picturesque bridge, I could have joined them. I could have sat in the sunshine more often and fed the beautiful swans and geese that came for food instead of sneaking out at dusk to feed them when I thought no one would be around. At the end of the lane stood a small 13th-century church and graveyard. It wasn't a Catholic church, and I never went inside, but I did hear the church bells on a Sunday morning which were plaintive if my hangover wasn't too bad, and a nuisance if it was.

There were many tall trees surrounding my little cave, but I didn't hear the happy tweeting of birds, only the doomfully raucous cawing of hundreds of crows as they congregated in their penthouse nests and which the landlord used to shoot early on Sunday mornings. While the noise of gunshot was disturbing it also felt appropriate. I was a regular visitor to the graveyard, and the tragic history of my little home seemed apt, and I felt I deserved the morbidity that lingered in the air around me. My memories of the little cave are as dark as it was. Was I aware then that my soul was slowly dying? No, but I can see now that I was severely losing hope, and my soul sickness was getting much worse.

One Sunday afternoon I had a rare visitor, and we went for a walk and visited the graveyard, and I gave us both a terrible fright. I was mournfully staring at an ancient worn headstone trying to read the inscription for the dead person buried beneath my feet. I could make out the dates were in the 1800s but couldn't decipher the full name and epitaph of the headstone's owner. The lettering was worn and hardly legible. Determined to read the ancient words, I stepped backwards for a better perspective and leant against the tall, sturdy headstone behind me so that I could focus more attentively on the inscription. I didn't notice the headstone moving at first but when I realised it was too late to try and stop it falling because it was far too heavy. I instinctively jumped out of the way and cried out. The cold stone headstone crashed to the ground with such a thud that I imagined all the ancient bones in the ground beneath me rattling in their decaying coffins. My companion and I got such a fright that we both looked at each other startled and then started running, and we didn't stop until we were inside my front door. When we were breathing normally again, I replayed what had happened in my mind and imagined that the headstone might have disturbed the ground and laid bare the grave's contents. I even asked my companion if I had committed a criminal offence by desecrating hallowed ground (although it was an accident). With all the courage I could find, and before I changed my mind, I went back to the scene of the crime and saw that the headstone had fallen intact and didn't seem to be damaged and looked as if it could be re-erected. I saw the vicar's telephone number on the board outside the church and called and left a message on his answer machine confessing my crime. I never heard any more about it.

Looking back I can see the funny side of what happened and smiled at the memory as I wrote this, and although I might have laughed a little (mainly with relief) just after the event, my recollection is of dread that I did something to disturb the sacred peace of the dead. This doom is a reflection of my state of mind at the time. I was serious, self-punishing and always expecting the worst, but worst of all, incredibly sad at where life had taken me. It makes me sad now to realise how forlorn I had become.

Yours,

Michaela

Chapter 27

12th August 2009

Dear St Thérèse,

While life in 'the cave' was subdued, professionally I had landed a prestigious, high-profile job. The ordeal of Glasgow had reduced my self-esteem to an all-time low. So I played even more of an act than I had before.

Every morning I put on the mask of a competent professional woman to arrive at work appearing bright and committed, but personally, I spent hours in the phone box crying to my small circle of confidants (mainly my ex-boyfriend and my mum). I felt lost, and I wanted to know how to feel better but feared that my inability to cope would lead me back to the psychiatric hospital. I believed that to survive, I just needed to try harder using the strength of my willpower. It was just a case of mind over matter; if only I could overcome the sadness and weariness of trying so hard.

I spent most weekends alone. One Saturday instead of making my lonely trip to the shopping mall, I decided to go into Edinburgh city centre, but I couldn't have told you where I intended to go when I got there. So I was surprised to find myself standing outside Edinburgh Catholic Cathedral, which I had never been to before. I felt too troubled to go in and stood outside for ages; but eventually, the need for peace overcame the fear of entering the cathedral. Once inside, the smell and quiet and peaceful presence that only exists in churches overwhelmed me, and I felt the hot tears streaming down my face and quietly sobbed as I went into the first empty pew and knelt down. I prayed from my heart and without shyness implored God for help with the inner pain I felt. While on my knees praying, I felt the gentle pressure of a hand on my shoulder and turned to see a kind face asking me if I was okay. I didn't know who the stranger was, but he spoke to me with compassion, and I shook my head to indicate that I wasn't okay. He sat down beside me and through tears I poured my heart out. I told him about all the pain I felt, how ashamed of myself I was, how hard it had been trying to make a success of my life, and how I seemed to be too sensitive and unable to deal with some of the difficulties I faced. After listening to my story intently, the stranger gave me some comforting words and then told me that he was the parish priest asking me if I wanted to say confession, so I did. I left the church less troubled, and I didn't feel so alone.

Finding myself in church that day came through a rare moment of following my heart. Whenever I do that, I always make good decisions, and the outcome is always positive. But a lifetime habit of being disconnected from my heart and only being aware of its neglect in a crisis meant my buried feelings had to scream to get my attention. My longing to reconnect with my faith took me to Edinburgh Cathedral that day, and the effects lasted, but I was still just scratching the surface: dealing only with the symptoms of what was wrong with me and not the causes. My heart had opened enough for me to know that I was wretched, so I looked within and realised that one of my heart's desires was to be a writer and decided to see what it felt like to write.

I did my HR manager's job from Monday to Friday, and I sat alone at the weekends in my lonely cave. By now it felt like the perfect home for a troubled writer. I sat staring at the wall wondering what to write about and trying to get something on paper, limiting myself to small measures of whisky but refilling the glass often. There was a small gap of optimum productivity which I used to aim for, not like an archer, skillfully aiming his bow at his target, more like a punch-drunk wrestler lurching clumsily at his opponent. My target was the small gap of time where I had drunk enough to have loosened up sufficiently to write something coherent but before I was too drunk to have any clue what I was writing. I always wrote longhand. The following day I would try to read what I had written. I could see the tight, tense writing ease-up into some brief luxurious lucidity and then the writing would decline into tortured, liquid scrawl. The pages would be patterned with circles of ink where there were no words only mini blotches of colour where tears had fallen.

I went to Mass at the cathedral every Sunday, and I tried to pray too, but I felt so unworthy within myself that I didn't believe that anyone would be listening to my self-pitying whimpering. I know now that God was listening to my prayers, and He did help me to move on. But the one thing that I needed a respite from wasn't getting better. The pattern of drinking didn't improve, it just changed, and I know now it was for the worse, but at the time I thought I had made a massive leap forward. In the efforts to control my drinking, I thought I had solved all my problems when I started drinking at home, alone. I had cracked it! It made much more sense. No one to offend and no one to apologise to the next day. It seems pure madness now to have welcomed this change in my drinking as progress when it was deteriorating to the dangerous zone that many alcoholics have experienced. Drinking alone, in secret behind closed doors. I felt unattractive on the inside and outside. Although I wished to be left alone, I managed to be involved in three painful friendships during this time which I regretted. I knew that they were harmful either to the other person or me, but I felt powerless to finish them until they reached their unhappy ends in the most painful of ways.

These are prime examples of co-dependency where instead of looking to what needed fixing within me, I noticed and responded to the need in another. While I was helping them, although painful, it was less painful than having to deal with my pain and defects. It is important for me to acknowledge that in the failure of these friendships, the fault was mine, and I still respect these people today.

It is sad to reflect now that I had given up on myself. I remember one day in the cave being so low that I couldn't get out of bed. I was doing what I usually did when I felt so low in spirit. I was reading for inspiration. The book I was reading was about angels. The central message was that angels are always with us and that one of the ways they make themselves known to us is through white feathers. I got up to make a cup of tea thinking about the last line of the chapter I had just read which was 'don't be surprised if you see a white feather very soon'.

As I walked into the kitchen, I noticed that something had blown under the door. I couldn't believe my eyes. It was the most beautiful large white feather half in and a half outside the room. The space that the feather had slipped through was very tight. It is hard to imagine that the feather hadn't been put there deliberately, but it must have blown under the door. I got such a lovely surprise, and the incident gave me hope that I wasn't as alone as I felt, but the glimmer of light wasn't strong enough to match the pitch-black darkness I felt within.

Yours,

Michaela

Chapter 28

13th August 2009

Dear St Thérèse,

It wasn't mental strength I lacked, and I had demonstrated enormous mental exertion in all the mini recoveries I made. What I lacked was honesty and insight into what was causing my problems. I was always running away from myself. Outwardly you would have seen a well-dressed woman with her make-up on and a smile on her face. Behind the facade was a lonely and frightened person who was finding it harder and harder to keep up the performance of normality.

I was never a daily drinker but a binge drinker; the main condition being that once I started drinking, I couldn't stop, whatever the circumstances. The outcome was usually devastating. I was a Mrs Jekyll and Mrs Hyde. If in the company of others, I would start off happy and then at some point I would turn from being on top of the world to being angry, distressed, and bitter or any combination of negative emotions. I got myself into many scrapes. I would usually wake the next day full of remorse and guilt, not just in a self-pitying way but full of fear and anxiety for the devastation and harm I had caused. Because I led a life that on the surface looked respectable and reasonably successful, people would be astounded to see me drunk. I had a lot of misconceptions about alcohol, believing that I couldn't have a really serious problem because I wasn't drinking alcohol daily. But I know now that binge drinking can be just as harmful to our health, both physically and mentally. The binge drinkers I have met in my recovery programme all mention the devastating effects of the mental and emotional side of their condition

As 1999 came to a close, I celebrated Millennium Eve at work as duty manager at the five-star hotel Edinburgh. Not long afterwards I was promoted to a regional role which covered Scotland to Birmingham and moving closer to home seemed sensible. It didn't take long to find a spacious flat in Southport, just an hour away from Liverpool.

Yours,

Michaela

Chapter 29

14th August 2009

Dear St Thérèse,

Moving from my gloomy cave in Edinburgh to the big flat on the promenade in Southport was like stepping from darkness into light, from night into day, such was the contrast externally and internally. I never tired of looking out of the window and seeing fabulous sunsets. It was like watching an artist paint the most beautiful pictures with colour and light in the evening sky. Life felt so much lighter and more peaceful.

I arrived in Southport engaged to be married to an ex-seminarian, but being comfortable living in the flat alone, I started to suspect that settling down in marriage wasn't perhaps exactly what I wanted. I experienced this as a small-nagging doubt, but I pushed the feeling down. I told myself that I was just weak and selfish to have such doubts and that all I needed to do was just try harder, I would make it work. It rarely occurred to me that the nagging doubts were gut feelings that were trying to get my attention. I was so used to believing that my instincts were wrong and not to be listened to – pushing them away had become habitual. My gut feelings were probably correct in the information they conveyed, but it felt safer and less risky to push on with the course of action I had willed. I understand now that a lack of self-love caused this lack of commitment to myself, and yet I felt that I was courageous and that I just needed to push myself harder.

I have read that many of our sins are not committed out of 'malice or bad intent, but out of despair' (Rolheiser 2004). This statement implies that our weaknesses comes from giving up on ourselves and describes my attitude at this time. The sadness is that my sins had consequences for other people too.

Although I had known my fiancé since I was a student, we had always lived in different places and had only spent 12 days in each other's company when I accepted his marriage proposal. We needed to get to know each other. I concentrated on what we had in common. I loved to ask him about his faith, and he answered many theological questions that I had secretly wondered about most of my life. I wasn't disappointed in his responses because I enjoyed getting to know him better, but often felt that I was missing something. I wondered why my faith didn't bring me the calmness and serenity that my fiancé appeared to have.

I understand now that it wasn't to do with the depth of my faith; part of my problem was perhaps that my longings were more urgent and hungrier than my fiancé's because they had been repressed and ignored. My feelings were volatile. At first, I found comfort in going to Mass together. There is a lovely church not far from where we lived, and the parish priest was young and vibrant, and the services were often standing-room only. But as much as I enjoyed the Sunday service, on our walk home along the promenade back to the flat I found myself suddenly becoming dissatisfied. In an instant, I would transform from peacefully humming the tune of the hymns we had just been singing in the church, to walking along the pavement shaking with emotion with tears running down my cheeks. I didn't have a clue what was wrong with me.

At first, I imagined that my fiancé's faith must have given him an insight into what was wrong with me and I wanted to shake him and say, 'Can't you see what is going on?' If he had said, 'No, you tell me what is going on?' I wouldn't have known what to say. I just knew that emotions hit me like a hammer, that I felt angry, but had no idea where the anger came from. After this had happened a few times, I became frightened of it. The impulses to say unkind things and the intensity scared me. So, as always, I focused on trying to hide rather than express the unpleasant feelings, and I tried to explain them away as frustration that things weren't working out quite as I expected them to. I just needed to try harder to be more positive, and I would be able to overcome the negative feelings.

Repressing this emotion was the worst thing to do. Although it was deeply unpleasant, I should have tried to discover what it was about, but I didn't. I did what I often did and buried the raw, angry feelings that were being stirred and tried to rationalise them away.

'I must just be under pressure,' I told myself. 'This will pass,' I reasoned. When I repressed deep angry feelings, I told myself that I was protecting the person that I was. My rationale was, why should my bad feelings poison another person?

Inevitably I damaged myself through another drinking incident at work and felt obliged to resign. In this subdued state, I was wandering around town on the morning of September 11th, 2001. I was in a phone shop, and the retail assistant told me that something awful had happened in New York and that if she were me, she would be at home watching the news. I went back and switched on the television and watched the twin towers crash to the ground. As with many other people, I was shocked and saddened by 9/11, but it also brought me to my senses, and I realised that instead of indulging in self-pity, I should be grateful for all the blessings that existed in my life. I had the strongest insight ever that my problems were of my own making. I didn't have strangers or terrorists destroying my life; I was doing it all to myself. So once again, I resolved to put the past behind me, cheer up and make another fresh start, try to be the best I could be, and learn from my experience.

The questions haunting me the most was: how and why did I keep pressing the self-destruct button? I couldn't fathom how in a few hours of madness I could destroy my life as I knew it. How could I reach the point of having no option but leave a job, a relationship, a city or even all three because I couldn't face the awful consequences of my behaviour? I drank to excess many times; but although my remorse was often huge, I would soon forget the resolve never to get drunk again, and in a few weeks I would start to think, 'Oh, it wasn't that bad' or 'I am a survivor.'

When you were 13 years of age, you experienced a significant experience on Christmas Eve which you called your 'complete conversion' after which you overcame your propensity to be oversensitive. On return from Midnight Mass, your father made a comment suggesting that it was the time for you to grow up and put childish things aside, and instead of being deeply wounded by the comment, you felt yourself react in a loving way. Your joy came from growing up overnight and in the strengthening of your soul; you felt God had done for you in an instant what you had been unable to do for yourself since your mother died, no matter how hard you tried.

Christmas Eve 2001 was like a conversion for me. We spent the last day on our honeymoon on the Isle of Mull in Scotland on 23rd December and arrived home in the early hours of Christmas Eve, and although I had to go to work later that morning, I stayed up all night reflecting on the past and the future. This experience felt like the fresh start I had always wanted. I wondered if, at last, I could just live a normal life. More than anything I longed to be normal. As I sat and watched my new husband sleep, I made every promise in the world to myself that I was going to be a better person and that life was going to be happier in the future. I was going to stop searching and settle down, and I prayed that in my new role as wife to a true gentleman, that some of his faith and gentlenesses would rub off on me.

Yours,

Michaela

Chapter 30

15th August 2009

Dear St Thérèse,

In April 2002 we were delighted to be expecting a baby. My husband and I agreed to do the cautious thing and wait until the pregnancy was a bit further on before we shared our news. But we couldn't hold on, and within a couple of hours, we had driven to Liverpool to tell my mum and dad. Sadly the joy didn't last long. One morning, I woke early and immediately knew that something was wrong with me. My husband was working nights so I went to the hospital alone and found out that I had lost the baby. My husband came to collect me from the hospital. I told him the facts, but beyond that, we didn't know what to say to each other. I felt guilty about the loss as if I had done something wrong and I assumed that he was upset, but he didn't say much. Typical of my conscientiousness (or stupidity) I was back at work later that day, and even later again that same day I was sitting on a plane to Belfast as we didn't even cancel a trip to see my husband's parents.

After the miscarriage, I was amazed at the number of people who told me in confidence that they too had had miscarriages. I found some comfort in knowing that I was not alone. Miscarriages are a lot more common than I realised. I just thought, well there is nothing I can do about this, and my skills at taking care of myself were poor. Instead of taking the time to recover from the loss I just wanted to get over the profound sense of guilt and inadequacy I felt. The day afterwards, in Ireland, I lay on the bed in the afternoon and cried, but I was nursing a bad hangover from copious amounts of red wine drunk at the airport the night before. So, once again, emotional pain was numbed with alcohol, and afterwards, I threw myself into work again.

I got the job I have enjoyed most in my life at one of the universities in Liverpool within a Business Development Centre. It was my perfect job being based in an academic environment, but with a functional role advising local businesses. It also involved regular trips to America and Europe, which were experiences of a lifetime. My new boss was grieving the loss of a daughter to alcoholism and before that his wife had died of alcoholism. We shared an understanding of the devastating impact of alcohol, albeit from opposite sides of the table. I opened up to him about my problems. He encouraged me to look inwards, and he was one of the first people to suggest that the answer I was seeking might be found in spiritual realms.

When we went overseas, he often took me to a local church or cathedral that he had previously visited. One example is when we went to Portland, Oregon. My boss told me that he had a surprise for me. I was intrigued. He said he knew a place I would love (he had been there before). He took me to a beautiful place called 'The Grotto' which is a Catholic sanctuary and the US National Shrine of our Sorrowful Mother. We lit candles at the beautiful outdoor grotto, which is a rock cave carved into the base of a cliff with a marble replica of Michelangelo's famous Pieta at the centre. We took the lift to the top of the cliff and walked around the acres of beautiful gardens. I was bowled over by the peace and serenity, and just when I thought I had seen it all, we went into a spectacular meditation chapel with floor-to-ceiling glass walls and the most amazing 180-degree views of the surrounding area. The chapel was peaceful. I sat for a long time in silence and felt the presence of holiness. We finished our visit in the Peace Garden and saw some wood sculptures. I remember thinking I could spend the rest of my life here but after a few hours, it was time to go. I felt grateful to my colleague for taking the time to show me and for knowing how much I would enjoy it. He was a great boss and friend.

Yours,

Michaela

Chapter 31

16th August 2009

Dear St Thérèse,

The last time I saw my husband was a Saturday morning in February 2004 when he left our home forever. We had been married just over 26 months. I was too upset to take him to the airport, and after I had watched him leave our home in a taxi, I ran upstairs to our bedroom and paced the floor powerless over the pain I felt and totally possessed by it. I will never forget how I felt that day.

I now know that this was the moment that I accepted that my marriage had failed. Most of my life I had feared failure of any kind and to know it so indisputably felt almost unbearable. With a fervour I had never known before, I prayed. I knew that I wouldn't be able to bear the sadness and despair alone. I had an immediate response to my prayers when the idea to listen to a guided meditation to Our Lady called 'Divine Mother' came to mind. I found the brand-new CD still seal-wrapped on a bookshelf. I ripped the cellophane off the packet as if my life depended on it. With tears streaming, I listened to the CD and followed the guided prayers, and when the CD stopped, I started it again; and again; and again until my head hurt with exhaustion. And the next day, as soon as I got home from work I did it again, and the next day, and the next day.

It worked St Thérèse; I clung to the meditation like a frightened child clinging to its mother, and I will never forget the blessings of release, care, and comfort I received from my

Divine Mother at that time. It was beyond human power. I also prayed to the angels for support. In the days after my husband left, the complete emotional breakdown I expected didn't come. I felt carried by my prayers on good days, and bad days I would just cry trying to resist liquid support, but inevitably caving in and then being even more remorseful when the effects wore off.

In between the more prevalent hangovers, guided by my prayers, I started to write. I came across a technique called 'Expressive Writing' pioneered by Professor J Pennebaker (2004). It is an incredible technique designed to help ease trauma and proven to have emotional and physical health benefits. Writing things down on paper helped to ease some of the emotional pain. I also wrote letters to angels and then wrote replies back to myself as if they were from the angels for guidance. Although it sounds a little crazy, it's incredible the amount of truth and wisdom that exists in those letters. One letter proved to be particularly prophetic when I spontaneously wrote in the midst of a letter 'from' the angels, 'God grant me the serenity to accept the things I cannot change, courage to change the things I can and wisdom to know the difference.' I later found out that this was called 'The Serenity Prayer'. I have no recollection of what motivated me to write the prayer and only recognised its significance in hindsight when that prayer became one of the most important prayers in the world to me.

Another event which helped me enormously was the opportunity to attend a five-day NLP (Neuro-Linguistic Programming) course in London led by Paul McKenna, the world-renowned hypnotherapist with guest appearances by Michael Neill, and Richard Bandler the co-founder of NLP. I didn't realise at the time how much confidence I might have gained in those five days and how it was to contribute to setting my life on a brand-new track. The course was extremely enjoyable with the highlight being the last day when we were 'cured' of our phobias.

There were two main options for phobia cures, spiders or snakes. We received our hypnotherapy session from our fellow trainee hypnotherapist in one room and then led into another room where several tarantulas were waiting to be handled; and on the other side, there were two pythons (called Victoria and Albert) lying in huge glass tanks. I didn't need treatment for the tarantulas, and unlike many, I was happy to approach the 'spider stall'; up close they were hairy, almost furry, which made them look cute rather than deadly, but the pythons were another matter. I had stood on a snake as a child on holiday abroad and ever since I could easily terrorise myself with the thought of a snake.

The more I tried not to think of a snake, the larger and bigger the snake would appear in my mind's eye. One of the most common scenes was when I was in the bath. The idea of a snake would come into my head, and I would be powerless against the appearance of a larger than life image of a pointed snakehead hissing and tongue-flicking as it rose out of the depths of the bubbles ready to take a fangy bite of my bare flesh. When taking a fresh towel out of the airing cupboard, it had to be checked for any unusual lumps or bumps before I was satisfied it was snake-free.

I stood in the 'snake queue' with trepidation and watched the people ahead of me handling the huge pythons.

'How can they do that?' I asked my therapist who was standing beside me. I conscientiously repeated the mantra of magic words to my subconscious right until it was my turn. I listened to the instructions on how to hold Albert. I waited for my nerves to turn to fear, but they didn't. Instead, I noticed an unusual excitement, and I didn't flinch when Albert's 12-foot body was lifted onto my shoulders, and I sensed his warm heaviness around my neck.

'What's happening here?' I wondered as I enjoyed the sensation of silky rather than slimy snakeskin sliding over my bare arms, and wondered at the beautiful iridescent colours of the python.

'Wow, this is great. Albert loves me,' I said dreamily.

'Erm, I wouldn't go that far, but I'm sure he thinks you are a safe and comfortable tree branch,' said his handler, but I was convinced that Albert loved me, and I was in love with Albert. Too soon it was time to let the next person hold my new friend. When I saw the look of terror in her eyes as she approached the python, I realised just what a great job my therapist had done with me. My therapy was a complete success; all fear had gone. My snake phobia was cured, and the effect has lasted. To this day the sight of a snake awakens curiosity and a desire to caress one of nature's beautiful creatures.

Not long after this course and almost exactly a year after my husband left Liverpool, I experienced one of the worst nights of my life. The next day, I took one of the best decisions I have ever made and which probably saved my life.

I have already written about my first meeting in AA and the wonderful impact it had on my life. I haven't drunk a drop of alcohol since. For this, I am extremely grateful. In the early days of recovery, with the guidance of my sponsor, I learned that drinking wasn't the cause but a symptom of a deeper problem. The programme encouraged me to look at myself, and I could see that I had deep-rooted issues which needing treating if I was going to stay well.

Yours,

Michaela

Chapter 32

17th August 2009

Dear St Thérèse,

I wholeheartedly threw myself into staying sober. I went to several meetings a week and read as much as possible and met my sponsor regularly. JC's kindness struck me, and if I am honest, at first I wondered if he would want anything from me in return. Then he explained that it was part of the programme of recovery to help others and that one day I would help others as much as he helped me. One of his favourite sayings is, 'You have to give it away to keep it.' JC came to my home regularly, and he sat on my sofa while I usually sat on the floor. We chatted for hours at a time. I listened to him intently. Through his questions, I came to understand that the things which I took to be common thoughts, feelings and behaviours weren't as normal as I thought. He explained what I needed to address if I was going to stay sober and get well. I see them as three aspects of a trinity, important individually, but all affecting each other. They are my relationship with myself, with others and with my Higher Power. To me, the success of addressing the first two of these depends on the quality and strength of the third. Fortunately, my relationship with my Higher Power was perhaps the strongest and healthiest. My relationship with myself suffered from a lack of honesty. I was not intentionally dishonest, more in denial. Denial had helped me to survive some of the difficulties I faced as a child and young adult. When feelings and impulses were painful, I had been taught to try and control them or try and push them away.

I know now that repressed impulses don't disappear, they lie lurking and waiting for me to be vulnerable, and I carried them around like a time bomb waiting to explode. JC's advice is always to accept and embrace my feelings, but I don't find it easy. In recovery, I had nowhere to hide, and I experienced them in all their rawness.

Beneath this denial and repression was a sense of not being good enough. One of the key issues that JC helped me to see was that I had been more courageous than I believed and that if I practised more self-honesty and self-acceptance, my courage would grow in abundance. JC also helped me to understand that I needed to be kinder to myself, not in the sense of material indulgence, more in thought and attitude. I had been hard on myself in a judgmental way since childhood. I learned that addiction results in a disconnection or alienation from the 'real self' which results in low self-worth, and recovery is about recovering (or in my case) discovering an authentic self.

I learned how my relationship with others suffered from perfectionism, people-pleasing and approval-seeking. I also had a fear of authority figures. JC helped me to learn how to be more confident and assertive with others and to tell people the truth about how I felt. This approach was challenging because I found out that for most of my life I had played a role, and in doing so I had told lies about my feelings. I had hidden behind the mask of the person I thought people wanted to see rather than presenting the real me. It came as a shock to some people when I began to express my true feelings because they hadn't seen that side of me before. I had to take responsibility for this and understand that not everyone would be happy to see the changes in me and might not like the 'real me'.

My relationship with God was a more challenging topic to discuss with JC, but I tried to explain that I had a strong faith and that I had been travelling on a spiritual journey for most of my life. JC understood that I had been a seeker and a questioner, and when I recognised this in myself, I saw how true it was in a positive way. I am always seeking for a deeper quality in my relationship with my Higher Power.

Yours,

Michaela

Chapter 33

18th August 2009

Dear St Thérèse,

Your 'little way' of spiritual childhood tells us to go to God like little children, and I love this image of a trusting child. I told JC about the 'little way', and he gave me a great insight when he said that it is not just about how we approach God, but it is also about how we view ourselves that matters. Our goal is to have the same feelings as we would towards a trusting child i.e. to be a loving parent to our inner child.

While I can understand the logic of this: I find it hard to feel it. JC shared his experience of speaking to his younger self and telling his inner child with love that everything would be okay in the future, and I was encouraged by this revelation.

Contacting my inner child is something that I haven't tried to do often, and I am not going to force it. It is too valuable an experience to push, so I am prepared to wait for it to happen spontaneously.

I find it helpful to consider God as a loving parent, and this related to my image of God when I was young. But when I grew older I somehow lost my sense of God as a loving Father and saw him more like a distant Father, someone that I was often too afraid to approach.

Yours,

Michaela

Chapter 34

19th August 2009

Dear St Thérèse,

You were able to control and regulate your emotions very well and channelled these into your spiritual desires and your vocation of love. I aspire to have better emotional control.

In my programme, we talk about 'recovery' as a process, and in meetings, I heard people talk about how they were 'recovering' their lost self, which they lost during their addiction to alcohol. While I understood this concept, I couldn't fully relate to it. I mentioned this to JC, and he agreed that there were parts of me that I couldn't recover because I had never had them in the first place, but gave me hope that I would find those aspects of myself that had never fully developed.

There must have been a time in my past when I was close to being my authentic self, but it was hard to pinpoint when this might have been. Perhaps when I felt close to God and studying, and when I was writing. The goal of my recovery was to reconnect with those elements and even more importantly to find those hidden aspects of my potential self. So I have just realised that my 'recovery' could be more aptly be called my 'discovery'.

One of the ways that I have travelled this path of discovery is through recognition of my desires and longings. In early recovery when I felt the instinctive, physical force of desire or longing, my response was to hide it. JC taught me that this was the wrong approach. When the desires and longings came through initially, they felt alien and raw and often scared me. I remember crying often and saying, 'I feel awful. What is happening to me?' and JC would say excitedly, 'This is great. It is meant to be. You are connecting with your feelings and desires.'

I remember one of the first occasions in recovery that mum and I disagreed. It was over something simple. She wanted me to spend the afternoon with her, and I wanted the visit to be shorter. I told her that I would visit but just for a couple of hours. This is where the conflict arose. I believed mum had an expectation of me that I was unable to fulfil. It had never occurred to me that I was completely at liberty to say 'I don't want to do it' and that it didn't make me a bad person. So with nervousness, I told mum that I didn't want to do what was expected of me and she seemed displeased. Although I felt unyielding emotional tugs to give in and say, 'Okay I will do it', with JC's help I stayed strong. Eventually mum and I reconciled our differences. JC told me this was a significant breakthrough. I thought that I had temporarily lost the plot, and it took JC's helpful explanation for me to recognise that my emotions were completely natural. Although emotionally I am much more literate today, I am still not good at identifying and expressing anger. I either overreact or underreact, but I am a work in progress.

The urgent longing to understand myself came most alive when writing. I did journal-writing as often as possible, but the more I did, the more I wanted to do, and becoming increasingly frustrated at the times when I wanted to write and couldn't. The desire to write was so strong that I was considering leaving my job at the university to make time to write.

I mentioned this to my boss and he kindly said, 'Let's see what we can do to help you.'

At this time I was reading avidly, as I have done most of my life. When I left Cardiff, I had so many books that mum offered to look after some of them for me. Even though I would have liked my books and bookcases back, I couldn't bring myself to ask for them, and I consoled myself with looking at them when I visited – and 'stealing' the occasional one.

Over time some of mum's and my books became intermingled. One day I was perusing the bookshelves, and I noticed a book I had never seen before. I asked to borrow it, and mum said she had picked it up in a second-hand shop and that I was welcome to have it. It was called 'Footprints on the Path' by Eileen Caddy (1981). I couldn't put it down; it touched me deeply. I read the whole book over a couple of days and felt something opening within me. It was as if the most intimate voice I had ever heard was whispering the words that Eileen wrote, addressing my heart and soul. I had never heard of Eileen Caddy, so I looked her up on the internet and discovered that she was a co-founder of the Findhorn Foundation in Scotland. I also learned that Eileen Caddy had an experience when she was in deep emotional pain, after which she wrote daily, and 'received' guidance from a still, small voice within.

After reading her book 'Footprints' which contains some of these writings, I read others she had written and felt that they came from an incredibly loving source. I also found out that as well as being a spiritual, ecological centre, and publishing house, Findhorn also had a caravan site, and I mentioned this to my boss.

The following day when I went into work, my boss said, 'You've got three weeks off, and I have booked you into a caravan at the Findhorn Foundation.' I had just over a month to wait, and I was overjoyed. I told my friend where I was going, and she said that she had been there and that I would love it.

Yours,

Michaela

Chapter 35

20th August 2009

Dear St Thérèse,

It was a nine-hour journey to Findhorn from Liverpool. It is on the east coast of Scotland in the Moray Firth. I drove overnight with Molly, my cat, on the front seat beside me and she cried most of the way. The door of her pet carrier was open, and she got out a few times and crawled onto my knee. Not the safest thing to allow while driving at 70-miles-an-hour on the motorway, but she seemed to calm down on my lap and was quieter. At times her crying made me anxious but overall I was extremely excited to be responding to the call of something deep within, and I sensed something special was going to happen there. When we settled into the caravan, I felt at peace and excited too. I intended to write and write and write. I woke on my first day so eager to start that I didn't even get dressed first. I wrote about hope and what it meant to me. I had a vague idea for a novel about a girl called Hope and how she came to live up to her name.

Being in Findhorn felt completely indulgent, and for once I didn't feel guilty; I longed to enjoy myself and savour every minute. I wasn't lonely once; just the opposite, I relished the solitude. Findhorn is a world-renowned community which started in the 1960s by Eileen and Peter Caddy. It grew from adverse circumstances when the couple ended up penniless living in a small caravan with their children on the edge of a caravan site which was essentially a rubbish dump. The original caravan is still there today in the garden at the heart of the community. The Findhorn garden is one of the most spiritual and special places I have ever visited.

The first time I walked into the garden, I experienced a rare moment where all my senses heightened in sync with each other. I heard a chorus of birds singing. I could smell the pine trees. I saw all the different kinds of flowers. I sat down on a stone bench warmed by the sun, and I felt something special was happening. It was as if the garden was offering a spiritual embrace.

Whenever I am meditating and seeking a tranquil place, I visit the Findhorn garden in my mind and sit on one of the benches and look up at the canopy of trees surrounding the small lawn. Sometimes I kneel on the ground next to the small altar, or I roam through the vegetable garden admiring the huge sunflowers. I may sit still and let the dragonflies land on me or gaze at the small meadow area waiting for a bird to hop out onto the lawn.

It is a remarkable legacy that the founders have left, a foundation of guidance and learning for all souls and a practical blueprint for a more environmentally friendly way of life. No matter what time of year I go, the sun is always shining. Every time I have visited the garden, even on a dull day, the clouds will eventually part, and a ray of sunshine will burst through. I will lift my face to the sun and draw in nature's warmth and light into my whole being.

The outer petals of my heart opened in response to the warmth of the inspiration of the spirit of Findhorn. I didn't explore the community at all for the first few days because I was too shy and made the excuse of being too busy writing. I eventually ventured out and met a lovely girl called Gemma, also a visitor, who showed me the gardens, the Universal Hall, the original caravan, the Sanctuary and the eco-village. We laughed at the irony that she knew so much and had only been there a couple of days, and I had explored so little and had been there over a week.

I told Gemma that I had come to Findhorn to write, and Gemma said that she had come to explore the theme of 'connection' within her heart. She was planning to bring a new dance experience to the UK called Zumba which I had never heard of (but I know today to be very popular). We experienced a lovely connection with each other as we walked around chatting and I invited her back to my caravan for afternoon tea. Gemma told me that there was a going to be a talk later that evening by Marshall B. Rosenberg the pioneer of 'non-violent communication'. I had heard of him but hadn't read any of his books, and I was keen to attend.

The talk was brilliant, and I learned how violent my inner talk was. I also learned how to identify and develop a life purpose. Marshall said, 'Find something that you enjoy doing which will be beneficial to others.' I loved the simplicity and impact of this.

Halfway through my visit to Findhorn, Terry came to visit me. Terry was then my new 'boyfriend'. His mum and dad lived opposite me, and we also had mutual friends. I liked Terry from the moment I met him about nine months earlier, so much so that one day when I was in bed with a very high temperature, and a little delirious, I sent him a text saying, 'When I get better will you come for a cup of tea?' This approach was forward of me because it was unlike me to be proactive in these matters of the heart. I was in bed for quite a few days recuperating from the virus, but when I was back on my feet, Terry called with a huge bouquet of flowers, which was the start of our romance.

Terry travelled to Findhorn on the train, and I went to Inverness to collect him. I was nervous about him coming but excited too. He stayed for five days, and we explored the foundation, the beautiful Findhorn Bay and the magnificent beach and enjoyed the fabulous sunsets. While we were falling in love with Findhorn, we were also falling in love with each other. We have been back to Findhorn several times since the original visit. We go there to fill our hearts and spirits with its wonderful magic. I have read several books about Findhorn, and many people say that the place calls them there, and I understand what they mean.

Of the many blessing I received at Findhorn, one of the most important was responding to the challenge of my understanding of love. I knew it to be faulty: to love someone in my view involved being responsible for them. My childhood experiences encouraged me to be like this. Love consisted of finding out what a person expected of me and then working out how I could meet those expectations. I rarely thought about what I wanted from the other person, but if they were unable to meet my expectations (for whatever reasons), I judged them as 'unloving'. I never felt consciously resentful if someone didn't love me, I didn't blame them because I didn't deserve to be loved.

Back to Findhorn and my 'lessons in love'. I repeatedly listened to an audio CD of Eileen Caddy's teaching on unconditional love (2005). She helped me to realise that love is not a currency or a commodity or something that has to be earned or even something that you only give to receive. I realised how much conditional love I had experienced. 'I will love you if ...'; 'I will love you when ...'; 'If you don't do ... then I won't love you.'

I learned that to practise unconditional love was much harder than conditional love. I don't know if Eileen Caddy was aware of your teachings, but I am sure she would have wholeheartedly approved of them. I also learned that good things come from acknowledging and acting on our longings. Going to Findhorn came out of a desire to know myself better and a compelling need to write. I was expressing myself in a safe and spiritual environment, and I loved being present and the self-awareness this gave my whole being.

Yours,

Michaela

Chapter 36

21st August 2009

Dear St Thérèse,

In the sanctuary of Findhorn, I found the courage to face some painful emotions. There is one day that is prominent in my memory. Molly and I had a routine whereby she came into my bedroom and jumped on the bed to wake me when the sun came up, usually between 4am and 5am. I would let her out of the caravan and then she would wait on the doorstep for me to let her back in a couple of hours later.

On my second to last morning, I woke about 4.30am and let Molly out and went back to bed and woke again about 7.30am but I was tired, and I turned over and went straight back to sleep. When I eventually got up at 9.30am and went to the glass door to let Molly in, she wasn't there. I thought she must be asleep somewhere under the caravan as she liked to do most afternoons. Throughout the morning I waited to see her black-and-white silhouette behind the mottled glass, and I went outside several times and called her, but she didn't come. At lunchtime, the lady in the caravan opposite told me that she had seen Molly at about 6am waiting on the doorstep, but she hadn't seen her since. After lunch, I walked around the caravan site expecting her to come running to me at any moment. By mid-afternoon, I was really worried and phoned Terry to see if he had any advice. Terry was reassuring and said she was probably curled up somewhere in the shade as the sun was scorching hot.

I spent the rest of the afternoon walking around searching for her and calling her name. I even walked to the roadside half expecting to find her lying lifeless in the gutter having been run over. The image was so sharp in my mind that it was such a relief that she wasn't there. By this time I assumed that Molly must have lost her way as it was close to the weekend and a lot of touring caravans had arrived during the day, and I was concerned that she wouldn't recognise her caravan.

By early evening I had walked and called her name to exhaustion. I got several phone calls from Terry and each time reported, 'No news yet.' I decided to try and distract myself and started reading a little book about guilt. I don't know if it was my anxious state or heightened sensitivity, but that afternoon brought an insight that I hadn't had so clearly before. I realised that I lived in an almost permanent state of guilt and how much emotional energy it took up within me. For instance, I reflected on how much I was blaming myself for Molly's absence and the thoughts of 'If only I had got up earlier. It's all my fault. I have let her down by not looking after her properly. What if I have lost her forever? What if she dies through my neglect? I will never forgive myself,' went round and round in my head throughout the day. My efforts to stop the thoughts had little effect. It was a familiar experience to know that my thoughts weren't helping me, but the more I resisted them and fought them, the stronger they seemed to get. The 'guilt book' described a meditation exercise for expelling guilt through breathing techniques. I did the meditation, and it gave me some relief and the powerful realisation that I had been bullying myself for years, and it was time to stop. It was time to start trying to love myself a little more. This insight was a vital step in my recovery. I finished reading the book, and there was still no sign of Molly, so I prayed that the near permanent state of guilt would lift, and asked for guidance. I also prayed hard about Molly and said that if it was God's will that I go home without her, as much as I loved her, I was ready to accept it.

I carried on looking for her throughout the evening, except for a quick dash to the beach to watch the sun go down at about 10pm. When I returned to the caravan in the dark and saw that she still hadn't returned, I felt sad. Terry phoned me to tell me that he and two of my friends would be leaving in the morning to come and help look for her.

I said, 'You can't travel eight hours just to look for a missing cat.'

He said, 'We aren't doing it for Molly; we are doing it for you.'

One of the most helpful suggestions was from my friend Jen who suggested through Terry that I put some of my socks (worn ones) outside the caravan so that if Molly had lost her way, she might be able to pick up my scent and smell her way home. So in the moonlight, like Hansel and Gretel (using socks instead of breadcrumbs) I carefully laid a trail of about 20 worn socks around the perimeter of the caravan. By midnight, I had set up a makeshift bed on the sofa where I could see the glass door. I decided that I might as well write because I couldn't sleep with Molly missing. I had been writing for nearly an hour when I looked up and saw Molly's profile on the other side of the glass door.

'She's back!' my heart cried with joy, and then I peered through the glass to check that my eyes hadn't tricked me as they had earlier. Several times that day walking around the site, I had spotted something which looked like black-and-white fur in the distance only to find that it was a dirty plastic bag, or an old wellington boot, or a pair of baby rabbits playing in the sun.

I jumped up and opened the door, and yes it was her. Molly had come home! I scooped her up into my arms and cried with relief, and she seemed as pleased to see me, nuzzling my neck and purring.

I let Terry know that she was back safely and he passed on the news to concerned friends, and I thanked them with all my heart for their support throughout the day. We unanimously agreed that the smelly socks had worked. When I retrieved them the next morning, Molly joined me playfully jumping and sniffing from sock to sock. In between sniffs, she looked at me, and I imagined her communicating either her approval that the smelly socks had done the trick, or her disdain that I was a complete idiot to have gone to so much trouble. Didn't she deserve to have gone exploring because wasn't she on her holidays too?! I nearly lost Molly again on our journey home. She jumped out of the car when we stopped at a service station and ran into the path of a lorry and missed being run over by a millisecond, but that's another story.

I arrived home from Findhorn re-energized and grateful for all the blessings I had received like beautiful seeds planted in me. All I had to do was nurture them. I felt clearer about developing my path of personal development and spiritual growth and my vocation to write. I thought that I would continue to write about hope and love but was surprised that most of my writing and reading was around 'taking responsibility'. It reminded me of when I was in my twenties in Cardiff, I had taught a class called 'Psychology and Adult Life'. One of the most important elements of the eight-week course was how important it was to accept that while we might not be responsible for what happens, we are always accountable for our reactions: for how we respond to every circumstance in our life. I ran the night class several times and loved exploring this theme of personal responsibility with my students. The old saying that 'a person teaches what they most need to learn' seems true in my case.

But why had this theme become so prominent in my heart and mind again? Wasn't it an old lesson that I had already learned? My thoughts asked me why, after being in such a spiritual place and being so inspired, was I caught in the tangle of a past lesson. Then I realised that while I had intellectually learned its truth, I perhaps hadn't fully absorbed its truth into my heart? There was probably an important reason why I did so much writing about this topic straight after visiting Findhorn and sensed that it was important to continue with it, even though I wasn't sure why.

Eventually, my head won the battle over my heart, and I put the topic of personal responsibility aside and moved onto another interest that I thought would tease me with the secret of happiness. Today I can't even remember what that new topic was.

Yours,

Michaela

Chapter 37

22nd August 2009

Dear St Thérèse,

After you had heard your calling to be a nun, and your father and uncle had given their permission, you wanted to enter the convent as soon as possible. At 15 years of age, conventionally you were far too young to join, and influential people tried to persuade you to wait. When you went on a pilgrimage to Rome, you took the opportunity of your audience with the Pope Leo XIII to ask his permission to join the convent early (even though you had been told not to speak to him).

In the summer of 2007, I went to Rome with mum, not on a pilgrimage, more as a martyr. I had agreed to go out of duty and couldn't say no but did my best not to show how I felt so that mum wouldn't be upset. I intended to spend most of the holiday focusing on her happiness and putting my feelings to one side. This approach is a worthy thing to do if it is done willingly and with a good heart. Indeed it would be a lovely thing to do, but the root of my actions weren't loving, they were fearful. I felt frustrated at being unable to tell the truth about how I felt. This reaction was typical of how I reacted to mum. I was too afraid to be my true self with her. What stopped me telling the truth? It is a lifelong habit that I had developed from childhood. When I make a feeble attempt at expressing my true feelings, and they result in disapproval, I suppress them and pretend that they don't exist and that I am happy with whatever plans we were executing.

A few weeks before we were due to go, although I was frightened of upsetting mum I made a brave attempt to speak my truth and told her that although I wouldn't back out of going, I didn't really want to go. Her response wasn't as bad as I thought it would be and she seemed to understand and accept I would still be going so as not to let her down. What was wrong with me? I had friends who would have given anything to be going on a trip with their mum. What story was I telling myself? Primarily, that I was a wicked daughter for not wanting to accompany my mother to Rome; and secondly, she was a bad mother for forcing me to go in the first place. In the days before going, I prayed a lot to find the strength to overcome my ambivalence and not to let it spoil mum's holiday.

On many similar occasions, I wished I could wave a magic wand for people to change their expectations of me, but now I realise that the problem didn't lie with them, it lay with me. It was my problem. I also understand today that being honest would have meant also finding the courage to expose other untruths I had told in the past and facing the backlog of pushed-down feelings would have been too overwhelming. So I continued to play the role of being happy with my decisions with regards to my family when often I was screaming inside because the truth couldn't come out and it was causing me a lot of pain.

Once we arrived in Rome, I enjoyed it much more than I thought I would. I managed to stay attentive and considerate to mum, and she was attentive and considerate to me; in fact, she was lovely. I did what my programme has taught me to do which is to stay in the present. I took each day as it came and wasn't too overwhelmed. I enjoyed the sightseeing very much and being in mum's company. I genuinely enjoyed myself. Did this make me feel better? Yes, and no. I was grateful that mum and I had a happy holiday, but I felt incredibly guilty afterwards because I had been so reluctant to go in the first place.

I now I understand that not dealing with repressed emotions gives them power over me.

Yours,

Michaela

Chapter 38

23rd August 2009

Dear St Thérèse,

At Mass at the cathedral today there was more news about your relics coming to Liverpool. There will be a meeting for all the volunteer stewards nearer the time to find out what duties we will be performing. I am excited about your relics coming, like something special is going to happen. It is uncharacteristically confident of me even to be contemplating such a positive outcome.

At the end of 2007, my contract at the university came to an end, and I decided to do freelance training and consultancy on a self-employed basis. I was fortunate in that I was offered plenty of work but unfortunate in that I was unable to say no when I had too much work. Consequently, I was extremely busy with designing and writing courses and travelling all over the UK delivering them, and I often felt stressed in trying to do too much.

Eventually the inevitable happened, and my physical health was adversely affected. One day, I was doubled up with pain in my stomach and ended up in the hospital with suspected appendicitis. After three days of lying in a hospital bed in pain, nil by mouth, each day expecting to have an operation, the consultant said that I didn't have appendicitis and that I either had a burst cyst on my ovary or a virus in my bowel.

After a week in hospital I went home feeling very weak and, in my journals, I wrote that I suspected that I had contributed to the physical illness by overdoing it. I felt exhausted.

When I had recovered, did I slow down? No, not at all. Why is it so difficult to learn our lessons? I repeat the most painful mistakes. I am sure that I am not alone in this? What does it take for a person to say finally, enough! I know it takes a lot for me to surrender. What keeps me going on a particular path even though I know it is taking me in the wrong direction? It is usually self-will. Self-will often comes from being too afraid to admit that we might be wrong, so we keep going in the hope that things will change of their own accord. Pride plays a part too. It takes some humility to admit that we might be mistaken. This admission rarely happens, though. Usually, things just continue to get worse until the situation brings us to a place where we can't ignore the truth any longer.

It is a 'rock bottom' when we find ourselves in a situation where all our options have run out, and we have no alternative but to face the stark reality of our situation. But sometimes even then, real honesty eludes us, we still try and blame other people or circumstances, when the best thing we can do is to admit the facts, accept the circumstances we are in, and then take responsibility for the part we have played. I obviously reached a rock bottom when I stopped drinking, but how many other times had I ignored the warning signs and continued on a path thinking, 'I will fix it; I can do it; I will make things better'? It takes more than willpower. It requires surrender.

After being in the hospital, I had a great opportunity, if not for a complete surrender, to try and slow down a little and take a more balanced approach to work, but I didn't. Soon I was back on the road working and almost as busy as ever. I accepted all the work offered to me. I couldn't refuse and caved under pressure not to let anyone down. There was, however, a subtle difference between this situation and other times when I have ignored the warning signs; this time, I knew for certain that I was heading for another crisis. I just didn't know when it would come. As I expected, instead of improving, my health deteriorated. Over the next year, at different times I was diagnosed with anxiety and IBS.

To celebrate his birthday, Terry and I went on a river cruise on the River Nile in Egypt, and while the holiday was most enjoyable, I spent most of the time exhausted and then became ill and bed bound for the last couple of days in Egypt. I knew that the physical illnesses were symptoms of a deeper cause. What was driving me to work harder than I needed to or was good for me? I was aware of my habits of people-pleasing and approval-seeking and perfectionism, but I saw these also as symptoms of a deeper problem. I used my journal-writing and expressive writing techniques to try and uncover what lay beneath the physical symptoms as I approached my writing like a detective trying to solve a 'whodunnit'.

This clinical methodical approach served me well. I made helpful discoveries about myself. My lifelong habit had been to only ever dare to express hurt when under the influence of alcohol and so these expressions of hurt had been negatively and unfairly misdirected, exaggerated or distorted, so much so that I didn't believe them to be genuine. I convinced myself that they were just unpleasant feelings that were triggered by alcohol, and I would beat myself up afterwards for what I had expressed. I told myself that the feelings were just the product of self-destructive tendencies. I began to realise the extent of my self-deception.

For the first couple of years of sobriety, I didn't think I had any significant hurt to express. But painful emotions from the past kept reoccurring which told me that there was something within me that needed addressing. I didn't even know that it was unexpressed hurt that was lurking within me until my writing started to reveal some clues and then I was on a mission to find out what they meant. Guilt and anxiety were the main suspects, but I always felt that there was something else, just outside of my conscious awareness but it was elusive, and I couldn't name it, but I didn't give up.

My post-hospitalisation surrender came almost a year afterwards. It was April 2009. One day I was in my study at home with JC, and we were chatting. I had been unwell again and felt overwhelmed by the amount of work that needed attention on my desk.

I calmly said to JC, 'I have got to stop.' It was like I imagined Forest Gump would have felt when he had run for thousands of miles, and he suddenly knew it was time to stop running. I had made my decision. I told JC that I wanted to spend some time doing full-time writing and felt immense relief and as usual, JC was completely enthusiastic about me deciding to commit to what he called 'my heart's desire'. Unusually on this occasion, I didn't procrastinate about my decision. I felt firm but anxious about how it would be carried out. Indeed it seemed almost impossible. I didn't imagine that I would have the necessary courage to carry it out. However, with the help of Terry's support and JC's guidance and some other relevant and timely circumstances, before long all arrangements had been made for me just to write; and nothing else.

The future lay ahead like a blank sheet of paper. I was excited by its possibilities, and although anxious about the uncertainties, I felt sure that something more than my usual willpower was driving me. For once in my life, I didn't question it. I tried to accept it, and this was JC's advice. 'Follow your heart', and I tried to do so. Little did I know that one of the most significant events of my life lay just a few months into the future.

I have reached an important point in my story, St Thérèse. I have brought you up to date with my life so far. This letter brings us to where my story started in April 2009 and to the beginning of my journal entries at the beginning of this book where I wrote about making my commitment to being a full-time writer. From this point, I will write my letters to you about things that are happening in the present rather than the past. The most important event to be happening in the foreseeable future is the visit of your relics to this country. They will be arriving in a few weeks at the end of September, and I am so excited.

I have written to you as a pilgrim in preparation for the visit of your relics. I felt inspired by your example and your 'Story of a Soul', and in these letters, I have told you a lot about myself and my life. However, I don't know what to expect when your relics arrive. I am not clear about what and why I am reviewing the past. I am not sure why it is relevant with regards to your visit, but I have done it in good faith. I have faith that telling you about the sorry state of my soul has already brought me some healing. I am noticing particular aspects of my faith in you. I feel so close to you, not just as a revered saint but almost like a sister. Also, your parents Rene and Zelie Martin come to my mind often. The day that I went to Mass and found out about you was the date of the first anniversary of their beatification.

You loved roses and scattered rose petals as a child, and when you were lying in the infirmary when you were dying, you could see the rose bushes in the garden. You said you would spend your heaven showering the earth with roses. You have already sent me several 'roses'. I have been able to deal with difficult situations with much less anxiety. For example, mum and I are planning to go to Florence together in a couple of weeks, and I am not as anxious as I thought I would be (although that situation might change). Indeed part of me is looking forward to going there because I know that you visited Florence on your pilgrimage to Rome, and I am hoping to find somewhere in Florence that I know you visited.

I notice actual roses all the time, and each time my heart leaps a little in being a little closer to your perfect heart.

Yours,

Michaela

PART FOUR

'Soul Searching'

CHAPTERS 39 TO 59

Chapter 39

27th August 2009

Dear St Thérèse,

This morning, as I was waking up, I lay in bed for a while thinking, but the thoughts felt more like external guidance rather than inner thoughts. This experience is happening to me more and more recently. I know they are my thoughts, but it is as if they are coming from somewhere other than my natural mind. Today I 'received' some clear ideas about life purpose and guidance. I will try and describe the gist of the experience. In spite of conscious searching and often being compelled to do certain things, for most of my adult life it is true that I have been unable to define what I would call my undisputed purpose in my life. But through the reading and writing I am doing in preparation for your visit; I am closer to finding my true life purpose.

This morning I realised that I had a sense of vocation throughout my life connected to my faith. In my mind's eye, I felt guided and saw myself guiding others on how to find a vocation and life purpose. It was a strange image to see myself confidently encouraging and guiding others to achieve their goals and dreams with conviction when I am so unsure about mine. I felt tense, and in response, I heard in my thoughts the phrase, 'You are preaching.' The word 'preaching' didn't seem right, and then the word 'exhortation' came to mind, and I relaxed a little which was strange because I wasn't sure what it meant.

I have just looked up the definition of exhortation, and the dictionary says 'the ability to help others to reach their full potential through encouraging, challenging, comforting and guiding'. I had an 'aha' moment when I realised that this is what I have often yearned to do. This definition describes what people do in my recovery programme and describes what JC has done with me. 'Comforting and guiding' is what I aspire to do with others. For example, when I saw my friend yesterday he was in so much pain with his knee, I urged him to go to the doctors as he is going on an overseas holiday soon and yet he can hardly walk. He phoned me earlier to say he went to the doctors this morning and will be having treatment before he goes on holiday. He said he wouldn't have done this if I hadn't suggested it. I understand why. He was in terrible pain when I was with him yesterday, and I could see that it was affecting his reasoning. He is usually so practical and yet I could see that most of his energy was being used up in fighting the pain. There was no emotional energy left for him to work out the best thing for him to do to get better. However, I am not taking credit for this, but thinking back to similar occasions when I 'tune in' to a person and sense what is happening and what might be needed, although intuitive impressions for solutions often come with clarity, I don't usually offer strong advice to people about their health in case I'm wrong. Yesterday was an exception.

I was just wondering how these impressions come, and the best way of describing it is that it is like an auditory feeling. At times of need, I listen for information, but I don't hear an external voice, it is like my mind and body 'hear' a response. Am I being guided now? I intuitively don't like the word preaching. I see it as imposing your will on another. But exhortation is different. An exhorter is a helper, counsellor, and comforter. The meaning of exhortation includes motivating and offering hope. The goal of exhortation is 'transformation'. Would the modern word for 'exhortation' be 'coaching'? This idea is food for thought.

I have been thinking about goals recently and how important they are in reaching our life purpose. I am all over the place with my goals. I change them all the time. Why? Is it because I doubt myself? I want to commit to something and stick with it. Is it because I haven't found my purpose yet? Is my purpose to love more? If not it is certainly one of my goals. How can I put this into practice? Please help me to realise that it is through my writing that I will find/fulfil my purpose. I am not sure yet what it is. While I can 'feel' things I can 'feel' loving, but I keep thinking it is not enough, that I have to 'do' something useful. Am I putting too much emphasis on being useful? Am I expecting constant feedback on my efforts?

Please, help me to understand I could never do enough to 'earn' God's approval. Indeed, if I received what I deserved, I don't think it would be much indeed. I understand that all our talents are the gifts of grace. We don't need to earn them. It would be impossible. They are gifts of grace given to us with unconditional love. As much as I know this logically, I find it hard to know the truth of this in my heart.

Yours,

Michaela

Chapter 40

28th August 2009

Dear St Thérèse,

I am re-reading your 'Story of a Soul' and noticing how much trust there is in your faith. Approaching God like a trusting child approaching their loving Father as you describe in your 'little way' leaves no room for self-doubt. You seemed to have little self-doubt in your life and, if you did, you knew that it had no place in an open heart, and so worked hard to eradicate it. Just as light eliminates darkness, so can trust eliminate self-doubt?

I have had many conversations with JC about trust. One I remember in particular. I had just explained to him that I had hardly trusted myself for most of my life.

'Who have you trusted then?' JC asked.

'Only God.'

'What about other people?' he asked.

'No, although I have given a lot of my time and energy to others, it wasn't out of trust or love, it was most often out of fear and a sense of duty.'

Today when I was meditating I felt an uneasy sensation within my body, but I couldn't put a name to it. I was thinking about what stops me fulfilling my commitments, certainly fear, but I was wondering what particular aspect of fear holds me back? I focused on a particular problem that I felt 'blocked' about which was writing these letters to you – they will never be sent and obviously never read by you in mortal form – and I realised that I was experiencing self-doubt which has been familiar throughout my life. I have battled doubt with the super-exertion of my self-will on many occasions, but I have learned that this is not the antidote to self-doubt. What is the antidote? Is it self-belief? I have had little self-belief at any stage of my life.

In your 'Story of a Soul,' you don't talk about belief much, but you do speak of faith. What is the difference between belief and faith? Is belief more to do with thinking and faith more to do with actions? I see faith as meaning trust in a Higher Power or others, and it is not something that we have for ourselves (we don't talk about 'self-faith', but we do talk about 'self-belief'), and belief is that trust we can have in others but also in ourselves. So faith for me is the act of putting my trust in my Higher Power and others, and self-belief is putting my trust in myself.

I used to think that as long as I trusted God, it didn't matter if I didn't trust myself, but I am changing my mind about this. I have been wondering, how can I learn to trust myself more? It is necessary to be able to trust myself as well as God and others. Indeed my spiritual growth depends on it. If I trust someone and they let me down, while I might be upset for a while, it is an easier pain to bear than the pain of knowing myself to be untrustworthy. Is this what self-doubt does? Does it protect us from the deeper pain of seeing ourselves as a failure?

I remember the day when I realised my truth about trust. I was about a year sober, and it was a Sunday afternoon, and I was driving to see my dad, and I was late as usual. As I stopped the car at the traffic lights, I felt frustrated at the delay in my journey, and my inner response was typical of such times of not living up to my expectations.

'You are late again! Can't you be on time for once! Why do you put yourself through the stress of a rushed journey when it is easily avoided?' etc. etc.

In the middle of the tirade of self-castigation from my inner critic, my thoughts stopped abruptly, and I heard a single statement, both a revelation and the simplest of truths to why I couldn't meet the smallest expectations from myself.

'I don't trust myself.' I heard it once in my mind, and its truth so took me that I repeated it out loud. 'I don't trust myself.' I sighed deeply as if from relief at finally discovering the greatest of truths.

'It explains a lot,' I thought as I continued my journey.

'I don't trust myself and have hardly ever have trusted myself.' The impact of this statement didn't dwindle over the coming days, indeed the more I thought about it, the more I became convinced of its truth, and although it was a sad admission, I felt relieved to admit it finally to myself.

Doubt lives in me in the place where trust should have been. What is doubt? It is a feeling of uncertainty which might make me look for more evidence about something. Mostly it is a negative state. However, doubt might be necessary for me to believe in something and so can it be positive too? Why does self-doubt feel so negative? It is more than a feeling of uncertainty.

Self-doubt can cause us to deny the reality of a situation. We might have talents and abilities and qualities that we don't recognise or acknowledge within ourselves because of self-doubt which is a terrible waste of talent and potential. Even when others tell us about the good things they see within us, we still don't believe them. I have learned that this denial of our gifts is prideful. It is certainly not practising humility. Self-doubt stops me from being the best I can be and from reaching my potential because it stops me taking the actions I need to take.

How can your example help me to overcome self-doubt? Your example teaches me to be confident in my faith even when I am not confident in myself. You believed that Jesus was always with you even when you didn't feel his presence, you had complete faith that He was still with you. You described this as like being in a little boat with Jesus, and when you felt disconnected, you imagined that Jesus wasn't disconnected from you, but just asleep, and still beside you. Your example teaches me that although I might doubt myself, I can always put my trust in God.

Your selflessness also teaches me that I can overcome self-doubt when I take the focus off myself and put my energy into helping others. However, here I come across another sticking point, that of my intentions. I have recently understood how important intentions are. I was thinking about how when we repress feelings that some of our subsequent behaviour can be unconscious, and when an unconscious need drives action, we often don't know the meaning of the act. For example, if I repressed the feeling of being unloved I might unconsciously be seeking the love that eluded me, but I might not be consciously aware of this dynamic.

If we can make conscious what is unconscious through understanding the feelings that have been repressed and hidden, then can we start to understand our true intentions? Character comes from a person's intentions as much as their actions. If my action is helpful to someone else and my intention is loving, then I have done something useful. If my action is helpful to another, but my primary intention is not to do something good but to meet some other inner emotional need, such as seeking another's approval, then my action is less than it should be. In this case, I might have deceived at worst or pretended at best. We don't just delude ourselves; we are also victims of our self-deception.

I know that you understood this. You battled with scruples in your early life and always strove to be pure. After your Christmas Eve conversion did your intentions become more genuine? Did they lose their childhood immaturity? They did. This purity is why you are a saint. Your actions had no remit or ulterior motive other than love. My behaviour has not been as pure in intention as it has been action. I tell my brother that as children it looked like he was the naughty one and I was the good one, but this is incorrect. His intentions were often purer than mine. As I say to him, 'You often did the wrong things for the right reasons, and I often did the right thing for the wrong reasons.'

What has been my primary intention in my relationship with God: for him to love me and guide me in a useful life. Here my intentions have been the purest. I have wanted to discern God's will for me and to follow it. In recovery, I have had experience of how to do this. I have learned to pray, and my faith has developed.

What has been my primary intention in my relationship with myself? For me to find something within me that I am good at, that is useful to others, and that will help me find some self-acceptance. I have lived most of my life in a lack of self-acceptance and seeking the approval I needed externally rather than internally. Is this the best of intentions? I think not.

What has been my primary intention in my relationship with others: for others to love and approve of me, or at least to like me. This is the order in which I put most of my effort, my relationship with others, then myself, then God. I realise that my priorities are back to front. My priority should be my relationship with God, then myself, and then others. I am sure that I am not alone in putting external influences as a higher priority in my life than they should be.

If I follow your example, love should be my priority in intentions and actions in each relationship. While I might be able to work this out rationally, I find it difficult to know the truth of this. What stops me? Is it fear?

Yours,

Michaela

Chapter 41

29th August 2009

Dear St Thérèse,

You said 'I only love simplicity. I have a horror of pretence' (Foley 2000), and your motives were pure. It came as a disappointment to discover that my motives and intentions weren't as pure as I thought they were. Is examining our motives essential to a spiritual life? I have found it to be enlightening, and I'm sure there are more insights to discover.

Driven by the motivation of survival, of the fight or flight variety, much of my behaviour was fear-based, but I have tried to deny or repress fear by pretending that I wasn't afraid. We are like actors in a play, and sometimes the lines become blurred between the real person and the character being played. I was lost in the role of the professional woman dedicated to her work because it stopped me facing the emotional pain that was bubbling under the surface of the real me; it stopped me facing my true fears.

Thankfully, in the recovery process, we don't become fearless, we learn to handle our fears more effectively, and we become more honest. I have tried to stop pretending and to be more honest with myself; and although the principle is easy to understand, i.e. to be true to ourselves, this journey to our authentic selves is one of the hardest to make.

Honesty helps me to discover that my motives haven't been what I thought they were. When I thought I was helping others, there was a deeper motive of protecting myself, even if I wasn't conscious of it, I was avoiding having to look at my behaviour. It is easier to examine and judge the behaviour of another than our own because we don't have to directly experience the pain of what we find. I became adept at working out what others expected of me but rarely considered what I wanted from a situation, and if I dared to do so, I didn't believe that what I wanted was attainable or that I deserved it.

While you and my recovery journey are teaching me to seek my motives from within, this change in focus from pretending and compliance to being honest is one of the hardest things I have ever done. There are many obstacles that the ego will throw up to block the path to authenticity. The ego doesn't want us to be discovered as frauds, so it will fight to maintain the illusion for as long as possible. That's why the inner surrender required for the quantum change that we experience in recovery usually needs a 'rock bottom' to initiate it. Nothing else will do other than us being the most broken we can imagine being.

The growth in the positive circumstances of my life reflects the maturity of my motives. I am relieved that generally, my motives are much more positive and healthier than they used to be. I am doing my best, and I am putting a lot of effort into understanding my motives, but the more I learn about them, the less I seem to know. As my personal growth develops, it seems like an important piece of my life is missing. It is a heightened uncertainty about myself. Is the missing piece of me spiritual, physical, mental or emotional? I suspect that it involves all levels of my being, but most notable at the moment is the emotional level; there are certain feelings which I experience which I still can't identify. Some are positive emotions, others less positive. Are they connected with hidden or repressed emotions, maybe anger? I am not sure.

I have often thought that I have found what I have been looking for, but the sense of discovery is short-lived. Sometimes I see this as encouragement that I might be closer to finding what I seek, at other times I despair.

I don't feel at all brave in this search, but you are giving me hope that I will find 'freedom' from this endless searching. I understand that each time I confront and embrace the uncertainty rather than run away from it, I come closer to my release.

Yours,

Michaela

Chapter 42

30th August 2009

Dear St Thérèse,

Did you speak to me during the night? I experienced an unusual mixture of lucid dreaming and 'night time daydreaming'. I repeatedly fell asleep and knew I was dreaming and then awoke and continued with the same train of thought. It was as if I could 'hear' the thoughts that came from an inner voice.

My thoughts were about how life passes in moments, brief separate scenes, being played so quickly that you no longer see the still pictures, only what looks like real movement. We 'receive' impressions about the past, present and future, as single 'frames' and they powerfully motivate and influence us. For example, if I 'see' myself as responsible for others, then this is what I will believe and act upon. So I wondered, if I have more positive impressions, will my life will my life become more positive?

During the night this insight felt good, somewhat liberating, but there is a piece missing. There is something just beyond my consciousness that I can't fully recall – a sense that this can't be so simple! Do we simply act on simple single impressions? Then I thought about how much notice I take of impressions presented by others, but I hardly pay any attention all at to my subjective feelings. For instance, I thought about mum and how responsive I am to what she wants of me e.g. time with me, and yet I hardly think about what I want for myself e.g. time to myself; time to relax.

I also thought about how our impressions can change over time. For instance, if my opinion of mum at one time made me scared, today it might make me defensive, so I have made progress. What is the impact of how the 'internal representation' of my mum altered? She has less power over me than she used to. I am stronger. I am working towards the being whole. I am less guilty. But deep within there are other unaddressed emotions.

My thoughts also took me to the influence of these impressions. If I 'see' that someone is angry in my presence, I just assume that they are mad at me, I don't check it out and react accordingly. So I was reminded how important it is not to just respond to first impressions i.e. 'don't judge a book by its cover'. When I was 'experiencing' these insights during the night, I got the sense that God (or was it you St Thérèse?) was suggesting to me that I look at the 'impressions' and question them. Then I could understand that they may just be a matter of my perception and not always represent the absolute truth.

Writing helps me to explore and make sense of my impressions and perceptions. It takes me through a process where I can examine my perspectives and check that they are real. Is there is an absolute external truth about anything, or is everything just a matter of perception? I don't think I am a black-and-white person and for me, there are many shades of grey.

I was also thinking about positive and negative impressions. My dad has just come to mind, and how these days he works hard to create positive images, for instance by making people laugh. Oh my goodness, it's just come to me! I can see what was missing in my thought process during the night! Actions speak louder than words! It is not the impression that is so important; rather it is the action that we take in response. We must own our feelings rather than rely on others and it is vital that we act on the correct impressions; otherwise, we are not true to ourselves.

The phrase 'actions speak louder than words' reminds me of a conversation I heard yesterday on the radio about the people who were the most successful 'Big Brother' competitors. The presenter made the point that the winners had something in common. They all appeared to consistently (but perhaps unconsciously) repeat a small, simple action that often went unnoticed but may be an influential factor regarding the overall impression that person makes on others. For example, one person throughout the whole time he was in the house just kept making a fire; another winner kept pouring drinks; another just smiled a lot. It was a small, unremarkable 'selfless' habit that seemed to be the key to popularity with the other housemates and the general public. This insight reminds me of something else, doing for others in small ways, which is the essence of the 'little way': the spirituality of the significant impact that taking small, simple actions can have.

Later

I have just returned home from Mass, and there was an amazing coincidence in how one of the readings was so relevant to what I had experienced during the night. It was from the Letter of St James 1:17–18, 21–22, and 27 about taking action:

'Accept and submit to the word which has been planted in you and can save your souls. But you must do what the words tell you, and not just listen to it and deceive yourselves' (Solemn Mass 30th August 2009).

Also in the Mass, the reading was about how it is not what goes into to us that make us 'unclean', it is what comes out of us. This made me think about how we can't always choose circumstances, but we can always choose how to respond to situations and how they affect us. These teachings tell me that I must act on the spiritual insights and understandings that I receive. In this case, the lesson is trust in the guidance that is available to me, that I have been given, and act on it, and this will help me to learn how to be true to myself.

At Mass today it was announced that there was to be a talk about you St Thérèse at the Carmelite monastery this afternoon. When I heard the announcement, my heart sank with disappointment because I had arranged to go and see dad and didn't want to let him down so I said to myself that I would have to miss the talk.

I arrived at dad's house about an hour before the talk was due to start and mum was at dad's too. Because I usually stay a couple of hours, I worked out sadly that I would probably be leaving dad's just as the talk was finishing. For the first half hour, I kept thinking about missing the talk, but I was trying to put it out of my mind and concentrate on my visit. It is not usually difficult for me to put my concerns aside when I am with mum and dad because I have learned to do it so well, but on this occasion, it was almost impossible. I was like a cat on a hot tin roof. I couldn't settle. I kept standing up from my seat and looking out of the window as if I would find an answer to my restlessness in the garden.

After I had been there about 40 minutes, dad asked me what was wrong. I was almost bursting with the need to say, 'I'm sorry to cut your visit short and should have told you earlier, but there is somewhere I want to be this afternoon', but this is not what happened. Instead, my eyes filled up, and I was choking back tears and with a lump in my throat tried to explain that I didn't want to let dad down, but I wanted to be at the convent in 20 minutes.

Dad could see I was distressed because he said, kindly and encouragingly, 'Just go sweetheart.' Mum wanted more information about who, what, when and where but I acted immediately on dad's prompting and didn't wait to give mum all the details she would have liked. Within 10 minutes Terry had arrived to collect me, and we arrived at the church just as the talk was beginning.

The talk was called 'St Thérèse of Lisieux: Ordinary – Extraordinary' and it was wonderful. The sister who gave the talk obviously knows you very well and is passionate about you and your life's example. I was so absorbed by the talk and hung onto every word. Sister spoke about your childhood and how you came to be a nun and your spirituality and how we can never have too much confidence in God. I can't remember much else at this moment; it is as if the teaching was received not by my mind but somewhere deeper within me that I have less conscious access to. I have been in an almost dreamlike state since, and when I was reflecting on today's events just before I started to write, it seemed as if it had been more of a dream than reality.

Thank you for helping me today, I would have been devastated to miss the talk. There are going to be two more talks next week and the week after.

Yours,

Michaela

Chapter 43

31st August 2009

Dear St Thérèse,

My connection with you is growing stronger. I sense it in the people I meet, my conversations with others, circumstances which arise, and even the material that I read. I tell anyone that will listen that you have inspired me to write this account, not just the details of my life, but of the past life of my soul, and its current lessons and challenges. It is 51 days (31st August 2009) now since I received your divine inspiration and its thread weaves through my thoughts and emotions strengthening my soul.

At first, your presence was tangible, your name, your image, your story, your teachings, and it still is, but now I delight in the subtleties of your presence as it deepens within me. I even sense your presence in the books which have come my way. For example, one day recently I wasn't well, and Terry brought me home a book called 'Angels in my Hair' by Lorna Byrne, about how she sees and speaks to angels. I read it in one sitting and really enjoyed it. It reminded of the influence of angels in my life. I have experienced the sudden appearance of single white feathers (on the ground, floating on air, on a chair I was about to sit on, in my handbag, in my coat pocket, and even in my hair) each one a message of hope to remind me that I wasn't alone.

Another word of encouragement came from a book called 'The Guernsey Literary and Potato Peel Pie Society'. I devoured this book within a couple of days. It is delightful. I enjoyed identifying with the central character's life as a writer, and I wondered if you were giving me hope of success by providing me with an insight of an author on a book-signing tour. I imagined myself quite comfortably in the role and could picture myself relaxing in a hot bath after a long day talking about my book to fans and soothing tired hands exhausted from signing so many copies of my book.

It reminded me of another time in early recovery when I went to New York on my own to do some research for work. It was in September, the beginning of the academic year which always reminds me of fresh starts. On the trip, I felt a new freedom and excitement as if the whole world was mine for discovering. It was a new dawn of seeing hopes turn into reality and I even dared to dream about the real possibility of writing a book.

Before I went to New York City, I purposely visualised what might happen in New York if I ever became a successful author. I imagined myself attending an appointment with a New York bookshop to do a book-signing event. In the visualisation, I saw myself getting out of a car (chauffer-driven limo courtesy of my publisher) outside a New York bookshop and stopping to oblige the press photographers with a stunning smile and to take a momentary glance to admire the window display featuring my soon-to-be-a-bestseller book. Then I walk into the shop to a ripple of applause from the fans waiting for me to sign my book. Although it was a whimsical vision, it felt real and exciting.

On the Saturday morning of my actual visit to New York City, I went for a walk and found myself looking in the window of Barnes & Noble bookshop at the edge of Union Square. I felt torn between what I was going to do next, go to the bookstore or go into the square. From a peek into the square I could see a farmers' market was in full swing and the delicious smell suggested that there were hot freshly made pancakes to be discovered. I decided to have a walk round the market before I went into the bookshop. As I stepped into the square, a young woman approached me and with a lovely smile said, 'May we take your photo? We'll give you 20 bucks.' She pointed towards a photographer's white umbrella in the corner of the square ready with a vacant chair for subjects to be photographed.

'Oh,' I said, 'I don't mind.'

'Great … are your British?'

'Yes.'

'What's your name?' she asked as she led me to the umbrella and invited me to sit down. When she had taken the photo, she gave me 20 dollars as promised.

'Thank you, ma'am. Have a nice day,' she said when we parted.

'What's the photograph for?' I called back; almost forgetting to ask.

'It's a literary magazine,' she said.

Then it struck me how significant it was that only a few weeks earlier I had visualised having my photo taken outside a bookshop in New York City and that vision had just become a reality. I felt waves of gratitude and joy that something special had happened. In the farmers' market, I bought a cinnamon-scented beeswax candle which I still treasure to this day. Thank you, for inspiring me with thoughts of what it might be like to be a successful author.

At Mass, your presence feels stronger. It is less than a month until your relics arrive in our city for two days, and I will be a pilgrim on retreat in my hometown when they are here. I will be stewarding for both days at the cathedral, and I have volunteered to bake scones for the refreshment table. I have also booked a room at a hotel in Salford so that I can continue my pilgrimage when your relics travel to Salford Cathedral directly from Liverpool.

The cathedral bookshop has a whole section devoted to you with books and pictures and bracelets and rosary beads and bookmarks and prayer cards and candles and key rings etc. Each week after Mass I go and check out the new merchandise. So far I have bought three books, one bracelet, two bookmarks, four prayer cards and four beautiful pictures. I haven't kept these all to myself. Two of the pictures are for mum and dad, and Terry said I will be your biggest fan when your relics arrive.

It has been recommended that there is no better way to prepare for your visit than to read your autobiography. I love your story, and it has been helpful for me to tell something of my own story in these letters. I have learned a lot about myself which I didn't see so clearly until now. Viewing our life as a story can help us to gain perspective and to find meaning in what happens to us. There are many types of story we could be in: an adventure story, a love story, a thriller, a nightmare, a pilgrimage. In many ways, it is up to us what kind of story we are living. Our attitude can help determine not only the plot but also whether the story has a happy or tragic ending. Also, what happens when we find that we aren't the central character in our own life? Or if we are too busy playing the key role in our own stories, do we have the capacity to play a part in someone else's life. I am not saying that I haven't been too self-absorbed, but as a seeker, I have intuitively sought the guidance of wiser people and this has meant that life has felt complicated at times because I have been too involved in other people's stories.

I have sought guidance from others rather than trusting my inner guidance, and although I haven't always accepted the help people have offered me, I have experienced incredible benefits when I have. But I suspect that there is an even simpler way to find guidance. I need to pray.

Yours,

Michaela

Chapter 44

1st September 2009

Dear St Thérèse,

I am often amazed at how the past and present converge with apparent coincidence and synchronicity. For example, I was thinking earlier today about 9/11, and later read in The Sunday Times an extract of a new book about a British woman who worked as an HR manager who lost her husband in the attack on the World Trade Centre when she was nine-months pregnant.

The journey that people make from despair to hope intrigues me. I have been reading about resilience and post-traumatic growth (PTG), and I am particularly interested in the category of 'spiritual change' which focuses specifically on a 'better understanding of spiritual matters' and 'stronger religious faith' (Tedeschi & Calhoun 1996). Over the last couple of days, I have read an inspirational book called 'The Shack' by Wm Paul Young (2008). A story with a powerful image of God as a black American woman and is about hope and how tragic circumstances lead to the growth in the spiritual understanding and faith of the main character.

Coincidentally this was recommended by an ex-client following a chance meeting who said she wanted to meet to tell me about a recent special experience. Before she had the opportunity to speak, I said that I thought I had seen her at

Mass at the cathedral recently, and she said she hadn't been to the cathedral since June when she had attended a healing Mass with Father Collins. I immediately told her about my experience with Father Collins (but I call him Father Jimmy) about seven years ago.

I was invited to attend the 'healing Mass' by a friend. I didn't know what to expect at all. The church was so full that we couldn't find anywhere to sit. My friend uses a wheelchair, so we placed ourselves with a large group of other wheelchair users. As the only one standing, I felt out of place. The congregation seemed animated, led by the massive presence of the tiny frame of Father Jimmy celebrating Mass. My friend had told me that people often experienced miracles at Father Jimmy's healing Mass.

I was absorbing the incredible energy of the mass and the emotion of the congregation when Father Jimmy walked down from the altar. He was walking in my direction, but I assumed he was heading for the people sitting in wheelchairs close to where I was standing. Then he stopped right in front of me and put his hands on my head and closed his eyes and prayed but I couldn't hear the words he spoke. Then he opened his eyes smiled at me and said, 'Release your burden. Don't be frightened' and then ever so gently he tapped me on the shoulder at which point I fell backwards by the force of the energy which I felt zip through my body. I got back on my feet quickly, and when I looked around, I saw another woman also falling backwards as Father Jimmy stood in front of her.

'What on earth just happened?' I wondered, but something within told me not to question it and just to accept the warmth of the energy which was still tingling through me.

One of the two people who had helped me to my feet asked me if I was okay. This kind lady had a happy expression and said, 'How beautiful! The Holy Spirit has blessed you.'

I didn't agree or disagree with her, but I sensed lightness within and a peacefulness washing over me, not of my making. I thought I might have felt embarrassed about everyone seeing me falling to the ground, but I wasn't. I had observed people falling to the ground when I went to the evangelical church. I had remained sceptical about the cause of such phenomena wondering if people fell to the ground because they were expected to. But I learned from this experience that it wasn't the case. I was the first person Father Jimmy prayed over that day, so I wasn't following anyone else's example, it happened spontaneously. (And he certainly didn't push me over!)

While I was telling my ex-client this story, I noticed that she looked a little bit shocked, and I wondered if she didn't believe in such experiences. But when she spoke I sensed her amazement, 'You won't believe this, but that is the same incident I wanted to share with you. Father Jimmy prayed over me at his healing Mass, and I fell backwards just like you.'

What an amazing coincidence that I had an identical experience? And as if to confirm the significance of the coincidence, when I next went to my desk, the first thing I noticed was one of Father Jimmy's books.

Yours,

Michaela

Chapter 45

2nd September 2009

Dear St Thérèse,

Yesterday I wrote to you about coincidences and how important they are to me, and how I notice them as reassurances that I am on the right path.

Another coincidence occurred two days ago when chatting with a friend; we were discussing how we were both noticing the importance of the physical body (as well as the mind) and being present in the moment. We both described how in the past we had lived too much in our minds and intellect, and we have both been receiving reminders recently about the importance of the physical body. I had an interesting insight when I was trying to explain to her my ideal job. I told my friend that as well as being a writer I would have loved to be a priest, like you, and she said, 'What is it that a priest does that you are attracted to do?'

I said, 'Helping people to know they are not alone and to be present on the spiritual plane, particularly when they are anxious.'

I was shocked by my response. I had never heard myself say this before and didn't realise until that moment that I had the desire to do this, but then I remembered that in my prayers and journals recently I have noticed this as a dominant theme. How to be more connected to God, self, and others. Then my friend said, 'How can you do this in your life without being a priest?'

After thinking about her question for a few moments, I explained to her that when I am with other people, I strive to listen deeply. When I am praying, I try and look to the guidance God might be giving, and within myself, aim to develop awareness of all the ways in which I am connected to others. I also explained that I seek to listen to others, God and myself with presence and that to do this I need to be present to the physical, emotional, intellectual and spiritual elements of experience.

My friend said, 'Maybe you realise that these energies are all interconnected', and I wondered if spiritual strength comes from being in touch with all aspects of our being. What happens if we are 'blocking out' one of these aspects? Is it an obstacle to our spiritual growth? Can we experience spirituality without being present? I don't think so, but when we are present, we are naturally in touch with our spiritual nature. So to develop our connection with a Higher Power, we need to practise 'being present', and I know that one of the best ways to do this is through meditation.

Another excellent teaching about presence is in the work of Patsy Rodenburg. When I read her inspiring book called 'Presence', I cried at the part where she explains that presence is a natural energy of life and connection with which we are all born. She describes how children are usually full of presence. They live in the moment. Children don't self-consciously worry about the past or future. The author explains that although presence is essential to our survival, it can 'get knocked out of us'. I wept because I understood what she meant; I deadened my presence to avoid pain.

However, as much as I want to develop presence, there is a part of me which I am deeply afraid of opening. Is this my soul? Hidden there is my potential for spiritual development, but if I try to go too deeply into this place, will it leave me too vulnerable? It's as if the hidden contents of this deepest centre might be stolen from me at any time and if that happened, I couldn't bear the loss of it. What might be stolen? The potential for connection and growth. Who might steal it from me? I don't know, and therefore I can only conclude it is an irrational fear, but I need to get to the heart of it.

Yours,

Michaela

Chapter 46

3rd September 2009

Dear St Thérèse,

Last night I dreamed vividly about JC. In the dream, I was with a group of people, and we were collectively learning how to tell the truth without offending. The exercise was about who could be the most truthful and the most charming. Even though I was struggling (not with charm but with truthfulness) I felt okay. Then JC came along, and when I thought he would be supportive, he suddenly took all his support away and criticised me, but instead of being devastated and victimised and believing he was right, I turned the tables and said, 'I can see through you trying to hurt me. You are showing me your pain. You are showing me what was done to you. You were encouraged to seek to do new things and to learn, and just when you arrived at the critical point for learning/insight/accomplishment, someone took your confidence in your success away from you, and this is what you are trying to do to me. But I am not going to let you. I am not going to let you hurt me like this. You don't have the power to do this anymore. You aren't the authority in my life. God is.'

I woke up with healing thoughts because I realised that the dream was about how I deal with disapproval. For most of my life, I had thought that if someone is unhappy with me, they are right, even when something inside me suggested that I might be right too. The dream helped me to realise that when people are unhappy with me, if my conscience is clear, their disapproval is their responsibility, not mine. I am hopeful about this lesson that if I take on anyone else's pain, it is my doing, and I mustn't be victimised. I am not obliged to accept somebody else's pain. Thank you, for this realisation.

I also received some more guidance in my meditation this morning about actions, about your 'little way'; how focusing on small details of actions is so important: it's a spiritual service. I used to think, 'What's the point of trying to be good and do some little things when only big things count?' But I realise that the 'little way' works, doing small, things works and is worthwhile. Firstly, because regular, purposeful, focused actions are not small collectively; they build into big things, and it is also the way that we make progress, one step at a time. Each time I smile at someone in the hope that I will make myself more approachable to them, I am practising the 'little way'; and while in itself a smile is not a big thing at all, it could lead to bigger things.

In the past I have been dismissive of small things, looking for the big things that will make me feel good. Now I want to focus on the smaller acts of love and service. Also, I am learning that it is not thoughts and words alone that matter, they have to be put into action. This lesson is what you teach in your 'little way', and this is what JC often tells me. You lived a life of loving. You expressed your love in words and prayer, but you knew it was more important to put that love into action. Life is about loving action, even small actions, indeed the small selfless actions can have the most impact. You knew that however small, these actions were blessings, and you knew that the heart is set free by blessings. The 'little way' is an important path and one which I aspire to; it is not just making the decision to start the journey which is important, it is taking the first step.

Last night I was thinking about the importance of telling stories and the thread that holds them together. Your story was held together by your obedient response. Yesterday evening Terry and I watched the film, 'Walk the Line' about Johnny Cash. I wanted to watch it because I knew he was a recovering alcoholic, and I hoped Terry would enjoy the musical aspect of the film. Afterwards, I was firmly aware that the primary focus of the movie, or the thread which told the story, was Johnny Cash's (another JC) relationship with June Carter (and another!). The film told a life story which depicted details of his career and illness and recovery, but the primary focus was the love story of his relationship with June.

Your story also has the thread of a love story running through it: your love of your faith and Jesus, and your understanding of what love can teach us. I am telling you my life story too, but where and what is my love story? I don't think that I have discovered it yet.

Yours,

Michaela

Chapter 47

5th September 2009

Dear St Thérèse,

You said that you wanted to be a martyr. When I first read this, I was a little confused. I immediately thought of the modern view of martyrdom where we might see someone as a self-pitying victim, but I understand that the traditional definition of martyr is much more virtuous. To be a martyr used to be a position that was highly respected. Martyr comes from the Greek word meaning witness. A true martyr is someone willing to make sacrifices for what they believe in, like your heroine St Joan of Arc. Her actions demonstrated that she was completely ready to act on her beliefs for her higher cause despite the risks. St Joan made the ultimate sacrifice and died for her faith. It is humbling to recognise that when I said in a previous letter that I went on a trip to Rome as a martyr, I was wrong. Now I understand the difference, I won't use the term martyr in such a superficial way again. I want to use it in the more traditional sense, as someone who can bear witness to the truth of their heart and soul, like you did.

I am going to Florence tomorrow with mum for six days. I have been worrying about going on this trip for a few weeks. As usual, when I am worried about something I can't change, I try to put it to the back of my mind, or just work harder to get into the right frame of mind. In this case, I am telling myself that I should be grateful to be going to Italy and that I will be able to cope with whatever comes up. This approach must be working because I am not as anxious as I thought I would be. I only agreed to go to Florence to please mum. I know from my recovery programme that people-pleasing and approval-seeking behaviours are not healthy for me; yet again it didn't stop me agreeing to do something I didn't want to do.

When we went to Rome together a couple of years ago, mum enjoyed it and said that she would love to return to Italy, and she chose Florence because of its reputation for fantastic art and art galleries and museums, etc. In the flush of an enjoyable time in Rome, and seeing how happy it had made mum, just after we returned home, I agreed to go to Florence. So the motivation for this trip snowballed from my making a promise to go and feeling it would have been incredibly selfish to refuse. The best I could do to be true to myself was to try and be honest with mum before we go. When I felt some tension last week about going, I told mum as nicely as possible that although I would never back out, I don't want to go to Florence. Mum was okay about it which was a blessing, and it released some tension within me.

Maybe I am not so anxious since I discovered that you visited Florence on your pilgrimage to Rome, and I would love to find the church you went to. But I can't guarantee that the opportunity to do so will arise so I'm trying not to get my hopes up too much, but I am praying that it will. My faith in you is helping to keep me calm, and I am looking forward to returning home because then it will only be a matter of days before your relics arrive in the UK, and then come to Liverpool.

Yours,

Michaela

Chapter 48

12th September 2009

Dear St Thérèse,

I arrived home from Florence this morning. Although I felt your presence strongly with me most of the time, I have missed writing to you every day. Most of my letters to you take a few hours, so I didn't even attempt to write from Florence because I knew my time alone would be extremely limited. I did manage to write my journal a little.

The trip was both inspiring and at times heart-achingly painful, but I am so pleased that I went. It was healing. As much as I spoke to you and my Higher Power every day, for the first three days, even though I spent nearly every waking hour with mum, I felt alone. As we wandered from gallery to gallery, the loneliness got worse and worse. Knowing that I was worrying mum by my disposition ('stop frowning' she said!) I asked her if it would be okay with her if I spent an hour by myself, and I sat beneath the statues in the square Piazza della Signoria near the Uffizi Gallery. I wanted a few moments alone to face the despair because I was in danger of losing emotional control completely.

As I sat alone amidst crowds of people, tears ran down my face as I prayed for strength to bear the despair I felt deeply. I didn't even try to ask for the despair to be taken away because, as painful as it was, I sensed that it had an important message for me and, as sad as I was, I felt open to accepting the lesson. I tried to surrender to what had triggered the deep pain. What was it? I felt some relief from the tears I shed, but all too quickly it was time to return to mum. The despair eased a couple of times when I remembered to speak to Terry and JC on the phone. I often forget that talking to someone helps me to get better and know that I am not alone. But no matter how much I know that this helps I often 'forget' to do it until I am in crisis.

You came to my aid when I went to visit the Church of Santa Maria Maddalena dei Pazzi. More than all the famous churches in Florence, I wanted to see this church because it is the one that you visited when you were in Florence. The plan was that as it was mum's birthday, she was going to sit in a Piazza and have a glass of wine and relax while I went to visit the church. We would walk to the Piazza together and then I would continue to the church. I was excited at the thought of making this visit alone. However, as we walked together following the signs to the church, mum didn't seem ready to leave me, and I felt worried that we would arrive and she would want to come in with me. I didn't want to deny mum this because she seemed to pick up on my excitement, but I wanted to be alone. I said a brief prayer that mum would be happy not to come and at the next sign we saw for the church, we each had different interpretations of what the sign meant. I prayed another quick prayer and followed the inner guidance which came to me, but it meant we took a wrong turning and the signs for the church ran out.

Getting lost was a blessing in disguise because by this time we had been walking for a long time in the heat and when we ended up in St Ambrose Piazza we decided it was a good place for mum to stop and rest and I left her telling her that I would be back in an hour. I retraced our steps to the last place we had seen a sign for the church, and I understood how we had misunderstood it the first time. I took the path we had initially rejected, and in the new direction I soon found two other churches and a beautiful synagogue and stopped to admire each and took some photographs, and then continued along the road. Within a couple of minutes, my heart leapt when I saw the plaque on the wall which said 'Church of Santa Maria Maddalena de Pazzi'. I was delighted and stopped for a second thinking, 'I am retracing the steps St Thérèse took when she was present in this place.'

I looked into a beautiful courtyard and wondered if it was a private building and if I would be allowed to enter. The signs told me that the convent was now a school and pointed to an entrance to the church beyond the courtyard. Nervously I walked into the beautiful courtyard with pillars and walkways (like a cloister) and felt an incredible sense of presence and peacefulness. A man was sitting on a chair with his feet on the wall reading a newspaper. He was the only person I could see. He looked as though he was guarding the entrance to the school. I walked a few more steps, stopped, and drew in the stillness, and the hairs on my skin rose with the sense of awe that embraced me.

'St Thérèse was here,' I thought looking all around. I caught sight of a movement in the sky about twenty feet above me, and I saw a beautiful white feather, not falling or drifting but dancing in the air, as though it was speaking to me.

I felt so joyful and grateful for this blessing and just knew that I was in your presence. It felt like an entirely personal 'hello'. I have often seen white feathers at poignant and meaningful moments in my life, and I wholeheartedly believe that they are 'messages' to tell me not to give up hope and to know that I am not alone. I was enchanted watching the white feather dancing in the breeze. I often chase white feathers when I see them falling to the ground, but this one danced upwards, and I stood and watched it float higher and higher upwards until I couldn't see it anymore.

With a joyous heart, I walked into the church. Compared to the ornate and impressive buildings we had visited in Florence, this church felt spacious and immediately gave me a great sense of peace. As I walked towards the altar, I heard a sound and looking behind me saw a young woman sitting at the back of the church. Then I heard voices coming from the confessional, so I guessed she was waiting for her turn to say confession.

I walked along the left-hand aisle looking into the side altars, and then I saw you. The altar held a larger than life-sized statue of you, on a high plinth. I felt the same surprise and delight as when we unexpectedly meet a friend, and we smile and embrace at the happy coincidence. I knelt at the pew in front of your altar and gazed at your beautiful face. When I look at your image, I often imagine that I see you smiling at me like Our Lady's statue did to you. It wouldn't have surprised me at all if your statue had spoken to me. I felt connected to you, and my heart spoke silently offering prayers of gratitude for this elevating experience. I just knelt and gazed at your face. I was brought back to reality when I realised that I only had a couple of minutes to get back to mum. I said 'Thank you' and 'Goodbye' and took a couple of photos and reluctantly left.

The following day we had planned to visit Siena where another Doctor of the Church like you came from, St Catherine of Siena, but unfortunately mum wasn't well in the morning, so I had an unexpected opportunity to return to the church. I couldn't believe my luck. I was sorry that mum wasn't well, but I was so happy to be going back that I almost skipped along the cool narrow stone alleyways. Again my time was limited, and

I intended to make the most of it. I sat at your altar and prayed for a while and gazed at your face. You seemed to be smiling again, and I thought that you are like an older sister to me. I have never had a sister, but I knew for a few moments what it might have felt like.

I lit a couple of candles. The precious time at your altar had passed so quickly. I had almost reached the exit when I remembered that I hadn't paid for the candles, so I rushed back to your altar to put the money in the box. As I was leaving, although the church seemed dark, something caught my eye as I was glancing at the altars. I stopped and took a few steps backwards to look closer at what I thought I had seen, saying to myself, 'I can't have missed this yesterday.' But as I looked more carefully, I said to myself, 'It is, I can't believe it!' There in front of me was a huge painting of 'Jesus in the Garden of Gethsemane'. This image inspires me hugely. I was overjoyed. St Thérèse, white feathers, your altar and now a huge painting of 'The Agony in the Garden'. I felt blessed, and my soul was joyous. I wiped away a few tears, took a couple of photos and left with my heart full of gratitude for the beautiful gifts of the Church of Santa Maria Maddalena de Pazzi.

Later that day, walking back to the hotel with mum after our afternoon outing to the Medici Chapel, I felt the cold despair creeping back into me. I was struggling for composure again. I was annoyed with myself that I was letting the joy of the previous day and that morning seep away so soon. I wearily spotted a church, and although I knew it wouldn't make me popular, I said to mum, 'I am just popping my head in.' Mass was in progress for a congregation of about ten people and there, just inside the doorway, was an enormous, beautiful painting of you. I dragged a tired mum inside the door and pointed. 'Guess who?' I whispered with a big grin. So again, your image appeared just when I needed you, and I felt you supporting and showing me that there is a way to overcome despair when life gets overwhelming. I popped in and out of the church so quickly that I didn't notice its name.

On the second to last day, I stood under a beautiful, comforting tree which I had grown fond of in the busy warm Piazza di San Marco when visiting for a few minutes every day for a brief meditation. I spoke to JC on the phone. I was close to tears, but my heart felt open. I knew that there was something that I had to let go of. The words I heard inwardly were 'I can't pretend anymore'. JC confirmed the words a few minutes later when he said to me, 'You have got to stop pretending. You have got to be true to yourself.' Neither of us stated what it was that I couldn't pretend about; it was as if he knew the contents of my heart without me expressing them.

As I walked back to the hotel to meet mum who was waiting in the lobby, I knew that there were two truths that I couldn't ignore anymore. The first was the truth about my relationship with mum; I wasn't a dutiful daughter, I felt like an abandoned girl who was constantly trying to earn the love that she had lost when her mother had left home for the first time when she was 11. But I also felt guilty because I knew that present-day experiences were not the source of the problem: they triggered unresolved pain from the past. The second truth was I couldn't pretend to know what was in my heart, as this was tantamount to abandoning myself. Denying the contents of my heart was contributing to my inner turmoil. I admitted to myself that there was love in my heart, and I was trying to hold it in. I usually did this with strong or unfamiliar feelings, just repress them or keep them at bay until it felt safer to express them, but this feeling of love was different, it was becoming more powerful as it bubbled up inside me. It reminded me of the desire and excitement that I cherished as a young girl sitting in church and looking forward to the life ahead of me.

Reviewing my journal written in Florence I can see that instead of being led by others, I have a strong new desire to lead myself. I am not alone, and never really have been. I need to reach out and connect with the sources of love that are available to me.

Yours,

Michaela

Chapter 49

13th September 2009

Dear St Thérèse,

I attended the final talk at the Carmelite monastery today about you. I missed one of the talks while I was in Florence, but all three talks will be available on CD shortly, and I ordered my copies today. The talks were brilliant, and I am looking forward to listening to them again. The sister has a strong understanding of your psychology and spirituality and gave me much food for thought about you. Today's talk was called 'Her Impact', and it was about your impact on your generation and your profound influence throughout the 20th century and the relevance of your message for the world today.

Your story is so uplifting. Your faith was fantastic. You loved God so much and so well. Your resilience in overcoming the loss of four maternal influences in your life is outstanding. Your compassion for others was extensive. Your self-discipline in your actions was awesome. Your mastery of your emotions was amazing. You must have suffered so much with an extremely painful death, and yet you vowed to spend your time in heaven sending down blessings in the form of a shower of roses. You said, 'After my death, I will let fall a shower of roses. I will spend my heaven doing good upon earth. I will raise up a mighty host of little saints. My mission is to make God loved' (Thérèse/Vernon 2008).

Your description of a saint sending a shower of roses is one of my favourite images. I notice physical roses much more these days. They have always been a special symbol for me, although I went through a dark period in my relationship with roses. At one time I almost loathed cut roses for their weakness. It appeared to me that these roses died far too quickly. The sight of the first droopy-headed rose in a vase which had so recently been blooming so beautifully would make me angry. I felt like shouting at them to straighten up and not let themselves fade so easily. My dislike of roses meant that I avoided buying them, and if I did see them in a vase, I would be sad for how soon their beauty would fade. Thankfully I am much more loving and positive about roses these days!

As a child, I loved the roses that my dad grew in his garden. There was one in particular called 'Blue Moon' which was a purple-blue colour and I thought it had the most beautiful fragrance imaginable. It wasn't a big rose bush and didn't have masses of blooms, but I loved it. I found peace as a child noticing the roses in the garden and the way my dad lovingly cared for them (and still does). After the death of Princess Diana, my dad bought two rose bushes, one for him and one for mum. I thought that it was lovely that Princess Diana had a rose named after her. I wonder if any roses have been named after you? One day I am going to plant a rose tree in my garden and name it after you.

Yours,

Michaela

Chapter 50

14th September 2009

Dear St Thérèse,

I am frustrated and wondering where writing to you is leading me and why I am investing so much in these letters? I enjoy writing to you. As your visit draws close, your presence in my life grows strong. It helps me to understand myself so much more, but today I am unsure about the path I am following. The hollow uncertainty is like the emptiness of craving approval. It is like an addiction, and unless I have my 'fix', I experience the hopeless withdrawal of self-doubt and self-loathing.

I am wondering about the 50-plus letters I have now written. I would like to collate them into a complete manuscript, but am anxious about doing so. I intend to continue writing until I have venerated your relics. I can't imagine I will ever be brave enough to let anyone else read them. But another part of me would love to have them published. Please, guide me through this painful ambivalence, and I pray that writing to you hasn't become a compulsion. I hope that I am writing from my heart.

On a more positive note, I am learning to be truer to myself and following the guidance of my Higher Power. I remember reading in Stephen King's book about writing that a writer's first draft of a manuscript is for them and that the polished draft is for the world. My fear is that although I would like to follow your example and produce a manuscript one day, I daren't believe that I will do so.

I sense an emptiness which is like a dark, scary nothingness; a space devoid of inner guidance and direction. But is this a bad thing? The void might not be a scary place after all. There might be a hidden opportunity within it. Rather than get lost in it, I might find myself. Although I want to know myself better and put a lot of effort into developing self-awareness and seeking guidance, I am frightened that if I look too deeply, I might find that there is nothing there. I might lose my fragile sense of self completely. A place of no guidance seems too awful to contemplate and, although it might be a place of freedom, I view it negatively because I don't trust myself. Why am I scared of inner freedom?

When I seek approval, I am not allowing myself to be authentic but presenting a false self to the world. When someone shows me genuine warmth, I don't appreciate it because I know they have only seen my false self. I often feel like a phoney but not just because I can kid others, but because of the extent to which I can also kid myself. It is one thing to pretend to others, it's another to deceive yourself. I want to develop self-awareness by honestly examining my motives and learning from the past and focusing on how best to be true to myself.

With my writing, I am following my heart's desire, i.e. being true to myself, but I am still trying to achieve it under the old regime, i.e. through approval-seeking. So what is the solution? To be true to myself I have to find new rules, new guidance, and new direction. Seeking approval occurs when we love conditionally rather than unconditionally. We believe that people will love us only when we are compliant otherwise they will withdraw their love. This makes it harder for us to learn to love ourselves. I recognise that the antidote to approval-seeking is love, loving myself and others and being real.

You tell us that we can love in a 'little way' and it is enough. We don't have to be perfect. Simplicity is good, and I want my writing to be simple, but instead, I try to make it perfect. Perfection is impossible. I need to keep it simple, and all will be okay. This inner emptiness is not to be feared. I need to embrace it, to be honest, and truthful with myself.

I am grateful for these realisations today. I need to love my writing. Writing helps me to know the difference between love and approval. When I am seeking approval, I turn away from God. Please help me to treat my writing as something to love and as a medium for learning to love to the best of my ability. Then I am fulfilling my heart's desire through writing in a new way: to love and to trust, to follow the example of the 'little way'. This insight is important. Thank you, so much for helping me.

Yours,

Michaela

Chapter 51

15th September 2009

Dear St Thérèse,

Today is a critical day in my preparations for your visit. I have just been to the cathedral house for the meeting for the stewards who will be working as volunteers during the veneration of your relics. It came home to me how soon your relics will be here when we were discussing the itinerary. It was good to associate with people who seem as excited as I am that you will be here in Liverpool in our beautiful cathedral in just over a week.

Today is the day that your relics arrive in the UK for the first time. Your tour starts in Portsmouth Cathedral on 16th September and ends in Westminster Cathedral on 15th October nearly a month later. Your relics will visit Portsmouth, Plymouth, Taunton, Birmingham, Cardiff, Bristol, Liverpool, Salford, Manchester, Lancaster, Newcastle-upon-Tyne, York, Middlesbrough, Leeds, Nottingham, Walsingham, Oxford, Gerrard's Cross, Aylesford, and London. I understand a visit to Wormwood Scrubs prison is also included.

Apparently, during your childhood, you drew a map of England and wrote the names of Portsmouth and London as two places you would like to visit. At the meeting for stewards, the Dean said that nobody knows how many people will turn up to venerate your relics, but he expects that many will come.

I took dad and mum a little plaque each with your picture on for them to commemorate your tour. Dad was delighted and said that you were beautiful and what a wonderful thing to have in the house. I expected him to be a little sceptical. He wasn't at all.

I am so excited about the tour of your relics. I don't have a precedent for what to do and what to focus on for the next month, but I have a few ideas; for instance, I will pray for you each day, keep fresh roses in the house, and let everyone know how special this visit is.

Yours,

Michaela

Chapter 52

16th September 2009

Dear St Thérèse

When I woke today, the first thing I thought about was that your relics are now here in the UK and will be in Liverpool in just over a week on 24th September 2009.

I know that I need to pray, but where do I start? I have been praying that all the people who want to find a way to know God better, can do so through you. I am learning from you that I don't need to approach God in suffering and through beating myself up. A much better approach is your way of loving and trusting. Not blind trust, but faithful trust and the aspect of love that helps us do what is right for ourselves and others. I have been thinking how much I like the word 'approach' because it incorporates the sense of moving closer; gaining access, and asking someone for something. My habitual approach to fearful situations is initially to resist and to then push forward, so I am torn and drained by the process. How can I be more confident in my approach? I will pray for courage and learn from your example.

I focused on my understanding of love when meditating recently, and had a flashback of remembering something that I keep forgetting. It is the insight that I experience love as burdensome and that love shouldn't be like that. Sometimes I confuse love for responsibility. My sense of responsibility stems back to when mum and dad split up, and I felt the burden was on my shoulders when we went to tell my brother David the bad news. I haven't felt confident enough to take any other approach. I have created certain expectations within myself about my family that if I was to try and break free now my fear is that they would feel abandoned by me. To me, this wanting my family not to suffer is a form of love.

I also understand that taking responsibility is an aspect of controlling behaviour. I am trying to avoid being hurt. I took responsibility as a palliative for facing the pain of the family break-up. Instead of facing loss and mourning it, I focused on the needs of my family but in doing so failed to meet my own needs. It was easier to deal with the external pain of others than the inner pain within. I might have successfully protected myself from some hurt, but I have also made it harder to access internal sources of self-worth, self-acceptance and positive feelings. This denial eventually led to even deeper hurt.

I also confuse love and judgment. Loving someone is finding them to be 'acceptable' and 'deserving'. If a person is found wanting, then they are not worthy of love. This approach has a fundamental impact on my behaviour. Here are just some of the consequences:

- I am responsible if other people are angry, sad and upset.
- I criticise myself harshly when things go wrong.
- I take responsibility for things that are nothing to do with me.
- I agree with other people when I know in my heart that I don't agree with them.
- I feel guilty if I stand up for myself, so I give in and find it hard to say no.

- Other people are more important than me, and I always put other people first.
- I let other people have power over me.
- I have no right to express my feelings.
- I let people 'dump' their bad feelings onto me.
- I let people treat me badly because their feelings are more valid than mine.
- I accept being abandoned by others physically and emotionally.
- I accept conditional love from others.
- It is my job to change how other people feel for the better.
- I must be able to know how others are feeling, even when they don't tell me.
- Other people's needs are more important than mine.

Having re-read what I have just written, I can see my current approach to love incorporates judgment, responsibility, control, guilt and shame, collusion, and the feeling that love is conditional. When I judge, I block love. My concept of love isn't just faulty it's harmful. This realisation is a huge insight for me. I am devastated by the truth of this statement. I am putting conditions on the value of love.

St Thérèse, please help me to understand love. After over 40 years of faulty thinking, please give me the strength to and courage to find a truer definition of love more in line with your teachings.

Yours,

Michaela

Chapter 53

17th September 2009

Dear St Thérèse,

I was dreaming about making choices last night and how they seem like a luxury to me. In one of my dreams, I was going on holiday and felt great anxiety about missing the plane because I hadn't packed my case, and it was time to leave the house to get to the airport. I keep going back to the same point of being nearly packed and trying to get to the airport on time. Each time the dream episode replays, there is a slightly different challenge. Usually, the one that I didn't overcome in the previous version of the dream is resolved, but then another obstacle appears, and I still fail to get to the airport on time. The experience is extremely stressful, and I wish I could overcome the insurmountable and arrive at the airport on time without being completely stressed. A detail which I am aware of in the dream, but seem to ignore, is that I don't even want to go on the holiday on the plane I am so desperate to board. But I know that someone else wants me to go, and that is enough for me to believe that I have no other option.

In another dream I had last night, I am at a buffet restaurant, and being watched as I try to choose which food to put on my plate. I am struggling to hold the plate because there is already too much food on it. However careful I try to be, the food is slipping off the plate and onto the floor. When I was given the plate, it was already full of food that I wouldn't have chosen.

Instead of putting the plate down and getting a clean, empty plate, I am obliged to keep hold of the one I have which has food on it that I don't like. I try to put some food that I like on top of the food that I don't like. This decision seems like a viable option. I keep persisting, trying to get more food on the plate, not because I want to eat it, but because I have to do it. I know I am being watched, and compulsively struggle to cope. The dream ends when I defiantly sit down in my seat with the overflowing plate of cold, disgusting food with the intention of eating the food I have chosen and leaving the food that I didn't select, but it is too late. The people in my party are going, and I am obliged to leave with them. I woke up feeling disgusted with the food and myself for both not coping and not giving in earlier to a fruitless pursuit of the compulsion to put others first.

Despite the frustration, stress and a sense of failure, my conscious non-dreaming self can clearly see certain themes in these dreams:

- Why don't I give up sooner on fruitless tasks?
- What is stopping me feel that I have a choice in each situation?
- Why do I persist in trying to make things right when the situations are so stressful?
- Why do I feel so powerless?
- Why is my thinking so negative?
- Why am I so hard on myself?
- Why don't I ask anyone for help?

Before I went so sleep last night, I was thinking about handing over those things which I am struggling with and trying not to feel so alone. I woke knowing that I need to let go and accept those things that I can't control. Sometimes I misunderstand acceptance and taking responsibility, and both feel like taking on burdens. True acceptance is about taking responsibility but letting go if necessary. That my view of acceptance and taking responsibility might be faulty is incredibly important. I have often bullied myself in the name of acceptance, and this needs to change.

Just as I am in the habit of earning approval before I can see myself as acceptable, so I take on as my burden the failures of others, as well as my own. I have a mistaken view of getting what I deserve. I am playing God believing that I can decree what I deserve and don't deserve. The power of God's love and God's grace far outweigh my decrees. Indeed, thank God we don't get what we deserve!

For so long I lived in a world not driven by love but by judgment, and I made excuses where I should have taken responsibility, learning from my mistakes. Am I too hard on myself when dealing with the responsibilities of others? What is the antidote? The ability to make loving choices; but more importantly, I need the grace to help me to achieve what I cannot achieve on my own.

Yours,

Michaela

Chapter 54

18th September 2009

Dear St Thérèse,

For most of my life, I have been a perfectionist. Perfectionists have high standards, and they focus on 'getting it right' and until recently it is something I would have been rather proud of, seeing perfectionism as synonymous with efficiency and high achievement. Now I am thinking differently.

At first glance perfectionists and high achievers might look quite similar, they both have high standards and strive for excellence, and when conditions are favourable, they both attain remarkable achievements. However, big differences emerge when they face setbacks or adverse conditions: crucially they each have different responses to failure. A perfectionist is threatened by failure and reacts negatively while a high achiever positively seeks hidden opportunities and uses it to learn and grow. Principles of false pride guide the former, and humility the latter. The perfectionist survives, and the high achiever thrives.

My perfectionism has been most common in my relationships. One of my worst habits is being unable to say no. In favourable circumstances, not saying no has led to praise for perceived commitment and perseverance (stubbornness in disguise); and in unfavourable conditions, it has resulted in people-pleasing and then anxiety and exhaustion (foolishness in disguise). The different outcomes between perfectionists and high achievers are caused not by high standards per se but on how resilient they are when things go wrong.

When I fail to meet the high standards I have set myself, I don't ask myself how realistic or achievable my standards were in the first place. Rather, I judge myself harshly and instead of perceiving what I have done well, I focus on what is still lacking. I don't learn from 'mistakes' but punish myself and push myself even harder. This cycle of low self-worth ends in tears of despair, self-condemnation, and then a renewed effort to find a new way to overcome my weaknesses. When I put alcohol into this situation, it is little wonder that it felt so soul-destroying.

I know that you had a time in your life when even the most commonplace of actions became a source of worry and anxiety to you, but then you grew to love your shortcomings as they were an opportunity to get closer to God. Theological writers describe your approach as a 'spirituality of imperfection' (Seelaus 1998), and the principles of my recovery programme have also been described as such (Kurtz & Ketcham 1992). I found relief in admitting that I was powerless to control many of the things I thought I could control: people, events, circumstances, etc. and within myself, I learned that I have many shortcomings and that some of these I cannot control. The key to serenity and well-being is accepting the things I cannot control and focusing my energies on what I can change externally and internally. This realisation didn't happen overnight, and it will be a lifelong journey of discovery and is welcome medicine for a hopeless perfectionist who consistently fell short of her ideals and projections of perfectionism into the expectations of others.

My perfectionism started as a survival technique when I was a child. Showing my true feelings was dangerous because my real self would be unacceptable to others, and the resulting abandonment or rejection would be too painful. When I feel that who I am is unlovable, I take proactive action against further hurt. I do this by hiding (and sometimes rejecting) who I truly am. I put on a mask of the false self which will be more acceptable, and I necessarily shut down my real feelings. I become so good at pretending to be someone else that I don't know who I truly am.

Perfectionists can take one of two emotional routes: either the path of compliance (as I did) where we try to be the better person we believe we ought to be – the one that our parents might approve of. Or we take the route of rebellion, our attitude being, 'I'll show you!' In both cases, the perfectionist puts the real self into hiding. We have learned that it is emotionally dangerous to be ourselves in the world. Unfortunately, perfectionism seems to be becoming more and more common as people face increasing pressure in everyday life. It takes a lot of mental and emotional energy to avoid failure. It can take its toll in the form of stress, anxiety, unhappiness, addiction and other illnesses. Perfectionists become trapped in a cycle of resisting, rejecting or even denying who they are. It is soul destroying.

How do we overcome this tyranny over our real selves? We take the path of uncovering, recovering and discovering the real self, which can be painful, but with courage, it is achievable and can become the most incredible journey imaginable. I can only tell my story, as you did, and I am learning that the story of my soul is both a spiritual path (for guidance) and a creative path (to heal) of writing. What needs direction and healing? All of me: my spirit; my emotions, my thinking and my physical well-being. Sometimes I can't tell the difference between the spiritual and creative energies; they seem to merge as one through a calling and inner-knowing. For years I overruled my inner-knowing, and in the future, my hope is that I will be able to respond to the call without shame or hesitation or doubt or negativity and get on with the job that my higher power has given me the resources to achieve. When will I stop being anxious about not being good enough? When will I adapt my wrong approach of trying (and miserably failing) to be obedient to others and God in the hope that my efforts will earn me rewards in this life and next?

You, are teaching me through the 'little way' that God knows we are imperfect and that all we receive from him does not depend on what we have earned because we could never humanly do enough to earn God's love. God loves us very much, but this is not on merit, it is a gift. Love is a gift of grace. This awareness brings me great peace and helps me to 'get over myself'. This gives me great encouragement to accept what I cannot change, especially my personal limitations, and gives me strength to get on with what is important in my life and that is to love to the best of my ability.

I know some people might think that if God isn't interested in our shortcomings, it means that we can take a 'what you see is what you get' approach to life. I don't think this is what you are advocating at all; you are telling us that freedom from the heartbreak of failure and liberty from the prison of self-consciousness and self-absorption exists in overcoming perfectionism. The value of my imperfections is that they provide me with an opportunity to learn more about myself, and they deepen my understanding of what I need to change in my life to be more loving. When we deny our feelings we deny our true self. When I am free from worry and anxiety about my shortcomings, I am more open to love.

When you were a young girl, you prayed for prisoner Pranzini to repent before his execution, and although it looked as though he wasn't remorseful just before he died, he asked for a crucifix and kissed it. Although I have never been in prison and can only imagine what it is like, I can relate to the idea of the prison of the troubled mind, and you are our guide in seeking this kind of freedom as much as any other.

Your teachings are helping me to understand love and how to love a little bit more. Again I believed that love is earned and is conditional on how right or obedient or self-sacrificing we are. To try and love by what we have earned is not love at all. You make it clear to us that God's love is vast and that it is not something external. I had a lovely experience when I was meditating about this, and understood the world to be a space filled with loving presence and that my purpose in life is to accept the energy of that love and help others to connect to it too.

One of my biggest barriers to love has been my disappointment in myself. I waste time beating myself up and bullying myself into trying harder and doing better next time. It is precisely the opposite of what I should be doing to encourage and motivate myself to improve and is certainly not coming from a place of love. It is a paradox that as a perfectionist in the pursuit of success I have spent so much time and energy in keeping up a façade of a false self when the path that can truly lead to success is the best version I can be of my true self. You show me the way for overcoming perfectionism. Your spirituality is an antidote to perfectionism. You wrote that your daily faults and imperfections were not significant to God. You understood that spirituality is not about excessive worry over the limitations of being human but that God is more interested in how loving we are. Your longings developed from the yearnings of the self to be good and the desires of your heart to love as much as you could.

So, your spirituality of imperfection helps deepen my spiritual journey to depths I never imagined. However, as much as I understand your theory with my head, the challenge is for me to let it sink deeply into my heart. I pray that you help my heart and soul become steeped in deep awareness of this profound truth for everyday living.

Yours,

Michaela

Chapter 55

19th September 2009

Dear St Thérèse,

I am wondering if my soul is the strongest and least damaged part of me and whether it has been the protector of my true secret-self, keeping it hidden until it is safe to express itself. I sense that my soul is not separate from my true-self. They are connected, and at the right time, my soul and secret-self will transform into a new whole person, like a butterfly emerging from its cocoon and taking flight in all its natural glory. My new wholeness will produce positive, creative, loving energies out of the transformational power of the struggle to overcome inhibition caused by negative, destructive powers.

The inhibition of behaviours, desires, impulses and feelings uses up valuable emotional energy, but it is what I am used to and is such a bad habit that I usually didn't recognise my true feelings when they came to the surface. Although there are feelings which are best left unexpressed because they are faulty and harmful, there are also positive things which I would like to express but I can't in case they cause conflict or hurt others, so this means that the good feelings are lost too. When we inhibit, we can lose our joy as well as our pain.

Inhibition might start as a survival technique: we learn to repress or deny who we are as a way of keeping ourselves safe, protecting the expression of deep hurt within. The cumulative effect of inhibiting is damaging. Each small incident in itself might seem fairly harmless or benign, but every time we inhibit we deny ourselves the opportunity for expression and authenticity. Over time this can be damaging. We lose contact with the truth.

One of the main effects of consuming alcohol is the loss of inhibitions, but this is only temporary. Once sober again the barriers come right back often even stronger. In the process of recovery, I have learned to see some of the good in me, and I have discovered a taste of what I love and enjoy as well as what I didn't like about myself. This understanding gives me hope.

The key to self-expression is a balance. Being able to find appropriate routes and means of self-expression rather than building up repressed feelings and getting drunk and then being out of control and ashamed and guilty about inappropriate behaviour.

Inhibitions are the link between my drinking and writing. They are both ways I have used to deal with what I can't express. Alcohol was a negative coping strategy, and writing is an incredibly positive one.

How does writing help my inhibitions? The process of writing allows me to start the process of discovering what has been suppressed and repressed and to allow it to see the light of day. The method of expression provides health benefits in reducing the stress of inhibition. Prof Pennebaker has written about this process in an excellent book called 'Opening Up' (Pennebaker 1997) where he tells us that inhibiting is stressful and that people who inhibit have more health problems because it is physiological as well as psychological.

Although self-expression and self-approval or self-acceptance might be the antidote to harmful inhibition, it is not an easy process. At first, we might not like what we express, and we won't like the process because it is painful, but we have to stay with it because it will pay off eventually.

What do I most want to express? What have I most inhibited? I want to be in a space where I am not compelled to seek approval or be perfect. I want to know what it would be like to be completely true to myself.

Thank you for these insights. I realise that with every letter I write to you I am expressing a little bit more of my true self, and pray that the hold of the habit of inhibiting is lessening with each sentence I write to you.

Yours,

Michaela

Chapter 56

20th September 2009

Dear St Thérèse,

I cried and cried and cried throughout Mass at the cathedral today. I have never cried so many tears at one time. I just couldn't stop so I spent most of the service kneeling with my head bowed and my arms folded on the pew in front and my head resting in my arms letting the tears trickle down onto the floor. Why was I crying? I don't fully know. Terry said it was tears of joy that your relics arrive in Liverpool this week. He might be partly right because I started crying at the thought that next time I am here in the cathedral, St Thérèse's relics will be here, and this thought stirred me in a particular way. I told Terry, and he laughed and said, 'If you are like this at the thought of being in the presence of St T's relics, what will you be like when they are here?' He has got a good point.

Is it part of the healing that I am receiving from you? Did the tears represent an emotional release? As well as the joy there is deep sadness behind my tears, and I can't identify the source of the grief. I can't remember ever feeling so outwardly emotional. I usually try and hide what I feel until I'm ready to burst. I haven't sought to repress or hide any of this emotion. It just is. It seems like a combination of excitement in anticipation of venerating your relics mixed with unexplained jitteriness.

As well as crying through Mass today, I was praying about how to speak to God, and the Holy Trinity came to mind and the decision to pray to all three. When I went for communion, my piece of the host was shaped like a triangle. The priest seemed to hesitate as he gave it to me. I told Terry, and he immediately said, 'Holy Trinity', so I saw that as a blessing.

I had a couple of attacks last week where I couldn't breathe properly, and I wondered if I had developed asthma. I mentioned it to my GP, and she said it was anxiety. I told her that I don't feel anxious. I asked her what to do about it and she said, 'Breath into a brown paper bag!' I felt silly when she said that, and cross too.

The cathedral piazza was festive and busy today because there was an art exhibition as part of the annual Hope Street Festival. After Mass, we met up with mum and Auntie Dorothy and went to a free concert at the Philharmonic. It should have felt like a wonderful treat to see the conductor Vasily Petrenko and the full Royal Liverpool Philharmonic Orchestra playing, but I spent most of the concert watching my mum.

I don't think she noticed me watching her, at least I hope she didn't because she would have thought me rude because I was staring hard at her, as if in a trance. I was wondering about my connection with her, and I realised that I didn't see her as a mother at all. Yes, I felt emotionally connected to her and know we have a strong bond, but I felt responsible for nurturing her, and I asked myself, shouldn't it be the other way round? My mind raced through memories and I realised that sometimes I am so afraid of her I shake and at other times she is like a little girl who I would do anything for just to see her smile. 'How could anyone evoke such a range of responses?' I told myself. There must be something wrong with me because I cannot be myself with her, I am always playing a role, trying to control my responses (fear of her) or trying to control her responses (trying to make her happy). I don't remember a single bar of the concert, and when we left I felt flushed, and I couldn't wait to get out in the fresh air.

I spoke to JC this evening, and he threw some light on what had happened today at the concert. It was a panic attack. He helped me accept that the GP didn't misdiagnose my anxiety. He said, 'The worst panic attacks are the ones where you don't feel any anxiety', which helped me a lot. JC said that I need to be brutally honest with myself about what I know to be my true calling. I have just realised that he didn't say what my 'true calling' was. Is it writing or something else? I think JC meant writing, but what do I believe it is?

Thank you, St Thérèse.

Yours,

Michaela

Chapter 57

21st September 2009

Dear St Thérèse,

What is spirituality? It is something we are born with and evolves as we do. Spirituality is not something we can choose to have or not have: we have it whether we know it or not. Like our health, even though we might not look after it well; we still have either a state of poor health or excellent health, and our spirituality can be in good or poor shape.

What state am I in spiritually? I am learning that to be truly faithful we have to keep the energy of our hearts and minds and our soul connected. When we allow ourselves this nurturing, we will naturally nurture others too. Nurturing is the primal role of the mother. I believe in the nurturing of the soul. Once when I was on a retreat, and I was thinking about love, one of the priests talked about charity as being an important aspect of love. I asked him, 'What does charity mean?' and he said confidently and simply, 'Think of the love between a mother and a child.' This explanation reminds me of you and your 'little way' of spiritual childhood.

The image of a child resting with complete security in its mother's nurturing arms is a great symbol for your 'little way'. The difficulty I have with this image is that instead of seeing a natural picture of a child being loved and cared for by its mother, my mind sees confusion. Does this mean that I can't relate to the 'little way'? Maybe not. Do I find it harder to identify with instinctive maternal love more than other people? If I do, perhaps in some ways it is a blessing because if I had been more at home with the most natural interpretation of nurturing, I might have been less inclined to seek and appreciate the spiritual understanding of nurturing.

Yours,

Michaela

Chapter 58

22nd September 2009

Dear St Thérèse,

You were familiar with your soul. You felt it strongly, and you could describe it. You knew your soul's destination was heaven, and its path was to stay as close to the shore of Jesus' love as possible. You also knew the feelings of your soul. It felt love, and love nourished it. Your example is inspiring and has raised within me lots of questions about what I know about love and my soul. I don't know much at all. I am fascinated by how well you knew your soul and how you communicated with it. I have read descriptions of people describing their soul as a place of peace, or love, or joy, or inner truth, and of being guided by their souls. I want to get to know my soul better.

What do I know about my soul already? Just as my heart is the source of my love, my soul is the source of my spiritual energy. What feeds my soul? It is nourished not just through how much I want to know God, but through how much I want God to know me; and not just by how much I talk to God, but how much I am willing to listen. In essence, my soul is at work when connected to my Higher Power. At these times I am guided through the harmonious synchronicity of my mind heart, thoughts and love. It is the most natural experience in the world.

I have been thinking about my soul for a few days and, inspired by your story, I meditated on these questions: What is my personal image of my soul? When am I most aware of it? How do I experience it? What are the feelings in my soul? So I closed my eyes and relaxed, and asked for help.

My thoughts went back to my childhood, and I remembered an experience when I was standing at the back door of our house looking out into the garden and felt both the external 'space' in front of me and an 'interior' space. I could see the coal bunker in my peripheral vision, and I avoided looking at it directly because I imagined something frightening in there, and I wanted it stay where it was. Apart from that, I felt peaceful and grateful for the gift of life ahead of me, and I asked God to help me use it to the best of my ability. I also felt a flutter of excitement in my stomach and another feeling which I couldn't identify then or now. My attention came back to the present.

I often think about this event, but I have never recognised it as a soul experience. I have also tried on several occasions to name the unidentified darker feeling which I want to keep hidden in the coal bunker, but it always eludes me. I have often wondered if it is a repressed memory. I can only describe it as a physical pulling in the centre of my chest which, if I am concentrating on it hard, can sometimes make my mouth dry and thirsty.

Meditating today, my thoughts went to various times in my life when I have been in sacred spaces, and felt connected to the presence of a Higher Power. I thought of the beautiful church in Prague where I saw the 'Infant of Prague'. I went to Prague for business purposes with colleagues, and we visited the Carmelite Church of Our Lady Victorious where the Infant of Prague statue is. From the outside, the church looks unremarkable so it was a surprise to see the elaborate altar within but the atmosphere remained intimate. I was also surprised at how small the statue was, I expected it to be much bigger, but I sensed it was much loved and special. I stood at the altar and prayed, but felt disconnected from goodness. I was still drinking then, and standing before the statue, I wanted to hide such was the discomfort. My conscience wasn't clear and I didn't know how to make it right, so I asked the infant Jesus to help me to get my life onto a happier and more carefree plane. After praying, I felt some relief from the burden of sorrow within me, and going for a meal later with my colleagues I felt more light-hearted and hopeful. I know you have a connection to the Infant of Prague and there is a photo of you with a statue; I have also read that St Teresa of Ávila is reputed to have at one time owned the statue.

I also thought about the awesomeness of St Patrick's Cathedral in New York City which is where some of my treasured experiences have occurred. The first time I went to St Patrick's was with my boss. He told me that St Pat's Cathedral was one of his favourite places and that he wanted to take me there. I was excited to go because I love churches and intrigued by his love of the cathedral. When we arrived and walked out of the sunlight into the darker interior, my first impression was, 'It's so big; much bigger than I expected.' I looked up at the magnificent ceiling and thought 'Wow', and then slowly looked around and couldn't take in all its beauty. I felt a lump in my throat and tears in my eyes.

'Wow,' I said. 'I see what you mean. This place has an incredible presence. It is alive with energy, not at all pious.' On subsequent visits to NYC, I always made sure that I visited St Pat's Cathedral to connect to the unique energy which I had never experienced in quite the same way anywhere else.

So it was with much excitement and pride that I looked forward to showing St Pat's to my dad when we visited NYC. As a retired police officer, dad is not at all whimsical or over sentimental, so his reaction brought me much unexpected joy.

We walked up the steps together into the dark interior, my dad seemed to have the same reaction I had on my first time. He just stood, looked up and around and didn't say anything.

'What do you think dad?' I asked.

'It's out of this world,' he said.

'Wow, that's how I feel', and we both felt a mutual joy of connection.

When it was time to go, we walked towards the massive doors to exit, and I saw tears in his eyes, and dad just shook his head the way he does when he is lost for words. 'Absolutely beautiful! What a place!' We stepped back into the sunlight, and as we were walking down the steps, a NY police officer asked dad if he had enjoyed the cathedral. Dad said he did very much, and I excitedly explained that he was a retired police officer from Liverpool. The officer immediately offered dad his hand, and they wholeheartedly shook hands. The police officer said what an honour it was to meet a fellow officer, and dad said it was his pleasure too. Now it was my turn to have tears in my eyes. I had never felt closer to my dad than I did at the moment. It was one of the proudest moments of my life.

Being close to the sea or water gives me a sense of spaciousness and connection. I thought of my many walks in all weathers along the Findhorn beach and around the Findhorn bay; the beautiful sunny day on Carmel Beach in California where the sound of the waves of the Atlantic Ocean crashing on the shore was one of the most beautiful I had ever heard. I recognised that at these special times in nature, the sense of spaciousness lessened the importance of my everyday concerns and my gratitude for the gift of my life was huge.

When I was a teenager, I had an operation to remove my wisdom teeth, and through damage to the nerves, part of my tongue was left permanently numb. However, I often know that something important is going to happen when I get a temporary tingling feeling in the numb part of my tongue. This sensation has become so reliable that I don't question it and just accept it. It happens when my Higher Power is trying to get my attention and I pay closer attention to what is about to happen with me or others. It often happens when I am reading too; it tells me that what I am about to read is of particular importance.

For the last four years, an important part of my recovery programme is the daily practice of maintaining conscious contact with God through prayer and meditation. I talk to God anytime or anywhere, but I haven't thought of the part that my soul might play. I simply ask God for freedom from self-will and knowledge of his will for and the strength to carry the vision of God's will into all my activities (but often failing).

My meditation continued and lulled me into a pleasant deep relaxation. Then a jolt like a mild electric shock made me jump and my heart beat faster. A feeling burst into my consciousness and then stopped before fully revealing itself. I held my breath asking myself did I want to know its name. Then recognition came with a crash of awareness and triggered a deeper, darker feeling which has characterised my soul for as long as I can remember. Its name echoed in my mind. Longing! I felt the ache of longing register throughout my body. When I felt calmer, I understood that the meditation had shown me that longing is the deepest part of my soul's experience. My first thought was, 'Oh no not that again; I thought I had dealt with longing!' Until four years ago I had lived with a profound longing to know what was wrong with me, but I thought that I had addressed this when I stopped drinking. But ultimately, in the presence of God my soul feels alive and spacious. It expands in sacred places and nature, making me grateful for the gift of my life and in the knowledge that while there is so much more to learn, I have faith that you will help me.

Yours,

Michaela

Chapter 59

23rd September 2009

Dear St Thérèse,

I am beginning to understand that my soul has been a secret place within the deepest part of me, and the place where I hide. Only God knows my soul intimately. He knows everything within it, even the things, or especially the things I don't know myself.

In your writings about your inner life, you convey a sense of internal space that I long for. You didn't over-analyse, which I am sure wasn't easy. Maybe it was because you were so committed to recognising your internal human conflicts that you were able to understand how important it was to keep the inner life as simple as possible. I have had so much mental confusion and conflict that I have hardly left myself any space to allow for my spirit just to be, and I sense that if I did allow my inner space to expand it would be liberating. But how do I do this? You did it through prayer, and I remember learning that the art of meditation was to 'be spacious' from Sogyal Rinpoche, a great Buddhist teacher and author. When I attended one of Rinpoche's talks at the Rigpa Centre in London, he repeated 'Be spacious' with a lovely chuckle and huge smile as if it was the only thing we ever never needed to know. I want to be able to develop my prayer and meditation to a point where I can sense more inner space, but how do I achieve this when my mind is so full and so constricted?

I had experienced healing before when I stopped drinking, and I believe that it can happen again. But what needs healing existed long before I drank and it is at a deeper level than the emotional and thinking problems that I have addressed in recovery. Something buried deep within me needs to be brought into the light. I have some ideas what it may be about, and my sponsor is guiding me.

I know that you will help me to continue on my soul's journey as I prepare for the arrival of your relics in Liverpool tomorrow.

Yours,

Michaela

PART FIVE

'SOUL SURRENDER'

CHAPTERS 60 TO 80

Chapter 60

24th September 2009

Dear St Thérèse,

Today has been one of the best days of my life and exceeded all my expectations. Your relics arrived in Liverpool's Metropolitan Cathedral of Christ the King this afternoon. At this very moment in the cathedral, the Carmelite nuns will be venerating your relics with an overnight vigil.

Let me start at the beginning. I arrived at the cathedral at 2pm, ready to be a steward from 3pm when your relics were due to arrive. I felt nervous, but when I saw how many other people had already arrived, I felt excited.

In the cathedral foyer the shop had set up temporary stalls, and the solemnity I expected didn't exist. Instead, people were three and four deep noisily trying to get to see what was being sold on the tables, and the Dean and Bishop and Archbishop in their striking colours strode up and down.

Anticipation crackled in the air like sparks of electricity. Although your casket hadn't arrived, 'St Thérèse is already here' I thought with awe, and imagined your spirit delighting at the many people gathered. The more pilgrims who come, the more people for you to shower with blessings. I knew without a doubt that this was what I had been preparing for since I came to know you.

I breathed deeply, inhaling the rich-perfumed incense, and the vibrant-coloured light from the stained-glass windows seemed to shimmer a fitting welcome for a saint. I dipped my finger into the holy water, its coolness contrasted with the warmth in my chest. It was like my whole body was unfurling into one big inner smile as I spontaneously smiled at the strangers milling around excitedly.

I wandered around the cathedral absorbing the atmosphere and relishing the opening within my chest; it reminded me of being at Midnight Mass as a child when I felt like I would burst with excitement. Steadying myself with deep conscious breaths, I instinctively knew that for once I shouldn't be pushing my feelings down, I should be embracing them. I knelt down in a pew and closed my eyes. I felt a palpable pulling feeling making my chest tight and uncomfortable for a few seconds and then a sudden bursting came like when you have been holding your breath and experience the relief of exhaling. I didn't feel like my usual self at all, but as if I had plugged into a new source of energy.

I surrendered to all the beauty, goodness and joy of the situation. Trembling slightly, tears welled up. As I went outside, I felt my phone vibrating in my pocket. It was mum. I answered.

'Hi Chaela, I just want to say, have a very special afternoon.' She spoke tenderly. More tears ran silently down my face. It was a few moments before I could say anything.

'Thank you. I'm sorry.'

'Don't cry darling,' said mum.

'It's all so moving,' I confided. 'I'll be fine,' I reassured her.

When I had finished that conversation, I decided to call Terry to share some of the experience with him. I felt more composed when I dialled his number, but as soon as I heard his voice, the tears were running down my cheeks again. 'What's happening to me?' I said.

'Don't worry; it is tears of joy,' said Terry.

'I know. I have been so excited about St Thérèse's relics coming, and they aren't even here yet, and I am so overwhelmed.'

'You are blessed, by St Thérèse,' Terry said.

Standing on the steps of the cathedral, I reflected on the all-encompassing glow that I was experiencing. It felt that it wasn't just coming from within me. Terry was right, your spirit was already present and had already touched me, and was still touching me. You were paying me a personal visit and filling my heart with the power of your love. I recognised that the deep longing I have been experiencing is a longing for love. It seemed so simple when I realised it, 'I have been longing for love', and somehow you were helping me to receive the love I had either lost or never known. I knew for a certainty that you were still with me as I heard an inner voice say, 'This is love. Open yourself to love. Receive love. Be love.' I repeated the words to myself, 'This is love. Open yourself to love. Receive love. Be love.' I sensed the words written on my heart, and although I felt an urge to write them down, I also knew I wouldn't need reminding of them.

I also realised how tender your love is; you had been preparing me for your blessing. In the last couple of weeks, every time I have thought or spoke of your visit I have felt emotional. It didn't matter who I was with – mum, dad, Terry, or alone – my reaction was the same. Powerful sensations swirled within my chest and stomach and I found myself crying for no reason, but the tears weren't sadness, more a release of the excitement bubbling within. Today the same thing had happened, and I understand with clarity and certainty what the feeling is: it is love. Love is filling my heart in a way I have never experienced so intensely before; thank you for this wonderful blessing.

I went and cleaned all the smudged make-up from my face and then went back into the cathedral. Evening prayers were set for 3pm, and I was told that I wouldn't be needed as a steward until after evening prayers. Many people had entered the cathedral, the pews were filling up quickly and I decided to go and wait outside to see your relics arrive. Standing at the top of the steps, my attention was drawn to a man standing close beside me. He looked to be similar in age to me. We smiled at each other and then he said as if we were in the middle of a conversation, rather than just starting one, 'St Thérèse is my best friend. I light a candle to her every morning. I have taken two days off work to come here.' He had an Irish accent but told me he lived in Liverpool. He seemed as excited as I felt and we shook hands and introduced ourselves.

'I'm David,' he said.

'I'm Michaela.' We smiled at each other knowingly for a few moments, and then he walked away, and I didn't see him again. Although it was a brief meeting, I felt that we had shared a significant moment with each other. It was like we both knew that we were in the presence of a soulmate as far as you are concerned. He didn't need to tell me how much your visit meant to him, I knew, and I am sure he knew how I felt too.

Then I bumped into a friend who had phoned me the day before to say he would love to see your relics arrive so we went and stood outside with all the press and photographers and watched and waited until the hearse arrived carrying the beautiful golden reliquary.

Although I had already seen your reliquary on television, my first sight of it in reality was moving. It was much larger than I imagined and exquisite, made of different shades of polished wood and gold. It looked like a large old-fashioned trunk protected by a Perspex dome. I could see that some of the engravings were of lilies and some of the gold filigrees looked like roses. Six pallbearers carried the reliquary on their shoulders, similar to how they would carry a coffin but without the solemnity of a funeral procession, the silence was much more festive.

I became overwhelmed with tears again watching the procession led by the Bishop and followed by priests, nuns and lay people winding its way up through the garden. When the procession became level with the outer doors of the cathedral, hundreds of patient pilgrims joined the procession. I wiped away my tears and followed too. There was an incredible moment of spontaneous applause as your reliquary entered the cathedral high on the shoulders of the pallbearers. The cathedral seemed even fuller, and the queues of people waiting on the steps seemed to get longer by the minute.

Just before the end of evening prayers, I was walking briskly through the crowds on my way to report for stewarding, and I felt someone touching my arm. I looked around to see an old friend looking smart and unusually wearing a tie.

'I am amazed to see you in all these crowds,' he said. I kissed him on the cheek and told him I had to dash and that maybe I would see him later. I wanted to ask him if he was wearing a tie in your honour, and although I didn't ask I guessed he was.

The organiser showed me to my steward's position which was just a few feet away from the reliquary. The route for the pilgrims wishing to venerate the relics was clearly marked out from the entrance, through the body of the cathedral, past the reliquary and then back through the body of the cathedral to an exit point. There were stewards strategically placed to direct and assist people along the route. I enjoyed directing the pilgrims in the procession as they walked past, slowly edging closer to the reliquary.

'Not long now,' I said as they passed me, and smiling with encouragement if people looked fed up with waiting. At every available moment, my eyes were drawn to watch the people when they reached your reliquary; most touched and some kissed the glass. I had known what to expect as I had seen people venerating your relics on TV at previous venues, but it was different seeing it for real. The reactions ranged from reverent, prayerful glances to awestruck adoration where people fell to their knees or seemed to cling onto the reliquary as if they were hugging a physical person. Those individuals who stopped for too long would be gently asked to move on so that the procession didn't stop moving.

As there were so many people in the queue, there was quite a long wait, and some people were less patient than others. I was frankly surprised at the brazen behaviour of some people as they approached me asking to be allowed to jump the queue; and how persistent they became if they didn't get their way. One woman physically tried to push me aside. Until this incident I was reticent, and a bit timid about refusing requests and I let people move ahead if they asked. Then I saw the security guard communicating with me from his position, and I knew what his non-verbal message was: be strong, so I was tougher and then he gave me a thumbs up when I politely refused and firmly told people they would have to be patient. For every impatient person, many waited patiently and joyfully.

After a couple of hours, an unexpected honour came to me. I was handed an ordinary yellow duster and asked if I would like to stand right beside your reliquary and wipe away the smudge marks that appeared as people kissed the glass or laid their hand upon it, and to ask people politely to keep moving. I was overjoyed and in disbelief. Amazing things like this didn't usually happen to me, but I know that you had a hand in it. I was so grateful and honoured.

When Terry arrived to collect me, I wasn't ready. I couldn't tear myself away from my wonderful duty of wiping kisses off the casket. From my position I could see him waiting patiently for me at the back of the cathedral. I waved and grinned at him, and he smiled and waved back and gestured for me to take my time. He knew I would be worried about keeping him waiting. I felt pure love for him as I watched him standing. I knew he would be absorbing the loving energy within the cathedral. It was a precious moment. He told me later that he was proud to see me standing there.

Reluctantly we left the cathedral. Terry had booked tickets for us to see a concert before we knew of your visit. I was a little sad to be missing the Mass this evening, but I will be attending Mass in the morning. Before we left, I went to the refreshment room to drop off the scones I had baked at 6am that morning. I met Claire, the organiser who told me she had been up at 6am too, baking cakes for the event. I was impressed by her dedication.

It was as if my spirit floated through the evening enjoying the concert. I felt physically light. Even though the Echo Arena is a stark contrast to the cathedral, the atmosphere within the concert crowd was similar to the cathedral today. People make their favourite musician/singer/band their source of elevation, pouring all their love and adoration into their favourite hero/heroines. Does this sufficiently meet and sustain people's spiritual needs?

Thank you for the most beautiful 'rose' you sent me today. I have felt my heart gently opening recently but my heart-petals bloomed today in a most profound way, and it is one of the biggest blessings of my life. Thank you for the blessing of understanding my longing for love, I pray that all the people who need your blessings receive them tonight and every day as you fulfil your promise to spend your heaven sending showers of roses.

Yours,

Michaela

Chapter 61

25th September 2009

Dear St Thérèse,

This morning, I was so excited. As soon as I arrived at the cathedral I bumped into a friend who introduced me to his friend. She was also a steward and in recovery. We chatted about how you had touched our lives and how popular your relics are.

Although I had been close to your reliquary yesterday, I hadn't had the opportunity to venerate your relics personally, so I joined the short queue to do so. It was moving to stand beside the reliquary and speak to you as a pilgrim rather than a steward. I thanked you for the beautiful experience yesterday and asked you to show me how to have a more open heart. As I was standing there, I realised that although I have always seen myself as a loving person, I intuitively know that there are 'blockages' in my heart, in the form of negative emotions. I had dealt with a lot of the apparent negativity from my guilt in early recovery and felt the benefit of surrendering to a higher power in my life, but there are still things that I know I haven't dealt with, and new perspectives yet to be embraced. I felt so blessed to have these few peaceful moments because afterwards I went outside and saw that the queue was now trailing down the steps of the cathedral.

Mum phoned to tell me that she and Auntie Dorothy were coming to the cathedral this afternoon for evening prayers. She also said that she had been in the cathedral yesterday while I was stewarding and that she had sat almost touching distance from where I was standing directing people. I was surprised that she didn't make me aware of her presence and that I didn't notice her. It would have been an entirely different experience had we made contact.

I reported for stewarding at 12 noon; however, I wasn't required until after Mass. More pilgrims arrived and the cathedral was packed full, with people standing at the back. I found a seat and just before Mass I noticed the woman I had met earlier. 'Are you looking for a space?' I whispered as she walked past.

'Yes,' she said.

'Squeeze in here if you like,' I said, and she did. In the ten minutes before Mass started, we had time to whisper a conversation. We found out that we have so much in common. We are the same age. Neither of us has children. We have been in recovery for the same amount of time. We are both suffering from panic attacks. We both get on better with men than women, and most importantly we both love you. We were joyful and felt the blessings of these amazing coincidences. 'St Thérèse has brought us together,' I said and told her how my heart had been opened in the days before your visit and about how emotional I had been yesterday just before your reliquary arrived. I described it as an opening to love, and she said something interesting, 'Maybe it was more a surrender than opening?' I suspect she is right. But whether an opening or surrender, it is one of the deepest releases in my recovery; it is interesting how it has affected me both emotionally and spiritually – I have mistakenly thought that the emotional and spiritual realms can be kept separate but now I understand that they can't. Indeed one of the most important aspects of my recovery is developing conscious contact with my Higher Power, and I understand now that we need our emotions to build this spiritual relationship. We engage emotionally in as much as we give of ourselves, and are open to receiving. It is a matter of the heart. The foundation of this engagement is love. I used to shy away from any loving relationship for fear of not fulfilling people's expectations of me but now I realise that my working definition of love has been deficient and severely faulty. You have helped me understand that love is not just about sharing or taking responsibility. Love is a gift given from the heart and received by the soul. Through love, you have accessed my soul. I want to learn to understand your approach to love, and to follow your example. I want to love as well and as much as I can and I know that this is the key to understanding my soul.

During Mass when we said the Our Father prayer, I realised that in it we ask to be shown our path and for the help that we need to follow that path on a daily basis, and how although we can't see our souls, we get glimpses through the visions we follow. Your vision was to love with all your heart, and through the guidance of the soul, you discovered the visions you were born to fulfil and to help others do the same.

After Mass, the Dean announced that it would be physically impossible to continue with the pilgrim procession past the reliquary for the personal veneration of the relics. There were too many people waiting, so the Dean asked that in your spirit, people be content to sit quietly and venerate in their seats. He assured us that you would still be answering prayers whether we touched your reliquary or not. He made the announcement sensitively, but I knew a lot of people would be disappointed; not least mum who would be arriving after Mass.

I sat quietly in the pew with thousands of other pilgrims and, as much as I tried to find peace within, a worrying thought kept intruding through my prayers: mum will be so angry when she finds out that there will be no further opportunity to file past and touch your reliquary. Mum had explicitly stated that she wanted to do so. I realised how much I was letting this bother me and tried to tell myself that I shouldn't feel responsible for mum's disappointment. As much as I knew it was irrational and unnecessary to be so disturbed, I couldn't shake it off.

'How brainwashed I am. I need to break this horrible habit of being over-responsible,' I thought. What I didn't admit to myself was that deep down my biggest fear was that mum would show her disappointment to me, and how would I respond to that?

The overcrowding situation then got worse because many people wanted to enter the cathedral and, for health and safety reasons, the decision was made to close the doors. All those who remained inside were locked in, and the thousands of people waiting to enter were effectively locked out. I stood for ages in the massive jam of people standing by the door waiting to get out and I imagined even more people on the other side of the door waiting to get in. I wasn't sure if mum had been locked in or out, but I dreaded it being the latter.

As soon as the doors opened again, I went looking for mum and Auntie Dorothy but instead I found Terry wandering around looking for me. We decided to take a break from the crowds and went down the steps into the café and joined the queue for some refreshments. While we were waiting for a cup of tea we bumped into mum and my aunt, and I could see that mum wasn't happy as she indignantly complained about being locked out of the cathedral, and now they had stopped the personal procession past the reliquary. 'How dare they …' etc. I tried to soothe her by telling her to go and find a seat and that I would get the drinks. Terry said he would help me. I asked mum if she wanted a cup of tea and then she said something in an irritated way which I thought was strange, 'Yes please, but don't put any sugar in my tea.' I knew that mum never took sugar in her tea and as far as I could remember I had never accidentally put sugar in her tea either. So why did she say this I wondered as I waited in the queue?

The café had made special arrangements so although the queue for refreshments was long, it moved quickly and people were good-humoured. I ordered the four drinks and was given four cups of black tea in disposable cups and directed to a table where I could add milk and sugar. It was still at the back of my mind what mum had said about the sugar in her tea. With Terry's help, I added milk to the four cups and put what I thought was the appropriate amount of sugar in three cups. We took the hot drinks outside to where mum and Auntie Dorothy had managed to find a free table and sat down. I was careful to make sure that I gave everyone the correct cup of tea.

'This isn't going half as well as yesterday,' I thought as we sat in silence drinking our tea. 'Where has all my happiness gone?' I felt anxious and nervous as if something dreadful was about to happen. 'What is different?' I wondered. 'Is it the crowds?' Yes it was busy, but it was busy yesterday too. 'Is it more commercialised today?' Yes, a little, but that's to be expected. I couldn't put my finger on the source of my anxiety. Then mum screamed, and I jumped spilling some of the hot tea into my lap.

'There is sugar in my tea! I told you not to put sugar in my tea!' Mum was angry and staring at me accusingly as if I had deliberately given her sweet tea. My mind raced backwards through my actions, but I had been especially careful given her warning.

'Maybe I have accidentally given you the wrong cup?' I said and looked at the others eagerly in the hope that they would say, 'Yes, there's no sugar in mine', but mine was sweet, and so were Terry's and Auntie Dorothy's.

'I will go and get you another one,' I said jumping up.

'It's too busy, just leave it,' mum said, but I went and bought another cup of tea. I tried to lift the tension when I returned by apologising and changing the subject by chatting about the morning's events, but that wasn't a great topic either because it reminded mum that she had been denied the opportunity of personal veneration.

My mind felt in turmoil. Did mum have a premonition about sugar in her tea? Did I accidentally put sugar in her tea? Did Terry accidentally put sugar in her tea? Mum's tight lips and frown told me that she wasn't at all happy. The day was spoiled. How can this have happened?

We were all a little subdued when we went back into the cathedral and took our places for evening prayer. I was aware of mum's vibes which were still saying to me 'I'm not happy' and although she hadn't said it was my fault, I felt responsible. It has only just occurred to me as I am writing this, how do I know whether or not there was sugar in her tea? I feel disloyal even having this thought, but after what happened later on, nothing would surprise me about my thoughts and behaviour.

Again the cathedral was full for the beautiful and moving service which celebrated the joy and hope that your visit had brought to the thousands of pilgrims. I tried not to let into my awareness the sadness I sensed that was nearby. Yes, I could be sad saying goodbye to your relics, and at the thought of the incident in the café. In the past I would have let the negative feelings prevail. But this time I was in deep awe when I remembered the opening of my heart which I had experienced when in the presence of your relics.

At the end of the service, with hundreds of other pilgrims, we followed the procession to where the hearse was waiting, and watched as the reliquary was placed into the hearse. There was spontaneous applause as the hearse slowly drove away and a single bell tolled. Although there were lots of people about, other than the imposing resonance of the bell, there was almost complete silence. I noticed that I wasn't the only person without dry eyes in the farewell crowd. Oh, St Thérèse, I am sure you were watching and saw how moving it was as your pilgrims said their goodbyes.

I felt tense sitting in the car with mum and Auntie Dorothy as Terry drove us all home. No one said much except when we said goodbye when we dropped them off at their respective homes. If we had all stayed together for much longer, I sensed that the tense atmosphere might have erupted into harsh words.

The relief of being alone with Terry was short lived. Within a few seconds, my main awareness was not with the thoughts in my mind or even my emotions; all my attention was being drawn to my body, firstly my breathing. I took a huge breath and felt familiar spikes of tension within my chest and stomach telling me that something bad was about to happen.

I then felt a surge of energy which in the past would have mobilised me to move swiftly away from the situation or prepare me for whatever adversity I was about to face. But instead, I just sat there in the car, wide-eyed, staring ahead, and holding my breath as if frozen.

I didn't feel afraid; it was quite a strange emotion in its intensity, but I knew that it was preparing me for action. The next thing that happened I am ashamed of, but I have to write about it honestly, and although I can't fully explain it at the moment, I hope that there was a reason for it happening.

Within seconds of the relief of being just the two of us in the car, Terry and I were shouting at each other. It wasn't a huffy tiff or a silly squabble; it was a full-blown screaming match which is dangerous when someone is driving a car. I can't even remember what started the row, but Terry made a comment about family tensions, and I exploded.

In the same way that I was overwhelmed by love yesterday, I was overwhelmed by a torrent of physical emotion in waves of heat and spikes of physical pain which I now believe to be a type of anger that I hadn't experienced so intensely before. It was a mixture of simultaneously controlled energy release and extreme lack of emotional control. I felt consumed with a rage that at moments was almost pleasant in the release I sensed in my body, as I shockingly observed myself repeatedly bang the dashboard with my clenched fist and every word was shouted at the top of my voice. Then when the car slowed down at the traffic lights, I leapt out of the car as if it was the best idea I had ever had in my life, rather than one of the most foolish. I landed clumsily on the pavement and took a few moments to take in that I had just jumped out of a moving car.

'What's going on? Yesterday was the best day of my life and today is turning into one of the worst.' I had to calm down.

Driving slowly alongside me for most of the rest of the journey, Terry patiently pleaded with me to get back into the car, but I stubbornly refused and stomped the rest of the way home. What happened to me? How could I go from being so inspired and joyful to experiencing such intense anger that I felt unable to control it? At first, I wondered, is it a lower power trying to steal my faith and the gift of love I received from you? For a few moments, this seemed like the best explanation. Then I realised that something within me had snapped. I wasn't furious about what Terry said at all. Although he was uncharacteristically critical of the 'sugar in the tea' incident, I was reacting extremely intolerantly towards him; the truth was that I completely agreed with everything he was saying. Was it this realisation that made me so angry? What would have been my typical response in this situation? I would have taken responsibility for mum's disappointment at the closing of the cathedral, the sudden ending of the procession past the reliquary, and the sugar in the tea, and then looked for a way to regain mum's approval. But something within me was significantly different.

Back at home, sanity prevailed once more, and we were both shaking, probably shocked by the suddenness of what happened. I can't say that I have never responded so violently and emotionally, but it was the first time that it had occurred while I was sober. Like an abandoned child I sat on the sofa and cried and then as I regained composure I apologised and hugged and kissed Terry, I was full of remorse.

When I calmed down, I explained to Terry that as soon as we were alone in the car, I was expecting to let off a bit of steam about earlier tensions and to have a bit of a moan. But instead, something felt as if it had snapped within me and that there was a huge, 'No, no, no, no, no!' screaming silently within me. Terry was understanding and philosophically suggested that sometimes to let in all the goodness, the badness has to come out. I agreed with this. Indeed a similar prayer had been said by me during Mass. I asked God to help me heal and let go of emotional obstacles. But I still felt the shock of how my heart, which had been so full of light yesterday, could bear so much heavy pain and darkness today. Terry proposed that yesterday had been so healing that maybe it had reached the cause of my sadness, and it had burst like a boil. Again as much as this made sense I still felt inconsolably sad about how what promised to be an exceptionally special day. The sadness soon turned to miserable guilt and then to mental and physical exhaustion, and I lay down and fell asleep wondering if I could trust myself to go to the all-night vigil we had planned at Salford Cathedral. When I woke I wanted to roll over and go back to sleep to push the despair away, but I felt called to write this letter. I sensed a promise that I would feel better for writing it all down, and there was a flicker of hope within that I might find some more meaning looking back over the day's events.

Unfortunately, at the moment, my mind isn't clear, and the best insight I can muster is the certain realisation that I am angry; genuinely angry; long-time angry; but angry about what and angry with whom? As I washed and dressed I wondered if the person I am most angry with at the moment is me. Each time I was disturbed today, it was caused by worrying about mum's reactions and what she was thinking. Why do I do this? The only conclusion I can reach is that I am a still a compulsive approval-seeker. Maybe I have even done this with you in writing these letters to you? Is that my underlying remit, to gain your approval? Yesterday I experienced an 'opening to love' inspired by you, and I pray that its effects continue and that my angry reactions today are the first steps in overcoming the inhibiting of my true self.

Today has been so different to yesterday, but I am not disappointed in you in any way at all. Indeed, my faith in you couldn't be stronger. Maybe I cannot see past the painful experiences of today at the moment, but I trust that these events have happened for a reason, and one day I will discover that you have sent me even more roses than you did yesterday.

We leave for Salford Cathedral in a few minutes to be pilgrims at the all-night vigil. I will be praying and asking for your help.

Yours,

Michaela

Chapter 62

26th September 2009

Dear St Thérèse,

Although I was much calmer when we set out for Salford Cathedral late last night, part of me was nervous, and in the car on the way I said prayers to you so that whatever happened I would be able to keep my emotions in check. I asked Terry how he was feeling and he reassured me that he was fine, but I imagine that we were both still a little bit raw from our contretemps earlier.

The decision to be part of the all-night vigil in Salford came out of my initial enthusiastic desire to follow you around the country for the whole month and visit every place on your relics' tour, but I knew that this wasn't practical. I was glad that we had booked a hotel room in case we were tired after the vigil.

We arrived just before the late-evening service began. The cathedral was warm and bright and my spirits lifted as soon as we walked in, and I felt the intimacy of the setting and noticed your reliquary on the altar looked even more impressive in the surroundings of a much smaller space. The cathedral was busy but not rushed, much more peaceful than Liverpool. We were welcomed warmly by a steward who led us to the front pew and told us that there was a queue to venerate the relics, but if we waited there, we would be called to join the queue shortly.

Just as we sat down, a young priest started night prayers, and I sensed the playfulness of your spirit through the priest who seemed jolly even while praying. I later saw him with some teenagers, and they were all laughing together. He appeared to be a lovely man. The prayers he said were beautiful and informal. As the final hymn was sung, we were gently ushered by a steward to join the queue to venerate the relics. The pilgrims' route was adorned with displays of you and your life. We stopped and admired the candles with your picture on. I noticed that the elderly man behind us in the queue was clutching an envelope with the edges of black-and-white photos peeking out. I was curious as to what they were and he explained that he had been an altar boy in the cathedral 55 years earlier. One of the photos showed him outside the cathedral with another young boy looking angelic and I felt honoured as the fellow pilgrim shared his precious memories with us.

We were in the queue for about half an hour, and we could see ahead that no one was being rushed past the reliquary or even asked to move on if they stopped. The reliquary was on an altar, and all around was a beautiful garland display of cream roses and green foliage. The scent of the roses mixed with incense was heady but beautiful. It was harder for people to kiss the reliquary than in Liverpool because the ledge of the altar acted as a barrier, but some people leant forward to do so. The pace was so much different. I saw pilgrims spending several minutes beside the reliquary with their hands placed on the Perspex cover, and their heads bowed, eyes closed, or just gazing at the reliquary alone in their thoughts. There were several petition boxes filled with brightly coloured pieces of paper. Also along the way were several hard-backed petition books for people to write their prayers and petitions. I stopped at one and made an entry.

As the reliquary was on the high altar, the Blessed Sacrament was on a side altar. Behind the reliquary were about eight rows of comfortable padded seats for sitting quietly. There was also a single pew at each end of the reliquary with space for one person to kneel and pray. The Dean told us that he wanted someone to be there throughout the night keeping vigil. As the hours passed, the queue eventually finished with only single visitors arriving. Terry and I sat for a couple of hours transfixed by the peace and holiness and saying our private prayers. I stood right beside your reliquary for about half an hour hoping for a place at one of the pews, but they didn't become available often, and people moved like lightening to get to them, so I decided just to sit quietly.

We went for a break and found that although it was the early hours of the morning tea was still being served, and there was access to a beautiful but small floodlit garden. Although it was cold outside, we sat in the night air and enjoyed a cup of tea and chat with one of the stewards (a young woman) who told us how busy things had been earlier and how impatient people had been to get to the reliquary. I told her that I had also been a steward in Liverpool and of the 'crowd response' there, and we both seemed reassured that our communities were not uniquely impatient.

After our tea, we returned to the reliquary, and I felt inspired to write a few words. This is what I was inspired to write.

Salford Cathedral midnight 25th September 2009

I am here St Thérèse, sitting beside your casket, in your presence, and I am blessed. I feel so close to you. I was praying before about vocation and purpose. You had a strong purpose.

Please help me to find my purpose. What do I mean by purpose? Mission. Something to pray for. I believe in prayer 100 per cent. I believe that prayers are not just said, but are also acted and written. Please help me to pray in my actions. Please help me to have a purpose. I am writing my story of my soul about resilience, but also about the source of my resilience. My faith. My life to date has prepared me for the graces I have received from you.

What am I hearing? Love and surrender, don't be too hard on yourself, the challenge is to accept your faults. What do I mean by faults? Shortcomings. How do I do this?

At communion at Mass today (actually yesterday now) I had a sense of clearing out the bad to let in the good. We have to clean out the bad to let in the good – don't pour new wine into old wineskins, but pour new wine into new wineskins.

This metaphor was important to me when I was younger. I am learning that each day is a new opportunity, another chance to make a fresh start. When we are making 'fresh starts' we are receiving the grace to start again. What stops us from making new starts or holding onto negative bad stuff? Fear and habit. But we can break habits if we want to. We can surprise ourselves. Negativity doesn't have to be a life sentence. But when we make fresh starts, for it to be a fresh start, we have to let go truly and fully and surrender. If we are in denial, it is not truly a fresh start – surrender. Complete surrender is a complete willingness to let go – we become empty; we hold onto nothing. When we are empty, we are ready to be filled with grace and love. But even when we feel empty we are never really empty, because God fills us up with love and grace. This process is what happens in my recovery fellowship. Surrender = letting go = making ourselves open to God's will – not our will.

Please, St Thérèse, help me to hand over and make myself empty for God's grace and God's will. Not to be afraid or angry or lash out. We lash out when we are resisting. We resist when we are afraid to let go. Please, St Thérèse, help me to stop resisting. When I do this, God's grace will come in, and I will have space for God's will and to know God's will.

Help me to be open, not to others so that they can fill the space, but to God. How can I be open and create space? Through prayer and meditation. Help me to write too. A life of service is good and positive as long as it isn't serving the ego but serving God. Thank you, St Thérèse, for these insights and all your help and guidance. I love you, and I am so grateful for your help. I love you and trust you; please help me to love and trust God too.

Amen.

When we were ready to leave Terry said he would have been happy to stay all night, and so would I, but we were both tired. I also felt that I couldn't be happier or more content if I tried. My heart felt full, and I didn't want to lose the positivity I felt through tiredness.

We arrived at our hotel and within a few minutes we were in bed. As I lay there expecting to fall asleep quickly I picked up a Holy Bible and sleepily opened it at random, happy to read for a minute or two wherever the page opened. My sleepiness was pierced by a jolt of surprise and recognition at what I read. Matthew 9:16, 'No one puts a piece of unshrunk cloth on an old garment, for the patch tears away from the garment, and a worse tear is made. Neither is new wine put into old wineskins. If it is, the skins burst and the wine is spilt, and the skins are destroyed. But new wine is put into fresh wineskins, and so both are preserved' (Holy Bible).

I was completely amazed. Only an hour or so earlier sitting beside the reliquary I had written the phrase about pouring new wine into new wineskins. What a coincidence! My surprise turned to a joyful presence of God and you, like loving parents would say to their child, 'We are here for you.' I felt like my pilgrimage had been a success.

Thank you for yet another blessing. Although it is significant, I'm not sure exactly what the phrase means yet, but I know it is important. It was important to me years ago; it came to mind when writing besides your reliquary and it was the first reading I came to when I opened the Bible. I pray that you will help me understand what it means.

Thank you with all my heart for an amazing time during the visit of your relics. It has been one of the most inspirational events of my life. I am full of gratitude for the hope that all the desires of my heart taking seed will grow into strong, loving and faithful actions.

Yours,

Michaela

Chapter 63

27th September 2009

Dear St Thérèse,

At Mass at the cathedral today I noticed that the excitement of your visit was still in the air. The congregation seemed to linger afterwards, and people seemed more cheerful and more animated as they left. I have to confess to my mind wandering a few times during the service as I gazed at the space where the reliquary had been positioned and remembered how special I felt standing and wiping the kisses off the casket with the duster. It almost seems like a dream now, but a happy dream and one that I am sure I will joyfully relive for the rest of my life.

After Mass, I went to the bookshop again, and there were lots of people crowded around the books about you. I wondered if they were pilgrims who hadn't yet read your 'Story of a Soul' and had come to buy your book, or maybe they were inspired to buy it for someone else. I am happy for those people who will receive blessings from the gift of your story.

As I am writing this, although I didn't notice it at Mass today, I am a bit despondent. Like the day after a special event when you gratefully recall how much you enjoyed yourself, but knowing that all too soon you will be back to the humdrum of everyday life. JC would call it an emotional hangover, and that's what I mean (not an actual hangover like I used to experience the day after the night before when I would usually be lying in bed both physically ill and mentally tortured with guilt and remorse at my 'good time'). Maybe 'anti-climax' is more apt (although not entirely correct). It is natural to be reflective and even a little sad after such excitement and enjoyment, and it feels ungrateful to wonder what next? But that's it; I am wondering, where do I go from here? I don't want to go backwards.

It's like the last day of a special event that you don't want to end. I used to hate endings. In my drinking days, I would do anything to keep a party going. I never wanted it to end. I understand now that it was the fear of being alone that propelled me to drink every last drop out of a social event. Thankfully today I am more accepting of endings, and much more appreciative of everyday life, but I still have a little bit of the anxious part of me that worries, 'Have I taken as much as I can from experience?' I don't like this about myself. I want to focus more on what I 'give' to situations. But I have to be honest and accept that this is still part of me at the moment. While I want to 'give' thanks for every second of the gift of your visit, another part of me wants to ensure that I can 'capture' the impact of your visit in such a way to hold it close to me forever and to make sure that I learn and grow from the experience.

I have just reassured myself that these letters to you will play some part in recording your visit, but they also feel inadequate, as if there is something that is knocking on the door of my consciousness waiting to be let in. I am going to pray and meditate on these thoughts. I am also going to pray for some more insight on the meaning of the parable of the wine and the wineskins. This intention has been on my mind a lot.

Yours,

Michaela

Chapter 64

29th September 2009

Dear St Thérèse,

I have been praying and reading about the parable of the wine and the wineskins and wondering about its meaning. I felt sure that there was an important insight for me. I intuitively felt that it is connected both to my heart-opening experience in the cathedral and why I was so angry on the second day of your visit. I wondered, 'Where did all that love come from and where did all the anger come from, and why?'

The first part of my question has been answered. Quite simply, you helped my heart to open. You helped me to accept the love that is within me and perhaps has always been there. But a lifetime of being burdened by responsibility hid the warmth of love just as the heat of the blazing sun is hidden behind grey clouds. You helped my heart and mind to open last July in preparation for your relics, and as if the obstacles were suddenly removed, I felt its full force on the day of your visit. So it is the second part of the question that I am more perplexed by: where did all the anger come from?

I came across an interpretation in an article (Osteen 2004) which explains that in biblical times, people used goatskins to store wine instead of bottles. When the wine was poured into the goatskin, they'd tie the top of the goatskin to seal the wine inside. These were known as wineskins. The interesting thing about wineskins is that even when they were new, they were soft and pliable, but as time passed and they aged, they would lose their elasticity. When this happened, the wineskins hardened and would no longer be able to expand. This response didn't have any adverse effect on the wine that was already inside. However, it did make a difference if brand new wine was poured into an old used wineskin. As Jesus says in Luke 5:37, 'And no one pours new wine into old wineskins. If he does, the new wine will burst the skins, the wine will run out, and the wineskins will be ruined.'

The article then asks what the point of the whole wineskin parable is, and the meaning behind it. As I was reading the article, a massive wave of recognition about the parable's personal meaning came to me. Jesus used the wineskins story to make a critical point; God wants our hearts and minds to be like the new wineskins, open and ready, but our faulty thinking can prevent us from receiving what God wants for us. The parable encourages us not to settle for anything less than our full potential and to do this we must enlarge our thinking. The wine in the parables is symbolic of our lives; and the wineskins symbolic of our attitudes. When He said, 'You can't put a new wine into old wineskins', Jesus was saying that we cannot have a spiritual life with restricted attitudes. We can't expect to have a life full of purpose and meaning if we have a negative attitude or continue to be set in our ways or to be bound by our faulty thinking.

I understood that although I have been willing to change to succeed in my recovery, I still have a major obstacle to overcome, and it is to do with my attitude and my emotions. I realised that the type of anger which came so readily just after visiting your relics has a special name, and it is something which is referred to in my recovery programme as 'the number one offender'. It is more commonly known as resentment. I understand a resentment to be the reliving of a perceived hurt, again and again.

I have never claimed to be free of resentment in recovery, but until today I didn't realise just how much resentment there is possibly within me and how much of a burden and blockage this might be. What made me think of this? It was when I understood that God has plans for everyone, and that is why he gives us talents. While He places certain dreams and desires in our heart; we will never accomplish them unless we're willing to trust him wholeheartedly and change our old ways of thinking and expand our visions. I said to myself, 'I find it hard to trust, and have a life-long habit of taking too much responsibility for others and repressing and inhibiting my feelings, especially anger, and I know that resentment is a form of repressed anger.'

Negative emotion and thoughts are like an old wineskin. Just as you can't pour new wine into old wineskins, God can't pour new desires, visions, and blessings into a closed mind that is full of untreated resentment and repressed negative feelings. I don't have as much sense of purpose in my life as other people have, and even if I do, something is stopping me recognising it.

I thought about the process of letting out the old and allowing in the new, and I recognised I am much more familiar with the 'old' than the 'new'. I know what the old is, negativity, resistance, fear, self-criticism, people-pleasing, anxiety, over-compliance, lack of faith in myself, lack of trust, and lack of self-belief, low self-worth, etc.; but what about the new? If it is having an open and ready heart and mind, how can I achieve this state? How do I become like a new wineskin? And how do I make sure that my attitude is renewed?

In essence, while I may have consciously put a lot of effort into letting go of the old, I have put a lot less conscious effort into opening up to the new. The parable means something that I haven't thought much about before, and that is that to let in the new I need to clear an inner space first. This space is something I long for. It isn't a place of safety but more a place of sanctuary. I need to find a place of stillness and calmness within, but how can I find this place of sanctuary within and how do I deepen and apply my heart-opening experiences?

Yours,

Michaela

Chapter 65

30th September 2009

Dear St Thérèse,

Your tour is about halfway through and today I have been reading more of the news reports about your visit so far. There have been thousands more pilgrims at each venue than expected, and every venue has reported queues of people waiting patiently to venerate your relics. It seems to have been a huge success and has stirred so many people.

Another important realisation happened today when I was reading an article about the message of Jesus in the Garden of Gethsemane by Father Ron Rolheiser (2005). I have always loved the picture of the Last Supper from when I first saw it as a mural on the ceiling of St Anthony of Padua Church; and as a child, I always wondered about what happened next. The agony in the garden is what happened next. The image of Jesus going to the garden with the disciples and kneeling down to pray can move me to tears anytime. Why does it affect me strongly? I imagine how lonely Jesus must have felt in his suffering. The disciples couldn't stay awake with him, so he was essentially all alone at perhaps his darkest hour. Father Ron says that it wasn't the impending physical suffering of his crucifixion that Jesus felt anguish about; but it was more about the emotional suffering, such as the loneliness He faced. I know that in my darkest times, it is being so alone that makes me suffer most. Separateness and isolation lead to intense loneliness and these are the times when I have felt most hopeless.

I also identify with the intimacy of Jesus telling the disciples how scared He was and then telling God his Father that he wishes that the 'cup be taken away'. He was obviously speaking from his heart and must have been really frightened. In his fear, Jesus is so courageous in his ability to say to his Father, 'yet not my will, but yours, be done.' In doing so, Jesus is saying I give my life freely, out of love and service, without resentment. He makes it clear that He chooses God's will rather than his will. He is both surrendering his will and accepting God's will at the same time. This scene is inspiring.

Father Ron says that this example helps us to be able to say and mean, 'Nobody takes my love and service from me, I give it over freely!' and meet the challenge of loving and serving others without resentment. It is the same message as the parable of the wineskins. I want to take these insights to heart. They might only be intellectual at the moment, but I pray to accept their truth.

Understanding that I might be rife with resentments has come as an emotional shock. How misguided I was to think that I didn't have any serious problems to do with resentments? I was missing the point when I thought resentment was just holding grudges against people and believed that I didn't hold grudges. Indeed, didn't I deserve a medal for how much forgiveness I have felt for people who have hurt me? But I realise today how much I need to accept in my heart the emotional and spiritual symptoms I suffer from are undeniably resentment. Here are some of the symptoms of resentment that I strongly identify with: the negative thinking and depressions it causes; needing to be in control; compulsive urges to seek approval; trying to please others and yet being upset that others have such a hold over me. I think about others too much of the time, and I feel guilty about my negativity towards people.

The idea that both the problem and solution lies not with the person I am resentful about, but with me, has had quite an impact on me. I thought that the blame lay with the other person and that I was doomed to be forever under their control, like a huge burden from which there is no escape. I didn't believe that it was within my power to change these situations.

It is ironic that I have spent many, many hours in self-searching and still I didn't realise that I was suffering from resentment. It is hard to believe. I didn't believe that I could be holding a grudge because I always tried to make people feel better by my actions. But what I was trying to do was to control and protect myself from future hurt. I wasn't being honest with myself accepting that I felt hurt and the extent to which I felt that hurt. For instance, when I had my breakdown years ago I had a breakthrough when I realised how angry I was with mum. I stopped contact with her but then when we started speaking again I wasn't honest, and I pushed down my angry feelings again. The pattern has repeated itself again and again. Because I am not facing up to the hurt, I am putting myself into vulnerable positions repeatedly, and then I am resentful in these situations. It is a vicious circle. I wanted everyone's pain to ease, so I took responsibility, but it has meant that I have been left with resentment towards others and myself because it was impossible for me to protect everyone from hurt.

So resentment is also a form of protection. By blaming someone else, I am protecting myself. Maybe I didn't realise that I felt resentment because I was so frightened of facing the hurt and pain? Or maybe I have given my power away so thoroughly that I don't feel entitled to be angry. I don't deserve to be angry.

I am aware that other people trigger negativity within me when they ask me or expect me to do something that I don't want to do, and I can't say no. But I thought this would be overcome by just trying harder. So why can't I say no? Because it will force me to accept my uncomfortable or painful emotions. When in pain, I am vulnerable and powerless and feel the threat of abandonment. It makes me panic. It makes me afraid but I didn't realise this was a process called resentment. I have read that resentment ties two people together stronger than most other emotional bonds and that the key to overcoming it is facing the hurt within and accepting the circumstances of the sources of the pain. I didn't understand this fully before.

Over the years I have read many, many books trying to find out what was wrong with me. I have searched hard for the key to feeling better. I thought that I just needed to work harder or pray harder to find the solution. But now I understand that resentment has given me restricted access to an important part of me. Bitterness and resentment make it harder to access and express my love. It is a barrier stopping me from being fully alive and embracing joy and happiness. When I am resentful towards someone I am laying all the blame on them and saying that they are the problem; it is their fault. Not mine. Letting go of resentment is not for the benefit of the person I am resentful towards, it is for me. I pray that I can be willing to feel the hurt buried under resentment and that I can accept it, whatever it is.

Please help me to take full responsibility for the inadequacy that I have been avoiding. Once I am prepared to accept it, I will no longer need the resentment. The antidote to resentment is not just forgiveness, but gratitude. I was wondering if your miracle of conversion on Christmas Eve was to do with the lifting of resentment. I have received my miracle in the last few days. When you mention being like a little child, this could also refer to being free of resentment.

At the end of my 'resentment study', I spoke to Terry and shared how much of a mammoth task overcoming resentments was starting to be, and he said something wise and helpful. You don't have to do it on your own.

Yours,

Michaela

Chapter 66

1st October 2009

Dear St Thérèse,

No matter how overwhelmed I felt yesterday, I can't be downhearted today. It is your feast day. I was agitated yesterday but calmer today. I want to accept the things that I can't change and have the courage to change the things I can, even if I'm not sure at the moment, apart from prayer, what the best approach is.

This morning I was looking outside from the first-floor landing window thinking about how I could celebrate your special day at the same time as noticing that the next-door neighbour's garden is like a wilderness. The grass hasn't been cut for quite a few months, and it has been left to go completely wild since the previous owners left. Before, when the lovely family lived there, it was a beautiful garden. They cared for it well, and it was a pleasure to behold.

I was looking out of the window for quite a few minutes when I noticed, standing tall in the midst of the grossly overgrown grass and weeds, a beautiful single white rose in as full bloom as any rose on a summer's day. As I was thanking you, St Thérèse, for sending me a rose on your feast day, I saw along the back wall almost hidden by overgrown grass and shrubs another beautiful rose, red this time standing as tall as the white one. I stood in awe and went and got my camera and took a photograph. I look out of the landing window most days, and I felt sure that I would have noticed the roses before. Perhaps you kept them hidden until today as a special present for your feast day.

The appearance of the roses got me thinking about the good things that we have in our lives that we don't always realise are there just waiting to be discovered, and equally, without being too negative, the bad things that perhaps we don't realise are within us or affecting us. As much as I want to focus on being positive rather than negative, I now know that there is a perspective that needs changing that stops my soul from developing to its fullness. Some of my resentments are from events in the past, but alarmingly there are situations in which I am creating new resentments on a daily basis through my current approach to life. There are people that I am not honest with. I am seeking their approval rather than being truthful. What can I do about this? These situations need to be dealt with urgently. As well as emotional pain, I feel the physical symptoms of my faulty approach. Sometimes I feel tightness in my chest, a knot in my stomach and a lump in my throat. But always accompanied by a sadness like an entirely calm lake that might look serene from a distance but if you were to plunge in it would be achingly ice-cold.

Resentment blocks the love and gratitude that I know is within me but is often hidden. I hide pain even from myself until it appears as a longing, like a cold draft in my soul. Increasingly in need of release, I defend most attempts at letting the source of the sadness come into conscious awareness. It scares me and threatens to wipe out all the goodness and light in my life, but until I face the darkness of this void, I will never be entirely free emotionally or spiritually. When I was drinking, the darkness was a profoundly destructive force over which I had no control. I felt victimised by the power that would force me to press the self-destruct button against my will.

Today I realise that it was too much self-will fuelled by alcohol abuse which caused my self-destruction. I believe wholly in the power of God's grace and healing, but I also know that I have a part to play in the growth of my soul. I have to take responsibility for the sadness and act. I noticed that I had called the blockage sadness because this is what I am familiar with, but now I know the sadness is a response to pain and hurt. Just writing that has made me tearful, but it is true. Underneath the resentment is sadness and underneath the sadness is deep hurt which hasn't been dealt with yet.

Thank you again for the gift of the beautiful roses in the garden today, and as my gift to you I have written this special feast-day prayer:

Prayer to St Thérèse, 'One Petal at a Time'.

Dear St Thérèse,

Often when we feel despondent or in despair, we can wish that our disposition would change from one of sadness to happiness or from being broken to feeling whole in an instant. Thank you, for teaching me that our hearts and minds will open like a beautiful rose, in God's time.

Please help me to remember that the process of the growth to fullness is just as important as the flourish of our full-bloom. If we unnaturally blossomed too quickly our dying would be sooner, and so the gift of any beauty and fragrance would also be shorter lived. Please send me a rose of gratitude to help me fully appreciate each moment, hour and day of my journey, one petal at a time.

Amen.

Yours,

Michaela

Chapter 67

2nd October 2009

Dear St Thérèse,

I have been thinking about something positive for a change: innocence. It reminds me of the purity of children and their right to be protected from any damage or corruption. Innocence also suggests the power of simplicity and blamelessness. It is about goodness and the virtue of being childlike as opposed to childish. However, innocence is not popular in society these days. It seems that children are encouraged to lose their innocence far too quickly. Sophistication and worldliness are seen as the prizes of overcoming innocence and are highly valued. If innocence is noticed in an individual, it can be classed negatively as naivety. The innocent are also accused of being gullible and inexperienced. One of my favourite writers, Father Ron Rolheiser, describes innocence as being in a state of un-woundedness, and I strongly identify with the idea of the opposite of innocence being 'wounded'.

The 'little way' is all about the simplicity of innocence. You tell us to go to God as simply and innocently as a child would go to their father. My recovery literature tells me that I should hand over my will to the care of God. Why is this so profound to me? It tells me the ideal state the soul should be in for spiritual strength and to be spiritually well. We don't need sophisticated and complicated souls to be able to hand our will to God, indeed the simpler, the better. It is also written in the Bible that we go to God as little children. This message is powerful.

I have lived a life which has been in direct opposition to innocence at many levels. I strived for sophistication and worldliness at a young age to survive my circumstances. I felt damaged by the break-of up of my family, but I felt myself to be the guilty party. I had carried a sense of shame for I don't know what. All my life I thought 'gaining experience' was always beneficial when often it was harmful to me. As I got older, my behaviours when I was drinking put me at much higher risk of damage. At another level, I earnestly sought to understand the cause of my wounds while at the same time doing everything I could to hide from my woundedness and to hide it from everyone else. My persona of competency and worldliness hid a naïve inner world, prone to and often accused of gullibility. However, I know that my longings have been pure, and I sometimes wonder if my shame and guilt have been unfounded? Did they belong to me; was I so at fault?

Can we turn back the clock on lost innocence? This morning when I meditated, I was focusing on what needed healing within, and I sensed in my chest an unwelcome knot of hard knowledge. I tried to breathe the tangles loose but the harder I breathed, the tighter the knot became. My heart beat harder and faster, and my face flushed with the struggle to resist the painful strangling feeling. Then I felt a ripping sensation in my chest as if something ancient was being pulled out of me. I stiffly stopped fighting then my insides relaxed. Tears streamed down my face in the knowledge that although I didn't know what it was, something had shifted emotionally and changed within me. After a few seconds of a widened void of emptiness, of nothingness, I felt a new knowledge within my chest, and I weakly sensed that my inner space seemed somehow lighter.

I was exhausted after the meditation, but I also felt the release of something that had not only been trapped in my psyche, it had also been physically stored in my body. I wept with the insight that my emotions had been robbed of their innocence earlier than they should have been and how I had carried this wound around with me for over 30 years. I reflected on my emotional scars and thought about how a butterfly emerges ungainly from its cocoon and how the struggle is part of the process of transition from its grub-like state to its beautiful delicate-winged state. If you were to interrupt this process, to drag its struggling body out of its cocoon too soon, even if your motive was to be helpful, the butterfly would emerge weak with the deformity of underdeveloped wings, and it would probably die soon afterwards.

As I reflect on the meaning of the meditation, my mind flits through the years, and I recognise my damaged emotions in all kinds of ways. There is time enough to reflect back on the emotional immaturity that I have struggled through life with like a butterfly with a damaged wing. There is a fundamental question that lies underneath all the memories flitting around my head: how can lost innocence be restored or healed?

Yours,

Michaela

Chapter 68

3rd October 2009

Dear St Thérèse,

When I need to understand more than just with my mind and thoughts, I use a technique called 'Focusing' devised by Eugene T. Gendlin (2003). Focusing involves 'listening' to my body and being open to the information I receive through communicating with physical sensations. I have had many valuable insights through focusing, and I value the wisdom that comes from the 'felt sense' and understanding what it is trying to communicate to me.

Recently during a focusing session, I tried to identify a physical feeling that I have sensed for as long as I can remember. It is a mixture of tension, alertness and restlessness. As I focused on these physical sensations, I realised with clarity and certainty that they represented a sense of being unsafe. Feeling unsafe is a response to either internal or external threats. An example of an external threat might be how I respond to others making demands of me that I cannot meet. Internal threats come from the negative things I tell myself and the unpleasant feelings I experience as a result. Some of this process is probably unconscious. Safety needs are clearly defined in Maslow's well-known hierarchy and come above physiological needs and include security of body, employment, resources, morality, the family, health, and property.

When we perceive a threat or danger (physical or psychological), our response is one of fight, flight or freeze. I have spent most of my life in an almost constant state of vigilance of trying to pre-empt threats. Although I have done this to try and be more secure, it hasn't kept me psychologically safe. Even when I am not facing an actual threat, I am living in fear of it. We use protective strategies (this uses up a lot of valuable energy) which are thoughts and attitudes that put up a barrier between you and the threat or danger. These are also behaviours we engage in to make us feel better or to give us a 'quick fix' and include such patterns as alcoholism, comfort-eating, smoking, workaholism, people-pleasing, approval-seeking, perfectionism … anything which will stop unpleasant feelings occurring or intensifying. The problem with these 'protective' behaviours is that they might treat symptoms temporarily, but they don't address the cause.

I have been researching the term 'psychological safety' and understand it to mean being able to protect myself from any external or internal destructive impulses i.e. keeping out of harm's way. It is also about self-knowledge and being competent in the world. To do this, I need to be self-aware, be able to direct my focus and attention on what is important to me and to be in control of my internal landscape. It also concerns my ability to express myself creatively and spiritually if we have experienced childhood trauma; it can affect the development of a sense of self that has clarity and purpose. We don't develop a strong sense of self-efficacy, and this affects our ability to protect ourselves and our psychological, emotional and physical boundaries. We lose our ability to relate to the world without abusing power or being abused by it. It also causes a lot of confusion.

How does an insight into psychological safety help me? In essence, it tells me that I need to develop a healthy sense of self. To do this, firstly I need to respect that the negative behaviours that amounted to self-abuse served a vital lifesaving purpose in the past. They helped me to survive the pain and confusion of my experiences. Secondly, as the past created dilemmas which have felt overwhelming and mystifying, I have to make some sense out of what has happened. I am learning that because reality can feel unbearable until I make sense of it, my patterns of perfectionism, approval-seeking, etc. are symptoms which will continue until I find their meaning. When I studied Freud at college, I was fascinated by his theory about how and why we re-enact (repeat) in the present patterns from the past until we make sense (remember) the trauma that caused them.

Since learning this as an 18-year-old, I have spent over 25 years trying to make sense of my life and find meaning in some of my responses to my childhood. I believe that there are no such things as coincidences and that everything happens for a reason and that my job is to learn from what happened to me and to put my learning to good use. Finally, I need to continue to develop strong, loving relationships with myself, others and a Higher Power.

Psychological safety is inextricably connected to spiritual well-being. One of the most profound experiences of my early recovery was the sense of security I first experienced. It came from knowing that I wasn't alone in my problem and that there was a solution i.e. the 12-step programme which also includes stages of spiritual development.

Today I can feel consistently safe in my relationship with my Higher Power. When I run my life relying on self-will, invariably I don't feel safe, but paradoxically when I surrender my will and rely on my Higher Power, I find real security in myself and my relationships with others. I want to stop expecting other people to provide the love and approval that I crave for myself. I need to learn to give it to myself and how to accept it. This also helps me to know meaning comes from my faith and the gifts of grace and in knowing that my Higher Power has done for me and will do for me what I can't achieve for myself. Finally, through spirituality, I can be creative and express myself and constantly find new meaning, as I am doing through writing to you.

Thank you, for your continuing to help and inspire me.

Yours,

Michaela

Chapter 69

4th October 2009

Dear St Thérèse,

I came across a quote a couple of days ago about loneliness by Albert Einstein: 'It is strange to be known so universally and yet to be so lonely.'

There has been a song running through my head for the last few days, 'Have you ever been lonely?' It is a song that my dad sings. I can't remember a time in my life when he hasn't sung this song. It always makes me smile because dad is usually happy when he is singing.

These incidents remind me that you felt lonely at times, but that you always sought to overcome it. Again, I strive to live up to your courage, but first I must admit the truth myself. For most of my life I have had a longing for a connection with someone or something that is out of reach or unavailable to me. Is this loneliness? I am not just talking about isolation from others where I wish for company or that I wasn't alone; I am referring to the profound loneliness that makes me disconnected from myself and separated from God.

I remember a powerful definition about loneliness by Dr Judith Orloff. She says that when people say they are lonely, they are usually describing only one aspect of what is missing. What they are saying is, 'I don't have full access to a whole place in myself or to a sense of spirit' (Orloff 2009). This definition is compelling. Dr Orloff also describes loneliness as 'a feeling of separation from a nurturing source from an inner and outer sense of home' (Orloff 2009). I am struck by the concept of nurturing in this definition. I experience loneliness as emptiness; feeling unworthy of connection; lack of nurturing, self-acceptance, self-esteem and lack of love. And yet if I was to look at myself through another's eyes, I might see someone who appears to have been a strong nurturer, and loving to others. I might also recognise her as generous with time and gifts. I would see someone committed to self-improvement and to being the best they can be. But only seeing myself through the eyes of others is not healthy. I want to see myself through my own eyes, through my unique perspective. But when I do this, what do I see? A seeker: someone who has been driven to find out what is wrong with her and to reach her potential, someone who has been courageous at times but scared and vulnerable at others.

I have faith. I need to focus on my purpose and not give up on myself. I am not weak, and I'm not a failure. I should be proud of this. I need to respect myself. I need to stop trying so hard and just be myself and accept myself as I am. I have always believed that I was deeply flawed and needed to reach a certain level of competence before I could be acceptable. God wants me to accept myself as I am and to use my gifts to help others and to stop trying to be someone or something I'm not. And I want to do it with love and self-encouragement rather than self-flogging and self-rejection. Please help me to find the wholeness within.

Loneliness is a sign that something needs to change. I grew up believing that I am powerless to change. My philosophy was to accept the pain which meant that I spent more time trying to deal with the pain than changing the cause. So it is helpful for me to know I can help myself most by understanding that moving forward is less about managing pain and more about embracing it.

How can I embrace rejection and feeling unloved and unwanted? I have spent my life fighting and resisting painful emotions. I need to stop doing this to see what happens. I did this with alcohol. I accepted that I was powerless and stopped fighting and resisting, and the reward was sobriety. I can do this with loneliness and move through isolation to a place where I feel connected again.

Where do I find a connection? I connect with myself through my writing. I can write when feeling rejected and lonely, and the result is making sense of what is happening; and through finding meaning, I gain a better and more positive perspective. I find a connection with God through prayer and meditation. I find a connection with others through nurturing them. Lack of self-nurturing is one of my biggest challenges

I have to practise self-acceptance and self-approval, stop playing a role and working against myself. I have to stop expecting others to meet my needs when I am not meeting them myself. It's my responsibility to fulfill my own my heart's desires. I offer others my complete attention. I want them to be comfortable with me and to know I am listening and I value their presence. How can I do this for myself? How can I learn to accept and love myself more?

I need to find the nurturing place of wholeness within me though the process of writing.

What does it mean to feel known? I think we are known when we are seen by another for who we are. Most of us don't want to be seen. We wear masks. We hide our authentic self, probably because we are afraid, but the more authentic we are, the more we can be known. I hide my authentic self. I don't feel that I deserve to be me. I am a writer who always thought that she didn't deserve to be a writer. That she could only be a writer when everyone else was sorted and okay. This deferring is not healthy. Through being our authentic selves, we tap into the divine and become more powerful. Please, guide my spirit to stop pretending to be someone I'm not, and to be who I am. There is a destination in this: being true to myself. Loneliness is the abandonment of self as well as by others.

I stopped writing to do some focusing and realised that rather than there being an emptiness within, my inner world is busy. There is 'bossy boots' me, and there is obedient 'compliant me', and they both fight each other for dominance; but underneath the fighting, I have just realised that they are both working together to protect 'the real me'. As much as this might have helped me in the past, I want to call a truce and allow the real me to feel safe enough to show her face.

I have also realised that this 'hidden me' might indeed be my 'inner child', the younger me that went into hiding when the world felt too unsafe for me to exist freely. I am eager to meet my younger self; does she hold the key to my heart's desires? Am I getting closer to connecting with her as I write to you and tell my story?

God has given me a job to do and I hope it is writing. I have realised that when I speak of the 'story of my soul', the keyword is not just 'soul', indeed the 'story' is becoming just as important. Through writing, I find out who I am and what I need to know in order to expand my thinking, my heart and my visions. It is always a journey inwards, a journey with a purpose. The purposes include learning about me and what my current challenges are about and how I can best serve myself and others. The more I write the more I discover on my journeys of exploration. I feel the colours of emotions, I hear the wisdom of words, I am soothed by the opening of truths and I am strengthened by the revelation of insights: I am empowered in prayer.

Yours,

Michaela

Chapter 70

5th October 2009

Dear St Thérèse,

Your 'little way' is the perfect model for teaching me that when I am weak, I also have the opportunity to be strong. I taught this in my resilience workshops, i.e., that coping with difficulties is good for us, as it is not in spite of adversity that we learn and grow but precisely because of it. At our weakest, we have the opportunity to become our strongest when we learn to change what needs changing.

You said that when people were afraid it was usually because their focus was too much in the past or in the future. I believe this statement 100 per cent. The key to change is to concentrate on the here and now because this is where change happens. Not in the past or the future but in the present.

You said that we only have to carry our cross feebly because when we are aware of our weakness, we become humble and are most open to God's grace. In seeing my weaknesses and inadequacies, I should not despair. It is an opportunity to surrender to God and say 'This is me' and 'I must accept this' and God will do the rest.

You said, 'If you are willing to bear serenely the trial of being displeasing to yourself, you will be to me a pleasant place of shelter' (Udris 2004). My faith has come from knowing that I am only human and that I can't expect to be perfect and knowing that God loves us as we are. When I am worried or upset it is because I am trying to be perfect or expecting someone else to be perfect.

Please help me to accept that I am not happy with myself and not to deny this truth but accept it now at this moment. I am powerless. In that powerlessness, all I can do is love and pray. You tell us to learn to love our defects because they keep us dependent on God's grace. So rather than self-accuse, I need to surrender. You describe 'littleness' as the ability to 'not to become discouraged over one's faults'. When I am humble, I am most teachable, most open to God's purpose for me.

Yours,

Michaela

Chapter 71

6th October 2009

Dear St Thérèse,

When I consider the question, how will I know God's will for me? I have almost been expecting an angel to appear with a set of instructions and say, 'When all these are done, God will be pleased with you.' You have helped me realise that I have been looking for inspiration externally instead of internally. When I look within I find my heart's desires! God tells us of his plan and purpose for us, through these desires. I am progressing from living in denial to living in hope and understanding what my desires are and knowing what to do with them. Please help me to be more aware of my heart's desires and how I can put them to work.

I remember the day earlier this year when I learned a new writing technique called Proprioceptive Writing (Trichter Metcalfe & Simon 2002) which is extremely effective as a therapeutic and creative-writing aid. I had an epiphany when I realised that most of my writing was quite prayerful. Not like old-fashioned prayers, but like you described a prayer, as 'a lifting of the heart towards heaven'. I hadn't realised how much I was praying through my journal-writing, not in a desperate way (although there is some of that!) but in a hopeful, faithful way. It was quite a revelation to me and a useful insight as a writer. I have longed for a vocation all my life, but I didn't allow this to manifest, suppressing it, along with many other desires, some of them too late to pursue now.

When I read what you wrote about God 'not putting a desire in our heart that couldn't be fulfilled' it started to make sense. The desires of our hearts have been put there by God. So doing God's will is not about venturing into a big battle between my will and God's will (I know I will never win!); it is about looking and discovering what desires are in our hearts and then with some discernment, acting on them.

With your help, I am finding my true heart's desires; they are becoming more familiar to me. The desire to stay sober, to write, to heal, to be happy, to belong, to know that I am not alone, to help others understand that they are not alone, to be loved, for acceptance and the willingness to love God with all my heart. Is this last one a new desire or a re-discovered forgotten desire? When in despair I used to say 'I want to go home': I meant to my heavenly home, not my earthly home. I used to feel homesick for a place I couldn't consciously imagine but was convinced existed. In God's presence I know who I am.

JC speaks confidently as if he knows what my heart's desire is and with the certainty that there is one ultimate purpose in my life and that they are one and the same thing. I used to think that I didn't deserve to have a heart's desire; it felt too frivolous and too enjoyable. The idea of a life purpose, however, sounded much more sensible and practical, and for years I consciously wondered what that purpose might be. I intuitively knew that what was at the centre of my life at any given time wasn't my true calling, and there were many false dawns. Today JC is convinced that my heart's desire is writing; but as much as I love it, I wonder if it is truly my heart's desire or it is in discovering what I learn through my writing. Maybe it is both? Am I writing to produce a book, or for the blessings of healing, insight and faith I receive. My desire is that these blessings should be passed on to help others. It is working beautifully for me.

I have just finished reading 'Daddy-Long-Legs' written by Jean Webster (2002) and first published in 1912. It is a book full of hope and inspiration, and I love it because it completely illustrates the healing model of writing letters to someone you love or who is important to you. Jerusha Abbott is an orphan who spent her childhood in an asylum. On the strength of her potential writing ability an anonymous benefactor pays for her to go to college; the only condition is that Jerusha writes a monthly letter to her benefactor. The book entirely consists of the letters to her benefactor who never replied. I will never receive an envelope containing a letter from you, but I will receive so much more from your blessings. I would recommend to anyone who wants to experience the benefits of therapeutic writing the following:

- Choose someone to write to who inspires you or whom you love (dead or alive, known or unknown).
- Write to them regularly telling them what you truly feel.
- Tell them about your life, desires, longings, successes, failures, hopes, intentions, etc.
- Notice what you learn and find out about yourself.
- Receive the blessings with gratitude and pass them on to others.

Also, I have just remembered that my favourite novel 'The Wrong Boy' written by Willy Russell (2000) is written in this style also. The letters are written by a troubled teenage boy to his hero, the singer Morrissey. I love that book so much. I have listened to the audio version, read by Willy Russell himself. It was one of my most enjoyable experiences. Indeed, I am sure that this was one of the inspirations for me to write these letters to you. I imagine that all aspiring writers have used their heart's desires openly and freely rather than hiding them and keeping them safe. Please help me always to be open and to listen to my heart's desires.

What is the energy of my heart's desire or life purpose that I aspire to? Passion. That word makes me feel uncomfortable, but it is the right word. What do I mean by passion? Energy, aliveness, enthusiasm, connection, and love. You weren't afraid to speak about your passion St Thérèse, but I suppress it. I compartmentalise it and project it onto other people so that I don't have to take ownership for it. The pattern goes like this: I recognise an attractive energy (passion) within another person (rather than myself). I engage with it, flirt with it, desire it and even fuel it. Then when things go wrong, I disown it. What makes things go wrong? Is it when I subconsciously realise that I can't control the passion; when it becomes too intense for me to handle. Because the passion has always belonged to another person, I somehow make them responsible for the loss and the pay-off is that I can avoid the devastating pain of failure. Until recently, this would have been the end of the process, and I would have just moved on seeking my next source of pseudo-passion. But in recovery, another stage has developed where although I still somehow disown passion, when it is gone, I miss it. I feel bereft. My heart feels as broken as if the passion had belonged to me, but I am not entitled to grieve for what is lost because I know it was never mine to have in the first place.

Another way of putting this is how I approach relationships: I make sure that I don't get close enough to people to experience real love. My actions say, 'I will love you from afar because I don't want to risk what might happen if I actually loved you and you loved me.' This process reminds me of the main character in Alfred Hitchcock's film called 'Marnie'. Marnie looks like a perfectly normal professional young woman, but she has a secret. She has the compulsion to steal money from her employers, and she does so successfully and clinically without any remorse. Each time Marnie has stolen a firm's fortunes, she starts again in a new position planning her next 'job', fooling everyone by looking like the most unlikely thief imaginable. Marnie is portrayed as emotionless except for her fear of storms and the colour red which trigger panic and anxiety for her and then she can't help but show her vulnerability.

The only thing Marnie shows any passion is for riding her beloved horse, Forio. Meanwhile, the character played by Sir Sean Connery becomes her boss and recognises her as a thief, and in fear of being reported to the police, Marnie is forced to agree to marry him. Her husband unsuccessfully tries to rehabilitate her. In desperation he eventually takes her to visit her mother, and Marnie faces a forgotten childhood trauma (the point at which I imagine the repression of her future passion might have occurred). Confronted with the truth, Marnie's hard façade crumbles, and for the first time she is released and able to recognise, accept and grieve the love that she has lost from her childhood.

'Marnie' is one of my favourite films and books because I identify with it so much, and it also gives me hope that the passion that I know is within me will one day be unlocked completely. I see more and more glimpses of it, but there is still more to be opened and released.

I am aware that passion is a strong emotion. It is hot, intense and urgent and essential to life. Recently I was talking with a colleague about people who live long and happy lives, and we agreed that what kept people going was their 'passion' and 'enthusiasm'. JC often says that I am like a bottle of uncorked champagne. At first, I thought it an odd metaphor (a drinking one!) and I didn't understand it at all, but now I do. He is referring to the potential release of my passion.

Passion is what I long to experience with others and yet at times when I have done so; I often feel guilty. To engage with passion and enthusiasm and the joy of living feels forbidden. So I fear and resist it, disowning passionate feelings because they are unruly, chaotic, uncontrollable, unacceptable and disruptive. Instead, I try to channel my energy in a non-passionate way of control and measure. This approach fuels perfectionism rather than the passion of being real and alive and living life to the full in the present.

I want to 'stop playing it safe'. I can be passionate about, and for, others; for instance, I work hard at being accepting of people and making them feel comfortable. I want people to be at ease and to able to be fully themselves with me and yet I can be 'formal' sometimes and too serious. These behaviours come from the most cautious part of me.

I want to be more passionate about how I live my life and how I work. How can I express and embrace passion more fully? Through doing what I love and engaging in my heart's desire. Writing. This statement makes everything seem simple. So why does it feel so complicated? Because being passionate energises me and yet frightens me at the same time.

I like the definition I found that 'passion is the energy that comes from bringing more of you into what you do' (Rosengren 2009). This definition holds great meaning for me. Firstly, I want to bring more of my real self into what I do rather than what I think I ought to do. Secondly, I have been holding back my passion for far too long. How can I allow more love into my life? As well as writing I can:

- connect more lovingly with others through listening with calmness and compassion
- relax and listen to music
- be enthusiastic rather than analytically intense about my feelings
- be true to myself rather than seek approval
- laugh more
- listen more
- do more physical activity
- meditate (passion is in the breath)
- just let go.

You were passionate and understood that passion involved the giving of yourself wholly to what you believe in. Please help me to follow your example and to channel my energies to be as true to myself as you were.

Yours,

Michaela

Chapter 72

7th October 2009

Dear St Thérèse,

One of the most important symbols of love to you was the Holy Face when you saw blood falling as tears from the face of Jesus, and you were so moved because no one was catching the tears. In compassionate response, you dedicated your life to bearing witness to the blood shed in Jesus' tears and to comforting him. You loved without resentment, and your 'little way' depends on giving love without counting the cost. You approach Jesus as a small child, in the same way as Jesus approached his Father.

My sufferings didn't bring me to compassion as yours did. My pain brought me to self-destruction and depletion. My sufferings haven't tested my love, they have tested my ego. How long can I continue to be a victim of my suffering? There is always someone to blame and I judge myself harshly. I thought I was learning from situations, but I wasn't. My heart wasn't engaged but hidden for protection.

I need to deal with the shame and guilt buried deep within me. I wonder if Jesus felt shame in the Garden of Gethsemane. Jesus didn't teach us to hide in shame, and it is not what you practised. I am inspired by how Jesus at first resists but then accepts his fate. Despair forces us to surrender and through this we find acceptance. Out of depletion comes courage and faith. In his time of need, God didn't send the disciples to comfort

Jesus in the garden, they were sleeping so He sent an angel. Even though Jesus lived as a human, how could the disciples have comforted Jesus in his darkest hour? I notice that the responsibility wasn't put upon them. All my life I have been over-responsible for others. The story of Jesus in the garden tells me that God isn't expecting me to take the weight of the world on my shoulders, but is giving me the opportunity to love others and to be loved in return. Self-will resists love and clings to negativity.

You have facilitated a conversation of love within me. My longing is for love. I want to be able to love like you, surrendering to love without resentment. Why do I still feel unworthy of love? I want to be able to love myself. How can I change my experiences of suffering into compassion? My understanding of your teaching is that this change can be achieved by:

- being more open to love
- consciously letting love into my life
- accepting love
- knowing that God's will is to love
- expressing my feelings and emotions
- following the 'little way' i.e. going to God with childlike trust.

The paradox of love is that it makes us more vulnerable before it makes us stronger. We can transform suffering into love in small ways. Please, help me to remember this and put it into practice.

Yours,

Michaela

Chapter 73

8th October 2009

Dear St Thérèse,

You were a visionary of love. What does this mean? How did this manifest? One way was through your courage. The parable of the wineskins tells me that I have to change my thinking; does this mean that I should be more courageous? How can I lead a visionary life? I have never really understood the true meaning of being a visionary.

Firstly I assumed that visions were unnecessary because they only concerned the future and shouldn't I just be living in the moment, or in the day? I also mistakenly thought that visions should only be positive and good, and therefore didn't apply to me because I didn't feel either, but I understand now that visions are to do with our explanation of how we view the world and what we expect from it. Anything that we expect to happen can be a vision, and so a vision can either be of darkness or light. Indeed my vision of what the future will bring, or of what I feel I deserve, has often been dark in that I have expected the worst to happen. I am realising through your help how to change a bleak future into one of light through prayer and healing. So visions are with us always. I suppose a dark vision would be more aptly called a nightmare or depression. Whatever we think about and focus on today will manifest in the future i.e. we will get what we expect.

Secondly, visions are about looking inwardly, and that is great if it brings wisdom, peace and serenity, but what happens if looking inwards brings fear, stress, and anxiety? You are helping me to see past these obstacles, and encouraging me to free myself of restrictions, and move through the darkness into the light that shines beneath fear and anxiety. I was destined to be a bit-player in someone else's life rather than being the main character in my own. It is exciting to think that I could have my own unique vision to consciously and intentionally guide my life's journey.

Visions help us to imagine what does not currently exist; giving us hope of a better way of being. One of my most cherished visions came when I received the strength to maintain the vision of a sober life. Until then, a fulfilling life had seemed utterly impossible but the experience of finding out that I wasn't alone – that there were other people just like me – gave me the strength to pursue a journey of recovery. Another example is the meaning of new wine into old wineskins. I am learning how visions can provide us with a bridge between an inspired world and the material world as I strive to discover the full meaning of the seeds that this parable has sown in my imagination. You are a true visionary, you have walked ahead of us and inspired us with your example in so many ways, most importantly through helping to awaken and direct inner strengths, as you have done for me.

Where do we find visions? They come from our deepest yearnings which make them difficult to discover, but access to this deepest place, the soul, is one of the fruits of a spiritual life. So, visions are available anytime, showing us not only a path but providing the motivational energy we need to press on and make the desires of our soul a reality. Creating and committing to new visions is a transformational process that can release us from the tyranny of our old selves and our old ways. It takes courage of course, but is achievable when we put these principles into practice. From our visions, we find our purpose and our goals.

Please, help me to accept that my vision is to love and to accept that love.

Yours,

Michaela

Chapter 74

9th October 2009

Dear St Thérèse,

How do we recognise our true self when our real strengths and desires are hidden? It's as if we create false selves to protect the core self. (Is my core self my soul?) These different selves all play a part in our psyche, but the false selves can't be ignored as what they tell us is not always in our best interests.

The false selves are like imposter energies, thoughts and processes that are allowed to rule our lives but they are only interested in our survival. For instance, the negative energy of self-doubt, which held me back, was an imposter for the self-belief I know exists deep within.

How do the imposters deceive me? They speak to me critically, anxiously and without love about how to treat myself and others. I allow the imposter energies to drain me because I don't have the courage to challenge them. I don't stand up for myself because I don't believe I possess the power to change the situation. I feel hopeless and defeated, and when I look within for guidance it is as if I am empty or dead inside. My voice is too weak and drowned out by imposter voices. I feel sick with the realisation that I have spent so much time listening to the negative messages and acting upon them and how much they have been persistent patterns in my life. I believed them to be 100 per cent right, but thankfully today I have hope that things can be different in the future. Some of these voices will be the effects of my sensitive response to my childhood, and while these beliefs helped me to survive difficult situations as a child, today they are no longer necessary and are certainly not helpful. The imposters will be found out for who they are.

You teach that ordinary people are worthy of being in friendships, and in a relationship with God, and this gives me high hopes for the possibilities within my relationships. Even when I can't trust myself or others, I can say to my Higher Power, 'Okay, I'll trust you.' My fear dispels when I discover that I am not alone.

Yesterday I was sitting reading and my cat Molly approached me with complete trust and sat down in my lap covering the book I was reading. How could I refuse her appeal for a cuddle? The power of her trust was overwhelming.

Please strengthen my hope that, through conscious contact with my Higher Power, I will continue on a path of transformation, where fear can become courage; resistance becomes acceptance; apathy becomes passion; mistrust becomes trust; resentment becomes gratitude and suffering becomes compassion.

Yours,

Michaela

Chapter 75

10th October 2009

Dear St Thérèse,

Being true to my 'self' is the hardest part of my inner journey. It is the deepest, innermost authentic part of me, guided by its teacher: my soul.

One of my biggest challenges is learning how to direct my life more from internal strength so that I am not so strongly influenced by external forces such as the expectations of others. I am used to looking externally for a sense of purpose, guidance, and validation through approval-seeking and people-pleasing, but I don't want to do this anymore. It doesn't work. It might bring me a temporary 'fix' to receive another's approval, but it doesn't bring lasting happiness and well-being, and it certainly doesn't contribute to a satisfying spiritual life. I am convinced that the key to making the 'U-turn' from an externally guided life to a more interior life is through the questions we ask ourselves. But intellectual questions aren't enough to sustain an inner life; even heart-driven questions aren't sufficient; we need to listen to the questions that come from the deepest part of us, our soul. Soul questions come from our deep need for meaning in our lives and that drive and desire is one of our deepest impulses.

Writing these letters has been a journey to my lost self and a pilgrimage of my lost soul. In this context 'lost' relates to the feeling of being abandoned. Much more devastating than abandonment by another is being abandoned by myself.

Looking back, I can see how the questions that have driven me have evolved. Prior to recovery, the life questions propelling me were:

- What is wrong with me?
- Who can help me?
- How can I gain love and approval from others?
- How can I prove myself?
- Post-recovery questions have included:
- How can I get well?
- How can I connect to my Higher Power?
- How can I be true to myself?

While the above remain valid questions, and I won't stop learning, there are deeper issues which concern me now which include:

- How can I stay consciously connected to the divine?
- How can I better follow my soul's journey?
- How can I best love and receive love?
- How can I share my gifts with others?
- How can I reach my full potential?

How do we access these deep-soul questions? The key to your soul was love, and your ability to listen to love. Despite hardship and losing your mother at such a young age, you were surrounded by the love of your father and sisters and surrogate mothers. Your life was defined by your love of Jesus and your fellow human beings. Your vocation was to love, and you loved so well as your autobiography reveals. You loved your way to heaven and send love back through the roses you promised to send.

Has love opened the door of my soul? I think so. My definition of love has changed. Love is not about being responsible and making my actions justifiable; a trusting child doesn't need to justify how it deserves love. Indeed a trusting child expects love without limits or justification and loves in return.

As grateful as I am that the door of love has opened, I know that when I am anxious and afraid, I slam the door shut again. It's an instinctive reaction to protect myself. When this happens, I feel like I am standing outside a door that I have knocked on. I wait anxiously and wonder many things. Do I look presentable? Will I remember to smile? How will I be greeted? Will I be welcomed? Will I know what to say to the person who opens the door? Am I expected? Will I be told to go away or will I run away in fear as we used to do in games we played as children?

I don't trust myself about love yet, but I am willing to love. Indeed I want to be able to love with all my heart, and I want love to be my vocation as it was for you. You are my role model, and I can't shake off the doubt sitting over me like a constant cloud that maybe I am too damaged, and therefore will prove to be inadequate in love or even incapable of true love.

I can sense two different places within. One place feels safer but isn't a peaceful or joyful space. It is logical and helps me to weigh up the pros and cons and decide the right thing to do. But I am not fully alive in this place. I am not fully awake. The other is a deeper more 'squirmy' vulnerable place where I can't see things clearly, and is raw and exposed. There are things here partly hidden from me. However, for all its fogginess, I am drawn to this place with a longing I can't put into words. I want to access it. I am sure it holds the key to passion and aliveness, but I am afraid to go forward in case there is nothing there or what is drawn out of me is selfish or wrong. What do I mean by selfish and wrong? What is the feeling behind this?

I have just stopped writing because I could feel the word I wanted hovering around me but couldn't name it, and then it disappeared like catching a glimpse of a familiar face in a crowd and when you look again the face has gone. So I closed my eyes and relaxed and then without realising that I was crying, I felt tears on my cheeks, but I didn't care about that because the right word had come and stayed. It was shame. Shame is a painful place where I feel unacceptable to others, and deserving of punishment. I feel flawed and unworthy of acceptance. I am trapped, powerless and alone. Shame has been described as 'spiritual bankruptcy' (Bradshaw 2006). I agree with this definition. For me, it is the source of my soul sickness. The thing that hurts most about shame is disconnection.

How can I heal this habit of shame? I paused, and I hear you encouraging me to keep telling my story. Now I hear you saying, 'Claim yourself!' How can I do this? I have been here before, on the brink of a breakthrough, but something stops me. I am more hopeful this time and it would be a significant breakthrough to achieve this. I desperately want to feel as if I belong to myself.

As if in answer to my prayers, amazingly I have just received an email from JC telling me to listen to the voice within and allow my Higher Power to use me rather than allowing others to use me and reminding me to have trust in myself and my instincts and strengths.

My goal is to be comfortable, validated and true to myself. I want to be less submissive and not wait for permission from others by trusting my inner guidance and my intuition. I will then have faith in myself.

Learning to love is a journey in itself, and although I haven't thought about it in this way before, I have been on this journey since I was a little girl.

Thank you for this realisation.

Yours,

Michaela

Chapter 76

11th October 2009

Dear St Thérèse,

Your 'little way' is sometimes called the 'little way of spiritual childhood' which means acting in your spiritual life as a small child would (Johnson 1997). I was wondering if there is a connection between the qualities of spiritual childhood and the popular idea today of the inner child? It seems that innocence and lack of pretence are essential qualities that they both share.

The idea of the 'child within' has for years both fascinated and frightened me because I have long suspected that my inner child has been hidden if not lost from me, and yet I wonder if recovering my inner child is something I should pursue? I have read about the psychotherapeutic and spiritual benefits of inner-child work and have found some of the ideas fascinating. I have particularly identified with the concepts of the wounded child and the abandoned inner child. It is entirely plausible that there is a child within that I have limited access to because she is hiding. When mum and dad split up, I had to grow up and can imagine that I left behind a lonely frightened little girl.

Today I had an important insight in my prayers. I was thinking about my inner child, and I felt the familiar back pain that comes when I am focusing on deep emotions and trying to do healing work. I have focused many times on the back pain and have never discovered its significance or meaning in a way that I could link/reunite directly between the certain physical feelings to their emotional counterparts.

As I focused inwardly, tentatively and as slowly as a frightened young child hiding behind its mother's legs peeking out to see if it was safe to come out, I sensed a presence behind me, close enough to be holding onto me, and then I felt the familiar back pain but with it came a fascinating image. It was as if a small tearful child was hiding behind me, but every so often her tears of frustration were compelling her to throw her tiny fists into my back. I have observed young children in frustration hit their mother as if to punish and at the same time urge her to make everything better. Was my inner child trying to communicate with me? Was she trying to tell me that she was frustrated and hurting and at the same time pleading with me to make things better? It seems very much like it. This image of distress didn't bring me comfort, but the idea of my inner child trying to communicate, even demanding my attention, was reassuring and it may not be too late for us to be reunited.

The feelings I associate with the inner child are the obvious ones of childlike joy, playfulness, light-heartedness, freedom, confidence, living in the present, and curiosity; but also the wounded feelings of abandonment, fear, frustration, depression, anxiety, helplessness, anger, etc. In trying to spare and protect myself from the latter feelings, have I diminished access to the positive emotions?

I suspect that if I can heal some of the anxiety and helplessness, I will have more joy and other light-hearted feelings. How can my inner child help me to achieve this? I sensed today that my inner child has been trying to get my attention for a long time. Is it because the voice of my inner critic also acts like a critical parent and is so loud that it drowns out the voice of a child? No wonder my inner child is too scared to reveal herself. I pray that she grows in courage and that her little fists continue to pound into my back until she gets my full attention.

Yours,

Michaela

Chapter 77

12th October 2009

Dear St Thérèse,

Earlier I was thinking about my inner child and trying to remember any occasions when I was consciously aware of her presence. I was prompted to go back to my journal, and I came across an entry from when I was at the writing centre in May. I remembered the incident as healing, but it is only now that I truly understand how significant it was. This is what I experienced and wrote up afterwards:

Journal extract May 2009, Writers' Centre, North Wales

At the beach, after a long walk I sat on a large rock to rest and was soon mesmerised by the sound and smell of blue waves crashing onto the beach; each wave confidently and naturally announcing its presence as if it was the only wave that had ever existed. Noisy gulls joined in the excitement of each new arrival. I felt at peace and grateful for my time at the Writers' Centre.

A fluttering sensation in my stomach told me that a strong feeling was about to be revealed. I sat as still as possible so as not to frighten it away but not knowing if it would be pleasant or unpleasant. At first, the feeling seemed reluctant to reveal itself until I felt an unusual sensation as if my tummy was being gently tickled and I knew that something was about to happen. I waited for familiar anxious feelings, but they didn't come.

Then a fluttering in my chest made me expect my peace to be shattered by anxiety. Was it going to be a sneaky anxious feeling I wondered? I reassured myself that it wasn't going to be a full-blown attack of anxiety because those feelings don't send advance parties, especially ones that tickled.

'It's a playful feeling,' I thought, relieved that it wasn't an unpleasant feeling that was about to reveal itself.

'It's like a child,' I thought. My heart lifted as if on tiptoes. 'How can a feeling be like a child?' I wondered. Then I felt warmth across my chest as if a child had just thrown its arms around me. I am not used to children hugging me, so I felt slightly stiff at first, and then I relaxed into the feeling. 'A little one is hugging me,' my senses told me. And as I wondered about the feeling, it hit me, without a doubt, I knew who the child was: it's me! It's young Michaela! She has come. I bowed my head in awe and respect and felt tears run down my cheeks.

I felt her presence for many minutes with the waves still crashing in an ovation to a reunion. Afterwards, I sat on the rock hardly moving, treasuring what had happened until I realised that if I had just felt the presence of my inner child, sadly I hadn't spoken to her.

I had almost forgotten this incident but reading it again inspired me. I found myself writing not to you St Thérèse, but to myself as a child.

Letter to myself as a child

Dear Michaela,

You are sitting up in bed, tears trickling down your cheeks, with ears pricked for sounds of activity downstairs. A few minutes ago, the front door closed as your mother left the family home. You are waiting to hear the door open again, expecting to hear footsteps in the hall and back up the stairs and hoping to see your mum come into the bedroom and tell you that she has changed her mind and won't be leaving.

But you don't hear the door open again. The silence tells you that she has left for real, and will not be coming back. Your mum has gone to her new flat and although you couldn't see her face as she left, you knew she was crying.

You wonder where she is now and imagine her driving to her new flat a few miles away. Is she is still crying? Thinking about your little brother brings on a rush of new tears. He is downstairs with your dad. Thinking about how they are feeling is unbearable. Your mum must be really unhappy to want to leave her family. She and your dad have arguments, but they also have happy times together, so she can't be leaving because of him. Your little brother needs his mum too much, so he can't be the cause of her leaving. It must be your fault. You must have done something terrible for her to want to leave. Thinking about your dad and your brother again, another wave of pain crashes in. Because of you, your dad has lost his wife, and your brother has lost his mum. You have to make things right again. You decide to try and get your mum back home, and you vow to look after your dad and brother until she returns.

Oh, young Michaela, how I wish I could go back to you, my 11-year-old self. I want to scoop you into my arms and comfort you. I want to dry your tears, alleviate your fears, sit on the bed beside you and tell you the truth. Although the truth would hurt, it would be less painful than believing that your mother left home because you did something wrong. You were not responsible.

With all my heart, how I wish I could go back in time, hold you and console you by saying, 'I am here for you. You are not alone and everything is going to be okay. Please don't be anxious little one, it was never your fault and please don't spend the rest of your life trying to make things better for everyone at the expense of your soul, future happiness, and sanity.'

I stop writing. The lump in my throat hurts and I let the tears flow. I am desperately sad for the abandoned child who is sitting and worrying about what she will have to do to support the family. It is time for my abandoned inner child to be reunited with her parent.

I hope that writing the letter will bring me closer to my inner child. I have some new understanding of her needs. Firstly, young Michaela is very real; secondly, she is my responsibility, and thirdly I know what she needs to heal: it is love. How could I have abandoned such an important part of myself for so many years?

These are precious insights, I am grateful for them, and I pray that I can take action on these understandings.

Yours,

Michaela

Chapter 78

14th October 2009

Dear St Thérèse,

When I woke this morning, I had no intention of going to London. Your relics have reached their final destination, Westminster Cathedral, and I imagined thousands of pilgrims filing past your casket, but I didn't think I would be one of them.

After breakfast, I couldn't settle and felt extremely restless, as if there was something I had promised to do but had forgotten. I sat down at my desk but kept getting up and wandering around, mainly staring through the window and thinking about you. JC phoned and said he would pop in for a coffee.

When he arrived we sat on the sofa together and again, I couldn't sit still. I squirmed about trying to give my full attention to our conversation about how I stop myself from doing things that I enjoy. JC said it was because I feel I don't deserve enjoyment, and as he said the words I knew them to be truer than I would have liked. I wished I was different.

Eventually, in exasperation at my fidgeting, JC said, 'What is wrong with you today?'

'I don't know,' I replied apologetically. 'I feel so restless, and I don't know why.'

Perhaps in an attempt to distract me from the difficult topic we had been discussing, JC asked me to tell him again about the visit of your relics to Liverpool. I smiled and started to tell him my story which he had already heard several times when I felt my eyes welling up.

JC didn't say anything about the tears but asked gently, 'Where are the relics today?'

'They are in London for the last night, and they return to France the day after tomorrow.'

Then he said seriously, 'Why aren't you in London today?'

Immediately, I knew he was right. 'Yes, yes, that's right. I want to go to London. Now!' I realised that all morning my impulse had been pulling me towards your relics.

'I want to say goodbye to St Thérèse,' I said and jumped up excitedly with this revelation; but just as quickly, I stopped myself and sat down again deflated. 'I want to go, but something is stopping me. What is stopping me?' As I said this I looked at JC, and he didn't have to say a word, I knew by his look, and the feeling inside me: a flood of relief, nothing was stopping me, except me. 'I'm going to London JC!' I shouted joyfully and leapt up from the sofa. JC laughed at my antics and said he would go and let me get on my way.

As he left, we hugged, and I said, 'Thank you for helping me yet again. I was so restless today and didn't know why but as soon as you said "Why aren't you in London?" I knew that is where I had to be.' He said, 'Go and say goodbye to St T; enjoy it; you deserve it!'

Within two hours I was boarding the train, and booking a hotel room, just in case I needed it, but the cathedral is open all night, and I want to stay as long as I can.

I feel so excited about being a pilgrim again. I have spent my life stopping myself and holding myself back, but I am now finding the faith and confidence to express what is within me. It reminds me of something I heard recently which apparently comes from the Gospel of Thomas: 'If you bring forth what is within you, what you bring forth will save you. If you do not bring forth what is within you, what you do not bring forth will destroy you.' My new purpose is to discover how to 'bring forth' that which is within me.

Yours,

Michaela

Chapter 79

15th October 2009

Dear St Thérèse,

When I arrived at Westminster Cathedral yesterday afternoon, I stood in the piazza and watched the thousands of people milling around and the hundreds of people in the queue waiting to enter the cathedral. I wandered about for over an hour, just absorbing the atmosphere which was electric. Looking at the huge screen in the piazza I could see and hear what was happening inside the cathedral.

At approximately 8.30pm I joined the queue of several hundred people. It started at the side of the cathedral and gradually worked its way to the cathedral entrance. The other pilgrims in the queue were friendly. We stamped our feet and rubbed our hands together to keep warm in the cold-night air. Some seemed to be praying silently and I prayed, thinking about all the pilgrims as being an individual soul. The feeling of goodwill was apparent in how unreservedly people chatted to each other, and I overheard some deep spiritual conversations which people didn't seem to mind sharing in the public.

'People feel safe here,' I thought, recognising that we are all connected in body and spirit. How much harder it is to relate to each other as spiritual beings when we are in a traffic jam, rushing around the supermarket or at work. I was surprised at the number of children in the queue and wondered how much they would have preferred to have been tucked up in a warm bed, but they seemed to be enjoying their adventure. Indeed I remembered that in terms of your 'little way', we are all children.

At about 10.30pm after a couple of hours in the queue, patience was rewarded with warmer air; beautiful candlelight; the unmistakable smell of the incense; and the sound of ethereal music. The atmosphere of anticipation at reaching the entrance was palpable, and I was just as excited as others seemed to be.

Inside the cathedral, the queue of pilgrims filed past the casket. As there were so many people, there wasn't time to stop and pray, but afterwards, there were plenty of empty pews for silent prayer and meditation. I sat down about 11pm, and for the next three and a half hours I sat and prayed and listened to intermittent music, prayers, and readings. I thought about my life and how that I might have done lots of things, but I haven't achieved much spiritually. Then I thought about your 'little way' and how it isn't the big things that matter but the ordinary everyday things and that these can be offered to God if they are done with love. Then I wondered what acts (small or large) could I categorise as done in the name of love and I realised that I have been at times a dutiful daughter and a caring sister, so I offered these, and gratitude for my recovery.

The music was beautiful and moving and I felt connected and open to its healing nature. I prayed about 'stopping' and 'blocking' myself and asked for the strength not to do this anymore and for the courage to bring forth the love which I know is within me. I thought about what stops me engaging fully, and I knew the answer, so I prayed for the blessing of deeper trust and confidence in myself, God and others. At 2.30am I walked to the hotel slowed down by stiffened limbs.

Although I noticed the cold, it didn't bother me for a second. Eventually I lay in bed shivering until some warmth seeped through my body and I slept for a couple of hours.

At 7am I returned to the cathedral and after Mass I visited the casket for one last time (there was no queue). After that, I sat in the Holy Souls Chapel which was in an archway and contained a beautiful altar. In the shadowy darkness, there was a large beautiful photo of you surrounded by candles, which bathed your image in the most serene light. I sat at the back of the chapel and prepared myself for the end of my life-changing pilgrimage. As I sat and prayed, I couldn't help noticing people who came into the chapel and walked around. Then I saw a scene which was ordinary but at the same time so striking.

A young, confident, attractive woman came into the chapel holding the hand of a child who looked to be about four years old. They looked so alike that I had no doubt that they were mother and daughter. The child's thick curly blonde hair reminded me of the child on the photos I have of myself at her age. The mother seemed relaxed looking around, and guided the child by her hand. The child seemed in awe as she looked up and around her. Both mother and child appeared to be completely at ease with each other and their surroundings but the way the mother held the child's hand made it clear that the mother was lovingly in charge; she led the way, and the child followed obediently.

While the mother looked at the altar and bowed her head, perhaps in prayer, the child noticed something on the ground. In the candle light I couldn't see what it was at first, but eventually, I saw it looked like a small statue-like figure which had fallen on its side. Without unclasping her mother's hand, the child leaned down and made several attempts to place the figure upright on the ground in front of the altar, but each time it was straightened it wobbled and fell onto its side again. Perhaps aware of the strain on her arm as she attempted to reach down without letting go of her mother's hand, she made her mother look down to see what she was doing. Her mother watched her trying to straighten the little figure into an upright, stable position for several moments but didn't intervene. After a few more attempts the child managed to set the figure upright – standing on its own without falling – and looked up at her mother with a huge smile of accomplishment. The mother smiled back and leaned down so that her face was at the same level as the child's and whispered into her ear. I didn't hear what the mother said, but the child looked up at her with the most beautiful smile and the mother gazed back and nodded as if to say, 'Go on, go ahead.' In an instant, the child bent down and swept up the figure with her free hand.

I watched them walk out of the chapel with the little girl clutching the figure to her chest. The mother and daughter did not let go of each other's hand once. I was enthralled at this scene, amazed at how tenacious and focused the little girl was in achieving her goal of setting the small figure straight and how pleased she looked when she succeeded.

I tried to imagine what the mother said to the little girl to make her swoop up the figure, and my heart told me that the mother had said, 'Go on, take her, you can have her', and the child had willingly accepted her mother's 'gift'. I watched them leave the chapel until they were no longer visible.

My first response was a momentary flicker of shock that the serene couple had possibly just stolen a sacred figure from your holy chapel. But it passed quickly when another thought came to me so powerfully it pierced my soul and I felt my heart thumping in my chest.

I understood the significance of the little cameo scene with the mother and child. When the little girl without question or resistance willingly accepted what was offered, I realised there was a deeper meaning and message. It was as if God was showing me that although I have doubted it, I too am being offered a gift, something I have always longed for, and all I need to do is to accept. What is this gift? Am I being invited to receive the gift of the trusting child that you tell us to be? Yes, for sure. But I know the message is much more powerful than that. God knows what I want more than I do. He is telling me about something more important than the child within. God is saying to me, 'You can have what you want; don't resist, just accept.'

I sat and wondered for a few minutes, what is it that I want above all else and feel that I don't deserve? As if internal barriers within my heart were falling swiftly, one after the other resistances melted away, and all the things that I had ever wanted and never achieved flashed through my mind. One thing that came to mind was my desire to be creative. God knows how much I have wanted to be an author and how much this desire has been inhibited by my fears, false beliefs, and insecurities. I wondered if God is telling me to take care of my inner child, but also to nurture the gift of creativity which I have used to write these letters. The best way to do that is to follow the example of St Thérèse: St Thérèse the creative. However, my intuition tells me that's not the full depth of the message. Writing is certainly my heart's desire, but there was something deeper meant by this understanding. I thought for a few minutes about how you have opened my heart, and then I asked you what is more important than my heart? My prayer was answered when I realised with clarity the name of the deeper place within me. It is my soul! And then with a rush that ran through my veins like liquid, I knew the truth. Above all else, I want to be free of the anxiety I have suffered for most of my life; I want to heal the soul sickness that has blocked love like brooding dark-grey clouds and left me lost and longing. I want to know that sacred space within my soul. With this understanding, I felt a huge feeling of release and then my body relaxed, my mind rested in peace, my heart rejoiced, and my soul soared and all became one! At that moment I received the love that does not need to be earned and gave thanks for the blessings that had been showered upon me. My heart filled with gratitude for my life, gifts, talents, weaknesses, wrongdoings, longings, my past, my present and my future. All of it. It was as if every single hurt or suffering I had ever experienced had been washed away leaving me clean, pure and new, like an innocent child. And it was in that moment I was renewed and reborn.

I sat in this elevated state for many minutes until my awareness came back to sitting in the chapel. This understanding, whether imagined or real was so profound that I sat with tears of gratitude and joy trickling down my cheeks. My heart swelled with love, and my mind repeated the phrase, 'You can have what you want: don't resist, just accept.' I never wanted to forget this moment and to keep its truth forever within my heart and soul.

I eventually left the cathedral and made my way home from London to Liverpool with the image of the mother now transformed into a symbol of love, and the little girl, a symbol of my soul, embedded within me forever.

Thank you for another wonderful rose. The rose of recognition that my inner child is not just a lost, troubled child who wants to hide, but a lovingly created soul that wants to go to God as naturally and as innocently as you describe in your 'little way'. My soul will be nurtured by the many different types of love a mother and heavenly Father will provide. This love will guide and teach my little soul to nurture itself through acceptance, faith and gratitude.

Yours,

Michaela

Chapter 80

16th October 2009

Dear St Thérèse,

It is remarkable that you have managed to reach so many hearts and souls throughout the whole world over many decades.

Through your inspiration, I feel that the divine is much closer than I ever expected. When I used to think of saints I imagined a great distance between them and me, but you shatter this illusion; I often feel as if you are right here beside me.

You said 'heaven does exist' and you have shown me that my soul isn't just something conceptual, it is a real place, and you have helped me on the journey to furnishing it with love. You said that when you died your journey would begin to help souls on earth, so even in death you assure us that the distance between earth and heaven is as big or as small as we want it to be.

Your inspiration closes the gap between where I am and where I want to be; you give me hope that my dreams and desires are possible. Every time I feel that I can't achieve something you say yes you can! You give me the confidence to follow my new path. I can be trusting, I can be loving, I can be grateful, I can be creative, and I can aspire to holiness. No matter how impossible these journeys of the heart and soul might feel, you help to me to believe that they are not only possible, they are necessary and worthwhile. You have listened to me and understood me and indeed have come to my aid, and a part of me has truly grown up at last.

Your relics are leaving the country today, and I am both humbled and proud to be your pilgrim. I have written about my experience, strength and hope, and while there is so, so much more I would like to tell you, hope is a high point to end this stage of my pilgrimage. Living in hope is a beautiful place; it makes me present to the here and now. Your example of how to live in hope is one of the things that inspires me most about your life and your teachings. You suffered, but you didn't see it as such. In your darkest hour, your faith was tested yet you didn't act as if you were alone. You truly lived in hope.

Now I see that you weren't always like a trusting child, especially during your 'dark night' you must have felt like an anxious child, just like me, and this is where your example becomes most wonderful. Even in your worst suffering, you still trusted with faith and confidence that God was still there for you even when you didn't feel his presence. You accepted your suffering. You didn't resist it. Accepting doesn't mean being a passive victim; it means that we are transformed by what we accept. When I accept what I cannot change, it becomes a source of spiritual nourishment for me. I am renewed. It becomes an opportunity to be humble; to rise to the challenge of loving more; a chance to strengthen my faith; to reach out and to ask for help from someone and to know that I am not alone.

You help me to understand how to approach the suffering we all encounter in life. I can treat it like a loving mother would treat an anxious child. She would not try and hide from the child, she would not ignore the child, she would not try and pretend that anything was the child's fault; she would only want to provide love and ease the pain.

In the same way, I can be there for myself and my suffering. I can treat any anxiety or distress by speaking to it and saying like a mother would, 'I'm here, don't be afraid, you will be okay, you are not alone.'

As you know, for the last 20 years I have searched for a purpose for my life, and I now feel like there is a chance that I can become a strong woman who has one of the most remarkable visions for her life; to be lovingly creative. I have gained so much from our connection over the last few months and I cannot put it all into words. I have enormous gratitude; I am loved, and more importantly, more able to love. As you know, one of my realisations is that I was afraid to love, afraid to be hurt. I was scared that if I looked at myself with honesty, I would find out too many painful things about myself, but just the opposite is true. I am learning to understand and accept myself.

The burden of an irrational but overwhelming sense of responsibility to others is lifting, and it gives me a new perspective on people who have loved me. As my preoccupation with pleasing people lessens, it will free me to see their true love. I have been as hard on others as I have been on myself. The seeds of profound reconciliation are within, and I know that these will be nurtured and that I will be guided. When I think of mum, the heaviness in my heart has lifted, and instead of feeling scared of letting her down, I see her loving smile.

I have a new definition of love to help me so aptly epitomised by the creative, nurturing energy of the loving parent and it can be applied to all situations and all people.

Love doesn't have to be earned; it is something to be given unconditionally and accepted freely.

How will I cultivate this love? Through actions, writing, telling my story, empathy, compassion, self-compassion, understanding, acceptance, not judging, not resisting, living in the moment, being present to myself and to the world, being present to others, and through prayer. I am loved by you and you will always be listening and at every opportunity interceding, and continuing to shower your roses from heaven.

It feels appropriate to write my last letter to you as your relics return to France, but I am not saying goodbye because I will still be speaking to you every day and carrying your message everywhere I go.

As you know, I have been telling everyone about you. I give people mementoes of you, and the response has been incredible. Just a couple of days ago I took a card which had been placed on your casket to someone who I know is not well and has been going through a tough time and needs your loving presence in her life. She phoned me after my visit, and this is what she said:

'I thought it was sweet of you to bring the picture of St Thérèse, but I didn't believe she could help me. During the night, I got up, unable to sleep and I felt just awful. I went downstairs and sat down and wondered what I could do, but everything seemed hopeless. Then I noticed the card you left on the mantelpiece. I picked it up and looked at the beautiful picture of the young woman and remembered that you told me that she was a saint. I don't know what made me do it but I said a prayer, and as I did so I placed the card on my heart. The most amazing thing happened. I felt a rush of energy, like electricity, go into me through my heart, and as it did, something changed within. I'm not sure what it was, but it was very powerful, and

I know that this will help me go forward. For the first time in ages, I felt as though I wasn't alone. Thank you for introducing me to St Thérèse.'

I thought my heart would burst with gratitude that you had answered my prayer for this person and that you had made your presence felt so quickly and so strongly. I said, 'St Thérèse has sent you a rose.'

I know that you will keep sending your roses throughout the world. Thank you for my many roses, some of which I have described in these letters.

To me the roses you shower upon us from heaven symbolise your blessings, your faith, your love of God and for us all and I shall spend the rest of my life 'catching the roses' and helping others to do the same.

I am not sure yet how I will do that, but I know that you will guide me. My pilgrimage won't end here; it is the beginning of the next stage, the start of the story of a soul who doesn't feel so lost anymore.

Yours forever,

Michaela

THE END.

References

Bradshaw, John. (2006) Healing the Shame That Binds You. Health Communication. Rev Ed. Edition.

Caddy, Eileen. (1981) Footprints on the Path. Findhorn Press Ltd.

Caddy, Eileen. (2005) The Small Voice Within. Audio CD. Findhorn Press Ltd.

Cameron, Julia. (1995) The Artist's Way. Pan Books, London.

Foley, Marc OCD. (2000) The Love That Keeps Us Sane: Living the Little Way of St. Thérèse of Lisieux. Illumination Books, Paperback.

Gendlin PhD, Eugene T. (2003) Focusing: How to Gain Direct Access to Your Body's Knowledge. Rider, 25th Anniversary Edition.

Gumbel, Nicky. (2007) Alpha Questions of Life. Kingsway Publications.

Kurtz, Ernest & Ketcham, Katherine. (1994) The Spirituality of Imperfection: Storytelling and the Search for Meaning. Bantam.

Mgr Johnson Vernon. (1997) Message of St Thérèse of Lisieux: The Little Way. Catholic Truth Society.

Nowinski, Joseph. (2003) Six Questions that Can Change your Life. Rodale.

Orloff, MD, Judith. (2009) Emotional Freedom: Liberate Yourself from Negative Emotions and Transform Your Life. Harmony Books.

Osteen, Joel. (2004) Your Best Life Now: 7 Steps to Living at Your Full Potential. Warner Faith.

Pennebaker PhD, James. (1997) Opening Up: The Healing Power of Expressing Emotions. The Guildford Press.

Pennebaker PhD, James. (2004) Writing to Heal: A Guided Journey for Recovering from Trauma & Emotional Upheaval. New Harbinger Publications.

Rolheiser, Ron, OMI. Gethsemane – The Place to Give Up Resentment. www.ronrolheiser.com [Accessed March 13, 2005].

Rolheiser, Ron, OMI. The Agony in the Garden – The Place to Stay Awake. www.ronrolheiser.com [Accessed March 7, 2004]. Rosenburg, Patsy. (2007) Presence: How to use Positive Energy for Success in Every Situation. Michael Joseph.

Rosengren, Curt. www.passioncatalyst.com [Accessed 2009].

Russell, Willy. (2000) The Wrong Boy. Doubleday.

Solemn Mass Pamphlet on the Twenty-Second Sunday of Ordinary Time, Metropolitan Cathedral Christ the King, 30 August 2009.

Steindl-Rast OSB, Brother David. (1984) Gratefulness, The Heart of Prayer: An Approach to Life in Fullness. Paulist Press.

Tedeschi, RG, & Calhoun, L.G. (1996) Journal of Traumatic Stress. Jul:9(3) 455-71.

The Holy Bible. (2002) English Standard Version. Collins.

Thérèse & Johnson, Vernon. (2008) The Autobiography of Thérèse of Lisieux: The Story of a Soul. Dover Books on Western Philosophy, Paperback.

Trichter Metcalfe PhD, Linda & Simon, Tobin PhD. (2002) Writing the Mind Alive: The Proprioceptive Method for Finding Your Authentic Voice. Ballantine Books.

Udris, John. (2004) Holy Daring: The Fearless Trust of St Thérèse of Lisieux. Gracewing.

Vilma, Seelaus OCD. (1998) Spirituality of Imperfection (Part One) Finding Strength in Weakness. Spiritual Life, Winter.

Webster, Jean. (2002) Daddy-Long-Legs. Dover.

Whelan SM, Michael Fr. St Thérèse One Hundred Years On: Irritatingly Irrelevant or Profoundly Relevant. http://www.Thérèseoflisieux.org [Accessed 2007].

Young, William P. (2008) The Shack: Where Tragedy Confronts Eternity. Hodder Windblown.

24084387R00211

Printed in Great Britain
by Amazon